INDIA'S NATIONAL DEFENCE

Defining Defence Reforms and Military Modernisation

INDIA'S NATIONAL DEFENCE

Defining Defence Reforms and Military Modernisation

Lt Gen Gautam Banerjee, PVSM, AVSM, YSM (Retd)

PENTAGON PRESS

India's National Defence: Defining Defence Reforms and Military Modernisation
By Lt Gen Gautam Banerjee, PVSM, AVSM, YSM (Retd)

ISBN 978-81-8274-937-5

First Published in 2017

Published by
PENTAGON PRESS
206, Peacock Lane, Shahpur Jat,
New Delhi-110049
Phones: 011-64706243, 26491568
Telefax: 011-26490600
email: rajan@pentagonpress.in
website: www.pentagonpress.in

Printed at Aegean Offset Printers, Greater Noida

Contents

PREFACE

Beginning from the time India found her freedom in 1947 to be able to chart her native destiny, management of the nation's military institution has been mired with serious problems. Indeed, the leaders of Independent India then, and even those who ran the state later, notwithstanding their statesmanship and intellect, had neither found glory in understanding this crucial pillar of sovereign nation-state nor had they made serious efforts to attend to that leadership deficiency.

The result was that India lost thousands of square kilometres of her territories in Jammu, Kashmir and Ladakh, and continues to suffer various hues of military hostilities along most of her borders. As if that was not enough, in the name of peace and good neighbourliness, she had been strategically naive to let her military successes pass without securing commensurate advantages, thus allowing the ever-intransigent aggressor to resurrect. That indeed was India's narrative in 1949, 1965, 1971, besides her defeat of Pakistan's proxy war first in 1997-98 and then again in 2006-08.

It is strange that even after committing substantial budgetary expenditure in maintaining the world's third largest military establishment, the Indian state, apparently as a matter of premeditated scheme, chooses to keep her military forces but at partially equipped condition for warfare. It is no surprise therefore that India deters her adversaries just about nominally. The disconcert rises even more when it is found that even as India finds success in her mission 'Chandrayan', she is yet unable to produce a satisfactory rife for her soldiery to fight with.

The cause of systemic disorientation on matters of national defence is just one: for the Indian state, political management of the military institution, the most powerful instrument of the state, remains an amateurish business and a prejudiced priority. That flaw is starkly visible when military professionals and civilian experts remain excluded, more or less, from the system of management of national defence and strategic decision making.

Absence of institutionalised professional participation in the management of national defence reflects in India's political leadership remaining devoid of strategic, organisational and managerial acumen. The same reason causes the defence bureaucracy, bereft of any military experience whatsoever and beholden to misunderstood, if not misconstrued, priorities, to be wary of military professionals' articulations. Thus excluded over the decades from grand strategic decision making, Indian military leadership has reconciled to looking low and thinking small, while maintaining professional élan through display of extra-ordinary valour in the battlefield. Similarly, in absence of dedicated cadres of visionary and experienced civilian experts to chart a long-term course for defence preparedness, the infrastructure of the nation's defence science and technology, industry and fiscal management remain denied of the requisite level of professional accomplishments. All these debilities shore-up to raise the cost of national defence and in-optimal use of national resources. That leaves the nation having to reconcile to high expenditure to buy yet inadequate security.

There have been many well intentioned attempts to modernise the system of apex level management of national defence. But in the face of partisan afflictions and fears of change, these attempts could not achieve the purpose intended. The attempt in this book has therefore been to propose practicable and palatable restructure of that system while taking care of partisan concerns. Suggested herein are professionally construed options to reorganise India's apex structure for defence policymaking. In so doing, first the current systemic shortcomings are identified and the systems followed in advanced countries are delved into. Then taking note of native competencies and characteristics, outline structures as well as roles and responsibilities to be borne by the political and military hierarchies, the defence bureaucracy, and the rest of the state apparatus that have roles in furthering the interests of national defence are suggested.

Perusal of the contents with an open mind is solicited.

Gurugram
01 February 2017

Lt Gen Gautam Banerjee,
PVSM, AVSM, YSM (Retd)

PREAMBLE

> *"Military strength and political power are preconditions for lasting national greatness, the substance of the greatness springs from the hidden sources of intellect and morale, firm ideas and values"*
>
> – **Hans J Morgenthau**

The Burden of National Defence

Situated in a geo-politically contentious neighbourhood, the issues of escalation of territorial assertions, proxy war, conventional military power ratios, military deterrence and nuclear posturing have wide ranging implications on India's national defence. These implications have to be addressed by the custodians of national defence through innovation of appropriate strategic postulations. In this context, the impact of a new generation of conventional warfare, evolution of sub-conventional warfare through state sponsored militias, growth of multi-nation terrorism incorporate, rise in internal insurgencies and frequent deployment for disaster relief add up to necessitate a profound rethink on the way armed conflicts and other military exigencies of the coming days are to be managed by the Indian defence planners.

Further, national defence being a resource-intensive commitment, its efficient management within affordable costs has assumed added salience in India's overall national endeavour. Obviously therefore, formulation of judicious defence policies must be an imperative for the rise of a modern Indian State. And as a corollary, a system of perceptive defence policy-making becomes a noble objective of astute statecraft.

Purpose of the Book

Even if India does not wish to bank on military power to solve her sovereign issues, it is a demand of geo-politics that she prevent her adversaries from settling their issues by military force. Apparently however, in spite of heavy investment in defence preparedness, India has not achieved the desired level of military security. Actually, as the modesty of her military deterrence starkly indicate, the 'wisdom' displayed by India's national leadership in devising effective defence policies has been far from astute when viewed in light of the threats the nation continues to be challenged with. Further, even when competent defence policies have been adopted, when it comes to implementation, the execution has mostly been tardy and the results achieved have belied the potentials. Indeed, it is a fact that India's potentially strong military capability does not optimally translate into corresponding level of political-military security for the nation, and that calls for serious deliberations – the purpose being to reconcile the equation between the nation's political aspirations, and investments made and resources committed on military preparedness against the dividend reaped.

As for the rest of the rather humungous Indian defence establishment, over the decades after independence, barring few exceptions, it has been stagnating on its past competences. Thus the custodians of defence research and development have been intent on passing on what contraptions they manage to devise rather than what the soldiery requires to fight confidently, the defence industry has gone moribund under the Government's misplaced industrial policies which protect obsolescence while stifling innovation, and the defence bureaucracy, unaccountable guardian of national defence, is manned by officials who may hardly be better than novices on matters of defence. And yet, defence policy-making in India remains the exclusive preserve of such bureaucrats, scientists and economists, while a strategically uninitiated political leadership, guided by the former lot, presides over the whole affair. It is so that the *raison d'être* of India's humungous defence paraphernalia – that is, to achieve effective military security for the nation – is increasingly infringed by mounting obsolescence of weapons and equipment and deficiencies in men and material that lead to the 'hollowing' of the military's operational wherewithal. India's native military genius for tactical and organisational innovations and strategic articulation of military power thus stand stymied by a regressive system of defence policy-making which staggers under the monopoly of amateur 'strategists', and its poor manifestation through imposition of banal, even regressive, defence policies.

The results are unnerving. Once celebrated for manufacturing quality small arms and light guns, India's defence industry cannot produce even a reliable rifle today, and while blocking import of war equipment on the pretext of indigenous development, her managers of national defence fail to deliver, after decades of cost and time overruns, on even routine promises made to their fighting forces. The situation is further exacerbated by the disorientation within India's Ministry of Defence (MoD), wherein matters of hard military imperatives – modernisation, reorganisation, infrastructure build up and training, even recruitment, discipline and motivation – are either diverted into oblivion of red tape or tentatively attended through procedures that have long been abandoned by modern nations, including Britain, its former mentor. Thus in matters of fiscal management, environmental and other procedural sanctions, procurement of capital weapons and equipment, terms of service and personnel administration etc., India's defence managers often overlook the hoary principle of 'military necessity'. In contrast, most militarily active countries apply this principle to go to extreme lengths in their effort to strengthen their military power; India's innately inimical neighbours do so more deliberately, even clandestinely. Indeed, it is a self-defeating process of defence policy-making that inflicts regressive defence policies upon the Indian military institution, and that in turn prevents efficient utilisation of the allocated defence budget. Military modernisation is stymied thus. The result is that India's rather large military institution, maintained at high cost, cannot but perform well short of its potential.

The summation of the situation is that there are serious but avoidable debilities in India's national defence management structure which prevents her from deterring aggressive behaviour from inimical neighbours. That debility prevents the nation from reaping the right dividends from its investments on defence – that should, after all, must be the right purpose of maintaining the world's third largest military force. Indeed, a developing nation like India, with all its wants for poverty alleviation and socio-economic progress, cannot afford the 'luxury' of nurturing such an inefficient system of defence management.

The purpose of discussion in this book is to deliberate upon the situation as narrated in the preceding paragraphs and to discuss the possible manner of redress of the debilities that afflict India's defence planning.

But before proceeding further, it would be beneficial in fostering clarity to the discussions if a standard convention of terms is adopted to specify certain key aspects of defence planning.

Defining 'National Security' and 'National Defence'

In the modern era, a nation's defence against military aggression is inexorably linked to other quasi-military and civil challenges – like internal stability, economic wellbeing, access to energy etc. – the entire gamut being assigned into the term 'national security' – or better still described as 'overall or comprehensive national security'. Notably however, within the ambit of overall national security, a state's commitment to deter or defend against external aggression continues to be honoured by its traditional primacy. Here, the term used for that commitment is 'national defence' or its synonym, 'military security' which in turn is defined by the construct of a nation's military institution. In other words, under the ambit of overall 'national security', the cause of 'national defence' against military aggression (or 'military security') cannot but remain to be the state's primary concern. The purpose of discussion in this book would better serve if the convention to differentiate between these two terms is appreciated.

A nation's military institution is an exclusive organisation that is mandated by the state to engage in warfare for the achievement of the most emergent political purposes. Therefore, in the scheme of national security, the highest concern is invariably accorded to ensure that the military institution remains fully competent to plunge into its excruciating charter. This is not to state that the other constituents of overall national security are of any less import, but it is to highlight the universal fact that when every other effort fails to curb an adversary's unacceptable animosity, prosecution of war remains to be the ultimate recourse to the preservation a nation's sovereign interests. It is so therefore that notwithstanding the salient roles played by the other elements of overall 'national security', no country has ever diverted from its exclusive focus on 'national defence' (or 'military security'), nor have they compromised on nurturing their military institution.

In the perception of India's ruling establishment, however, that exclusivity of the cause of national defence seems to have been subsumed into the basket of other elements of overall national security. Military security is thus liable to be viewed in similar context as that of the civil elements of overall national security – to encompass the citizen's social, economic, legal, energy and water security, and so on, for example – rather than according higher prioritisation to the imperatives of 'military necessity'. Further, India's ever hard pressed governing establishment is liable to be enticed by the visibility and ready returns from such elements of overall 'national security' – development works and industrial progress, for example – and use these to conveniently rescue itself from having to bear the more complex, costly and longer term burden of developing the parameters of 'national defence'. This trend manifests in the managers of Indian defence attempting to cover their inability to upgrade military security by publicising their commitments in favour of other, civil aspects of overall national security – like energy, communications, employment etc. – the contrived clause of 'confidentiality' coming handy in diverting the focus. No doubt, it is most desirable to strengthen the quasi-military or civil components of national security, but when that is used as a diversion from the inadequate state of the national defence, the matter turns harmful.

Complementary Sectors of National Defence

As it would be seen during the course of the following discussion, in dealing with management of national defence in the contemporary period, it has been universally found necessary to distinguish a nation's defence structure into two complementary sectors. For the purposes of this discussion, we may refer to these two sectors as the 'military institution' and the 'defence establishment' respectively. Notably, since both these sectors are organised to perform complementary roles in nurturing the nation's military power, there have to be functional inter-dependencies built-in between the two at all levels of hierarchies. Resultantly, at the apex level of national defence management, the mandate for both the sectors is destined to merge into a singularity. In sum, the monolithic defence sector of the past has, in the modern era, bifurcated into 'military institution' and 'defence establishment', both converging at the delivery end of an all-inclusive military-civil-industry joint endeavour.

Military Institution

In this discussion, the description of 'military institution' – as it evolved over the thousands of years of existential experiences – must represent a unique organisation that is dedicated to the 'call' for preparation, posturing and prosecution of warfare in order to perform the role of a nation's ultimate leverage of political power. To that purpose, the military institution must remain wedded to its excruciatingly demanding role that the nation 'commissions' it for, and nurture its soldiery to engage in warfare across a wide spectrum of strategies and tactics that meets the national cause. Disposal of the nation's trust through that commission requires the soldiers, sailors and airmen to rise beyond the ordinary human instincts and to imbibe such exalted military ethos which the society itself is wary of subscribing to. Indeed, the act of devolution of national mandate upon the military institution is rooted at that sublimate spirit of mutual commitment in which the state and its soldiery celebrate each other's cause. The theme underlying this relationship is the commitment to the achievement of military security even at ultimate cost – 'goal-dedication', to wit.

Defence Establishment

As distinct from the term military institution, the description of 'defence establishment' is applied here to represent all such organisations and agencies which contribute to societal, techno-industrial, fiscal, academic, diplomatic and above all, political articulations to further the cause of national defence. Thus the defence bureaucracy in the MoD, the Defence Research & Development Organisation (DRDO), various Ordnance Factories (OF), defence-specific Public Sector Undertakings (DPSU), Department of Defence Estates (DDE), private arms industry and dual-use infrastructure like transportation, supplies, information technology (IT), communications etc. should answer to the broad description of 'defence establishment'. This description conforms to the vast range of quasi as well as purely military charters of defence preparedness that have to be performed through military-dedicated and dual-use organisations manned mostly by civilian personnel of requisite expertise. Complexities and consequences of such charters pose extreme challenges to these organisations and agencies in their endeavour to build up the foundations for competent national defence – the motivation coming from the theme of 'target-realisation'. Obviously, management of the 'defence establishment' requires realisation of native technological competencies, industrial resources, fiscal capacities and political ambitions in the backdrop of geo-strategic realities to deliver the requisite war wherewithal to the 'military institution' according to specified levels of quality, quantity and time-lines, for the latter to respond to its national mandate.

Principles of 'Military Necessity' and 'Unlimited Pledge'

The afore-stated distinction between the culture of goal-dedication in the 'military institution' and target-realisation in the 'defence establishment' makes it extremely complex for any nation-state to find an optimal balance in its defence management. This difficulty is a factor of a nation's, and of course its adversarial powers' political compulsions and the resources at hand to satiate those. Military conflagrations being extreme measures and adverse fallouts of these being irreversible, a burden of 'military necessity' is thus imposed upon the state's priorities, so as to ensure that no chances are taken in the achievement of right outcomes of military ventures.

Many times, when states are unable to balance their military security compulsions with the limitations of resources to bear that burden, they are pushed into adoption of short-term expediencies and to overlook that imbalance. They do so hoping to get away with the compromise. But in geo-strategic estrangements, many times such hopes come to be belied, and compromises made in military preparedness are rued. This is but a case exemplified by the scene in independent India's pre-1962 era, when a fairly competent military institution was deliberately reduced to psychological and material destitution, ostensibly for the cause of economic progress, and yet asked to "throw the Chinese out"! In contrast, Pakistan's adoption of underhand means to acquire nuclear status is an example of exercise of the principle of military necessity.

Notably, the concept of military necessity for the state is complemented by the principle of 'unlimited pledge – regardless' that is subscribed to by the men military, this being another extraordinary feature of the military institution.

Such indeed are the dilemmas that make it complicated to rightly manage the call of national defence. Even those countries who possess centuries of experience in political management of national defence, have many times failed to reconcile these complexities. Appreciation of the fundamentals highlighted above help in dealing with the subject under discussion.

The Theme and Layout of the Book

To present the right perspective, political philosophers are sanguine that national security rests upon three foundations, viz, 'political or societal security', 'economic security' and 'military security'. It is also considered that along with a defined geographical area and people living in it under a formal system of governance, military power to protect sovereign interests constitutes a third fundamental ingredient of a 'state'. In the context of sovereignty of the Indian nation-state, this perspective translates into protecting her way of life in a world order that is increasingly dominated by brazen economic exploitation that is overtly or subtly backed up with aggressive military power.

In that contextual salience, the purpose of this book is: Firstly, to recount the political purpose of the nation-state in investing on its military institution and the spirit that guides the state-military interdependency; secondly, to revisit India's national defence management structure, her organisation for defence policy-making and the imperatives for emanation of quality defence policies; and thirdly, to delve into the manifestation of these endeavours through all round transformation of the Indian military institution in tune with the goal of preservation of the nation's 'military security'.

The multiplicity of aspects that shape the system of the nation's defence management requires distinct lines of discussion, and accordingly, the book is divided into two Parts, as follows:

a) Part 1: Reforms in Defence Policy Making System. Proposition of a modern and efficient defence policy-making system is the theme of discussion in this Part. In the interest of logical build up, the discussion takes off from the necessity for the Indian State to undertake comprehensive defence reforms, takes cognisance of the modern systems of defence policy-making in various advanced nations and recounts the evolution of the system of defence policy-making in post-Independence India. The factual build up is followed up with a discussion over the necessity, goals and purposes of defence reforms. Finally, the discussion leads to logically considered propositions for a contemporary and customised national defence management structure, and its corollary, an efficient system of defence policy-making. Finally, such crucial policy issues which require foremost attention to initiate the full process of defence reformation are touched upon.
b) Part 2: The matter of military modernisation – or 'military reforms' as distinct from the overarching 'defence reforms' – is the theme of discussion in this Part. The course of military modernisation – and its all-encompassing version, 'military transformation' – however can only be appropriately charted when the national mandate upon the military institution and a corresponding package of fiscal commitments are spelt out at the political level. Thus between these two boundary conditions should the military professionals undertake to crystallise the nation's 'military doctrine' and translate that doctrine into native 'military strategies'. Finally, modernisation of the Indian military institution should be in conformity to such strategies considered. These therefore are the fundamental issues which are discussed in Part 2. Besides, certain key and contentious

features of modernisation of the Indian military institution, to turn it into a truly modern and cost-efficient bulwark of national security, have also been touched upon.

Finally, it may be appreciated that the issues are vast, and much beyond the scope of just one reading. The discussion here therefore has been confined to the identification of priority imperatives of strengthening national defence and the appropriate courses to adopt in securing the purpose of India's military security, defence reforms and military modernisation being the recourses to that end.

PART 1

REFORM OF NATIONAL DEFENCE POLICY MAKING SYSTEM

"Military strength and political power are preconditions for lasting national greatness, the substance of that greatness springs from the hidden sources of intellect and morale, from ideas and values."

– **Hans J Morgenthau**

Overview

The Course of Discussion

A system of competent defence policy-making must be the sine quo non for the emanation of effective defence policies that are devoted to building up the nation's military security. It would therefore be in order to start the discussion with the 'national defence management structure' and the 'system defence policy-making' in India before turning to the key features of appropriate 'defence policies'.

Further, competent defence policies must propound the means and methods of building up native defence capability that would protect India's interests within the ambit of resources which she can marshal. Therefore, the policies propounded have to be competently applied in enabling the nation's military institution to stand up to its political mandate. Necessarily therefore, the discussion in this part would also cover the fundamental aspects of affordable strategic options for India and the corresponding guidelines for military force-structuring.

The subject being vast and deep, it is proposed to focus the discussion to the core aspects and such purposeful endeavours which offer appropriate directions for the defence policy-makers to proceed with their charter in due spirit of enquiry and initiative. Accordingly, the subject matter has been discussed in five chapters as described subsequently.

Chapter 1: The Onus of Defence Reforms

There is a constituency of opinion-shapers in India who profess continuation of status quo in the system of defence management. The preference of this group is to take recourse to occasional, incremental upgrades of the system only when unavoidable. That the system has 'stood the test of time', including the greatest victory of Indian arms in a millennium, the 1971 War, is cited to bolster that argument. Given the social and economic priorities that the Indian governing class remains tied to, that is an argument rather pleasing, even if it runs contrary to the natural demands for organisational modernisation. Assiduous break-through across such myopic notions is a necessity to institute meaningful defence reforms. Arguments for 'why defence reforms?' is therefore the charter in Chapter 1 of this Part.

Chapter 2: System of Defence Policy Making in Some Advanced Nations

In order to catch up with the modern standards of defence management, it is incumbent upon India's defence planners to examine the features of defence policies as adopted by advanced countries as well as their mechanisms of defence policy-making. The purpose is not to copy these, but to understand the right nuances for customisation and application of these in the indigenous context of national defence. This matter is the theme of Chapter 2.

Chapter 3: Evolution of Defence Policy Making in India

The culture of post-Independence defence policy-making, post-1962 and post-Kargil War initiatives to reform the system, inefficient budgetary planning and vacillating state of military preparedness, and the shortcomings in India's present process of defence policy-making are the issues discussed in this chapter. The purpose is to seek guidance and identify pitfalls in instituting effective ways to uphold the nation's defence commitments in the contemporary era.

Chapter 4: Reform of Apex Level National Defence Management Structure–1

The overdue reforms in the management of national defence found the government's reckoning after the unsavoury experiences of the Kargil War. Since then there have been some deliberate government-sponsored initiatives to reshape the structure for management of national defence. However, when it comes to implementation, many of the desired steps have been languishing, partially or entirely, due to organisational fears and friction. More notably, except for few mild reorientations in the defence establishment, the initiatives have addressed only a narrow band of higher military and intelligence hierarchy, thus leaving the better part of the structure for national defence to stagnate.

Accordingly, the two distinct sectors of defence reforms – namely the military institution, and the nation's larger defence establishment – that are tuned to the contemporary era have been distinguished in this chapter. Thus to begin with, a modernised national defence management structure and a system of defence policy-making, to manage both the sectors, have been proposed. Following up, the reforms applicable to the first sector, for the best management of India's military institution in the contemporary native context, have been proposed in this chapter.

Chapter 5: Reform of Apex Level National Defence Management Structure–2

In continuation of the preceding chapter, and having defined an overall national defence management structure and its system of defence policy-making, the discussion in this chapter veers to the reformations in the second sector, that is the nation's rest of the quasi-military and civilian defence establishment – the term denoting all those national endeavours that support the military institution in the latter's fulfilment of its roles in preservation of the nationhood. Thus a control organisation dedicated to manage defence procurements, research, industry, logistics, personnel management, national mobilisation and reserves, fiscal provisions, management procedures etc. is proposed in this chapter. Further, a mechanism for reforms implementation and audit has also been touched upon.

Lastly, the ultimate purpose of the reforms, that is the core objectives of long term and immediate term policy-making, have been touched upon in this chapter, the purpose being to keep focus on results rather that the processes of reforms which had been our bane in the past. Accordingly, the characteristics, rather than the contents, of the long necessary defence policies to be emanating from that control organisation have been enumerated at the end.

Convention of Usable Terms

In analysing the cause of optimal defence management, the first step to take is to define a conducive and effective 'national defence management structure', so to say. To qualify further, that national defence management structure must be served by an efficient 'system for defence policy-making', which in turn must lead to emanation of focused 'defence policies'. Thus for the ensuing discussion, the terms to contend with would be: One, 'national defence management structure'; two, its corollary, 'system for defence policy-making'; and three, its product, 'defence policies'.

Next, at the second tier of defence management, there must be an empowered mechanism to ensure true implementation of defence policies that emanate from the said system of defence policy-making. Of necessity, such an implementation mechanism has to include the activities of monitoring, feedback, and course corrections. These aspects shall also be subject to discussed in this part.

Finally, for the purposes of discussion in this book, we shall consider 'military transformation' as a sub-set of overall 'defence reforms', and a larger, all-encompassing version of 'military modernisation' that goes beyond the tangibility's to cover conceptual and procedural progress.

*

CHAPTER I

THE ONUS OF DEFENCE REFORMS

"Begin, be bold and venture to be wise."

– **Horace**

Why Defence Reforms?

Many defence policymakers find it expedient to continue with status quo in the prevalent system of defence management, while taking recourse to incremental upgrades when unavoidable. Besides containing what is viewed as ambitious and unaffordable demands from the military institution, they find the persisting system to be reliable and time tested. Above all, they prefer to perpetuate the stranglehold of bureaucracy, finance managers and science community over defence policy-making, practically to the exclusion of military professional participation. Liberation from such regressive attitude towards national defence and corrective institution of modern concepts in its management is therefore the matter of discussion in this chapter. To do so, it is intended first to touch upon the contemporary challenges of national defence, followed by a count of the debilities that afflict India's defence management, and finally, answers to the dilemmas over defence investments that confront the national leadership.

Contemporary Challenges of National Defence

Geo-politics poses many challenges to India's rise as a developed and egalitarian nation, situated as she is between a claimant super power which intends to seek its destiny through articulation of military muscle, a neighbour who is seized of an obsession to undermine 'Hindustan' even if in so doing it has to asphyxiate its own society, and an Ocean which is sought to be turned into an arena for geo-political wrestling by its ever-ravenous transients. To complete the picture, there are smaller neighbours who, while enjoying many social and economic concessions from India, are yet compelled to indulge in India-baiting in the hope of extracting more. Then there is the true super power who, in order to uphold its commitment to the 'pursuit of happiness' for its own citizens, is ever contriving to push the rest of the world to sacrifice their assets in its favour. In this fiendish milieu – as evidenced by being drawn into five wars, two 'police actions' and four near-wars – challenges to India's external security are serious enough for a developing nation to commit nearly rupees three lakh crore annually – and rising – just to maintain a level of minimalist military capability to defend herself. The malediction however does not end here.

Having paid excruciatingly over the past millennium for the society's inability to control its short-sighted enticement in vivisecting the Indian nationhood, large sections of Indian citizens remain consumed, even after independence, by that same death-wish. In many parts of the nation, they have either exploited weaker sections to push them into armed rebellion or have sold their loyalty to anti-national forces – state-sponsored as well as non-state – to inflict insurgency and mayhem upon their motherland. Then there thrive many elements that, taking advantage of the nation's democratic dispensation, choose to abuse it through radicalism, terror and the farce of 'popular sentiments' to contrive secession and disintegration of the Indian nationhood. The result is that in nearly one fifth of the Indian landmass the state's writ runs but in exception. Indeed, these anti-national elements have to be restrained by force before they reconcile to better sense. In this instance too, when situation deteriorates beyond a point, exercise of military power becomes the ultimate recourse to preserve the nation's integrity. Activation of military power to control as many as six insurgencies over nearly the entire post-independence period, and numerous deployments on internal security are the testimonies of that necessity. In fact in the contemporary world, military power deters internal instability just as it does to external threats – even the United States of America (USA), so sensitive in keeping the military out of domestic involvement, has had to amend its constitution to permit that option.

Lastly, the vitiation of the global environment has imposed an unpredictable and uncontrollable burden of massive proportions upon the state in the form of management of natural calamities. Here too, military forces, professionally competent and mentally attuned to standing up to overwhelming odds as these calamities are, must remain the ultimate responder in bringing succour to the people, existence of disaster management organisations notwithstanding.

No doubt, to deal with such consistent impositions of destructive nature, farsighted foreign policies, competent diplomacy and good domestic governance need to be backed up with the language of universal power: a modern military organisation that is founded upon a robust defence infrastructure, and guided by a sound process of defence policy-making that leads to the adoption of farsighted defence policies.

Debilities in India's Defence Management

At independence, India was a nation that had been was consigned to extreme poverty by two and a half centuries of internal turmoil and imperialistic loot. Ever since, her national leadership has been engaged in a struggle to pull India out of that situation. Ironically however, that noble concern translated, except for a period between 1963 to 1987, to a conscious policy of overlook of the health of the nation's military institution.

Independent India had found herself bestowed with a great military institution. During her early years of nationhood, she extracted full benefits from that inheritance to preserve her integrity against external as well as internal threats besides earning accolades in service of the UN. However, seized by romantic notions of peaceful co-existence and by turning that notion to be dismissive of military power, her political leadership also consciously pushed this institution to the seeds. Thus, the period between 1948 and 1962 was devoted to rhetoric pronouncements of a peace-loving world order in which military power had neither the priority nor a purpose. Then, having been taught a lesson in 1962, there came a period when the moribund military institution was resuscitated. Indeed, for the next 25 years, full political dividends – in terms of 1965 and 1971 Wars, continuous internal insurgencies, regional interventions in Sri Lanka and Maldives, and above all, nearly three decades of effective deterrence against Pakistan's and China's aggressiveness – were earned from that investment. That spring period however, ended in 1991 when Indian economy fell into such distress as to the government having to pawn its bullion to save payment defaults. The military institution was again to suffer the brunt of that situation, and soon enough it turned into a 'hollowed' behemoth of little capability other than keeping insurgencies in check.

Meanwhile, the rest of the defence establishment – procurement, research, industry, estates and bureaucracy – was, in the misplaced notion of 'civilian control', gradually 'released' of accountability to their sole cause of existence – the military institution. Thus, these players of the defence establishment allowed themselves to turn autonomous, and much to the exclusion of professional military supervision, began to enjoy a licence to propagate their partisan motivations. That these players were grossly unequipped in understanding the military's concerns was not considered a matter of systemic disconcert. All this while, the political class remained smug in their rhetorical eulogy of the nation's military institution, while doing little of reckonable import to address its mounting debilities.

The result is there for all to see:

a) Even while maintaining the world's third largest military force, adversarial military impositions upon India – territorial encroachments, proxy war, terror attacks, and the ever looming prospect of military aggression – remain undeterred. In the post-1990 period, inimical neighbours have routinely attacked India with no fear of retribution; insurgency in Kashmir Valley, intrusions leading to the Kargil War, hosting and arming of anti-nationals, terrorist mayhem, and plant of traitor cells all over the country are some examples of that brazen one-sided abuse. In response, all that the nation's vast military institution can do is to prevent the assaulters from emerging victorious – nothing more; no deterrence, no retribution, just passive reaction.
b) There has developed a chasm between the military force and its sustenance with duly scaled compliments of war wherewithal – weapons, equipment, munitions, transportation and logistic infrastructure, and appropriate training and funding for these – for it to be at an acceptable level of operational fettle. The military institution therefore faces the wasteful prospects of being afflicted with low 'Usability Factor' in performance of its primary role – the factor that signifies an inability to deploy full military might to deter, or win, wars in favour of the nation.
c) For its main weaponry, tanks, guns, small arms etc., India's military institution remains yet at the mercy of foreign military industry. The situation is no better even in respect of performance enhancer accessories and medium technology back-up equipment. Thus with research, development and production confined just to replacement

hardware of the basic kind to sustain a stagnant military force-structure, and encouraged by the protection of a military-weary government, the defence industry had no motivation to compete, develop, export and earn profits. An industry which was fairly modern and reliable till the late 1940s, degenerated within three decades to a state when it could not produce even a good weapon or an accessory (1).

d) Poor civil-military relations, caused by abdication of political control in favour of bureaucratic control, have led to debilitation of the military institution by an aged, top heavy, stagnant and fiscally imprudent structure. Indeed, regular attempts made by professionals to reorganise the military forces in tune with the modern concepts of warfare and so to make the best use of the defence budget have been derailed by a disoriented defence bureaucracy and the ludicrously regressive procedures devised by it.

Indeed, objective evaluation of India's management of national defence indicates that:

a) One, enemies are only partially deterred from undertaking overt military aggression. But yet, they find ways to strike at her through other forms of warfare without any fear of retribution.
b) Two, only a part of India's massive force-structure is maintained in the state of operational readiness, a reckonable proportion of it being consigned to the condition of 'hollowness'. Consequently, a good part of the forces could be found to be unusable at the time of crisis.
c) Three, strategic naiveté in defence policy-making, exacerbated by ill-advised diffusion of ownership, authority, expertise and responsibility towards national defence, has caused the military institution to slide below its operational potential. The government machinery seems to have gone inert in its accountability over defence preparedness, and another operational debacle due to proficiency or material deficiencies may well be let go-bye, as it happened in 1962 and Kargil.

Strange but true, the fact remains that most of Indian post-independence defence policies have led to weakening of that very military institution which has played a singular role in keeping the spirit of India from being subsumed by self-destructive afflictions of our diverse societies and at the same time, kept predatory neighbours and their cheerleaders from dismembering the Union. Even if it is granted that in the early periods after independence there had been fears, false as it turned out, of military takeover, which the bureaucratic class could exploit to keep the military institution out of favour, and that there had always been the dilemma of 'bread versus bullet' in a country reeling in abject poverty, there is no denying that there were more competent methods of preserving that life-line of Indian nationhood without undermining its core competences. Indeed, the Indian state had consciously, if in culpable innocence, adopted strategically guileless policies to go by in its management of national defence.

Dilemma over Investment on Defence

A developing nation has many aches to balm. It is so that there are the commitments of social uplift, human resources development, economic progress and internal security, all of which have to be attended to with judiciously balanced alacrity alongside the matter of the nation's defence against external and internal threats. Indeed, a democratic government has to respond to partisan, if genuine, clamour arising simultaneously from all sectors for priority allocation of funds and facilities. With the spectre of five year accountability to the people looming overhead, it is only to be expected that under such conditions, the political leadership, both in and out of the government, would like to keep the defence expenditure to the bare minimum – relevance of military security is inexorably tied to the people's overall prosperity after all. There may have been some sense, therefore, in government's past procrastinations over incurring expenditure on its military institution, though arguably that may have been overdone during the last two decade or so to the extent of allowing the nation's so far stagnant military capability to be afflicted with disconcerting 'hollowness'. Viewed alongside the self-inflictions – like amateurish approach to defence research, industrial capacity building and harness of human resources– there is little doubt that want of strategic wisdom and foresight have been the bane of independent India's defence policymakers.

Lessons of political history tell us that while for any nation, preservation against external threats and internal turmoil both are equally salient, committal of national resources to the former is to be accorded a higher priority as compared to the latter. The reason is that unlike the constitution and penal codes through which a nation is governable, there are no exercisable laws in the international arena to contain injustice, highhandedness or aggression. Indeed, notwithstanding the facade of diplomatic practices to cover up international bullying and usurpation, 'might' continues to be the 'right' in the ultimate arbitration. Military power therefore remains the sole guarantor of sovereignty and relief from the ever-prowling predators and usurpers. That is the reason that even a yet developing country like India has to spend heavily on national defence.

Every nation goes through the dilemma of 'bread-versus-bullet' and social security versus military security. Actually, both being inseparable, this dilemma is an affliction of clouded mind. Indeed, mature governments, with due forethought and hoary wisdom, regularly find the right balance among these contending requirements. They do so by:

a) One, tuning their politico-military goals to be in compatibility with the resources allocable for military preparedness, as indeed Britain and France, among many others have; and,
b) Two, enjoining their military leadership to find, with equal measure of professional wisdom, ingenious ways to defend the nation through affordable combat power, as do Taiwan, Japan, Vietnam and Pakistan, among many others (2).

Regretfully, such is not the case with India; her huge fiscal commitment on defence remains anomalous on either count: One, the political goal remains ambiguous and incompatible with allocation of funds, facilities and wherewithal of war; and two, the military hierarchy, while having no option but to confine the scope of force-modernisation just to the acquisition of few of the current generation war-machines, remains satiated with old concepts and obsolete force-structures even when the adversaries, indeed all of the world militaries, have moved over to devise new strategies and organisations for prosecution of warfare in the contemporary era.

A defence policy that addresses the afore-stated anomalies and so reaps the benefits of cost-efficient defence capability must be the need of the day (3).

Signs of New Understanding

If the afore-stated self-infliction prevails today, visions of coming of a long overdue empowerment of India's defence capability seems to be on the horizon at last. This understanding is apparent by the government's pronouncements regarding redress of operational voids and modernisation of the defence infrastructure. Arguably, being subject to flagrant aggressive behaviour from inimical neighbours, the nation's rulers seem to be recovering from their weariness of military power, a search for international relevance acting as catalyst. If indeed India's defence policy-makers have been so sensitised, they may be better equipped in articulating that endeavour if:

a) The past system of policy-making as well as the policies made through that system, which led to the undermining the cerebral and material attributes of the military institution, is revisited;
b) A competent structure for management of national defence and a system of deliberate defence policy-making is instituted, and the role of military professionals in such processes are accorded due primacy;
c) Full range remoulding of the defence establishment, to accrual of advantages in wielding military power, is set in motion through promulgation of comprehensive and updated defence policies. These policies should be aimed at vitalising defence research, military technology, indigenous production of major military hardware, and better maintenance of operational and logistic assets.

No doubt, the Indian state's management of national defence has been far from astute. Even then, she has been lucky so far in preserving her nationhood – barring some territorial losses – without having to invest in military preparedness that should have been commensurate to her difficult situation. But time has come to accept that the emerging world order may not be so forgiving in the future. To restore the situation therefore, beginning may be made, first to find an appropriate structure for management of national defence, and designate that structure to operate an effective system of defence policy-making. There is hope that such a structure and the system it operates, would devise meaningful defence policies.

In this context, it would be interesting to see as to how other advanced nations go about preparing their defence capabilities, to address their challenges within resources affordable. This purpose would be attended to in the next chapter.

END NOTES AND SELECT REFERENCES

(1) This situation has its seeds in the self-pretentious policies adopted in the early years of India's Satayagrah-induced independence, which posited that: One, the defence industry need not produce anything but the most basic constabulary kind of hardware to maintain the military organisation in the state as it was, keeping

pace with military technological advancements being seen as contrary to India's advocacy of peace; two, it was despicable to earn 'blood' money from production and export of sophisticated military hardware; and three, as a corollary, defence industry could remain confined within state-control and out-of-bounds to private enterprise. This disoriented policy was one reason that India's progress in the field of pure sciences and technology remained well below par its actual potential.

(2) To cite some examples: One, Taiwan and Japan have prepared their tiny military institutions so optimally as to deter military adventurism of as powerful an adversary as the People's Republic of China (PRC); two, when confronted with the juggernaut of People's Liberation Army (PLA) in 1979, the Vietnamese Army resisted the aggression with its irregular forces while waiting on the home side of the mountainous terrain, thus forcing China to resort to a face-saving call-off; and three, Pakistan, unable to decimate her self-sworn enemy through conventional war, innovated the strategy of 'proxy war' to strike at the Indian nationhood. Thus while Taiwan, Japan and Vietnam have structured their military power with a potent mix of modernity and high quality manpower, Pakistan satisfies itself from thumbing nose to India's all round superiority through deft, if potentially suicidal, diplomacy and proxy operations.

(3) Air Commodore Jasjit Singh, "Security Environment in 2025: India's Interests and Strategies, USI Journal, Jan-Mar 2007, New Delhi.

*

CHAPTER 2

DEFENCE POLICY MAKING IN SOME ADVANCED NATIONS

"Only those who have strength, and are perceived to be willing to unleash it, can protect their interests without the use of force."

– **Luttwak**

Setting the Stage

A nation's defence capability is an exclusive investment that is dedicated to protect its interests when harmless forms of parlays fail to impress the adversary's quest for undue impositions. Political theory therefore mandates that enunciation of grand strategy, that is, as to when and to what extent a nation will choose to apply military power to protect her interests, and organising and equipping her defence sector for it to be able to secure those goals, is a role for the national leadership to undertake. These are the conditions which provide the foundation over which a nation's particular brand of defence policy is to be devised.

Obviously, an indigenous defence policy must harness the nation's intrinsic strengths, and at the same time cover its deficiencies, both these factors being conditioned by terrain, human resource, scientific temper and industrial capacity at the nation's disposal. Evolution of a best suited defence policy therefore requires conjoined involvement of the nation's political hierarchy, its military leadership and various contributing state-institutions such as those performing in the fields of science and technology, industry, education, transportation, and above all, the bureaucracy.

To see as to how competently have we been able to evolve our indigenous defence policies to address our security challenges in the contemporary era, it would be necessary to study the processes that have been adopted by leading powers in developing theirs in the post-World War II period. The intent is but to educate ourselves in devising our native brand of defence policies.

United States of America (USA)

Having found nationhood by the exertions of her citizen-soldiers, the United States (US) accords top priority to her defence policy-making through a constitutionally sanctified system. However, her military interests being inapplicable to India, we may confine ourselves just to the key processes followed in her post-World War II policy formulation, and learn from it.

The US Government is serious in regular issuance of formal mandates for her armed forces, so to keep her military institution in tune with the dynamics of her political goals. Thus was enacted the 'National Security Act of 1947' and its amendment in 1949, the 'Defence Reorganisation Act of 1958', and then the 'Goldwater-Nichols Department of Defence Reorganisation Act of 1986', the last one having been culled out of the thoroughly deliberated 'Locher Report' of January 1985 titled as 'Defence Reorganisation: The Need for Change' and the 'Blue Ribbon Commission on Defence Management', also known as 'Packard Commission' of June the same year. These Acts are followed up with defence policy amplifications at more frequent intervals, that is, whenever there is a revision of political dispensation that might call for reorientation of the nation's military objectives. Thus the US Department of Defence has evolved into a structure composed of the Office of the Secretary of State for Defence (Cabinet Minister) at its head, the establishment of the Joint Chiefs of Staff, the Service specific Departments of Army, Navy and Air Force, each having its own Secretary and Service Chief of Staff. The military forces are controlled through 'Specified' and 'Unified' Combat Commands, the former commanding the core service force-structure and the latter assuming command of joint operational order of battle as deployed to meet military objectives.

Another package of measures was adopted in the aftermath of 9/11 attacks, and then one again in 2005 after the Iraq War, which led to many initiatives on raisings, restructuring and interlinking of various branches within the defence establishment. Thus there is the system of promulgation of the 'Presidential Study Directives', the 'Presidential Policy Directives' and the 'Strategic Planning Guidance' for the defence policymakers to go by in managing the nation's military capabilities. Finally, there are the 'Quadrennial Defence Reviews' which are carried out at frequent intervals to enunciate the aspects of course corrections that might be needed for the articulation of military power in exercise of dynamic political choices.

Toned to contemporary perfection, the apex body for management of the military institution in the USA is the 'National Command Authority' headed by the President and Commander-in-Chief and seconded by two organs, namely, the 'National Security Council' headed by the National Security Advisor, and the US Department of Defence (DoD) headed by the Secretary of Defence. Notably, as a balancing forum, the Senate wields considerable approving authority over the DoD as well as the fundamental matters related to the military institution. Chairman, Joint Chiefs of Staff is the top military advisor to the political leadership including the Congress and the final authority for formulation of joint forces doctrines and strategies (1).

The next rung of defence hierarchy is divided into three streams, as follows:

a) The Departments of the Army, Navy and Air Force. These Departments are headed by the Secretaries of the Army, Navy and Air Force respectively. The next tier consists of two components. One is headed by an Under Secretary and performs bureaucratic staff work, while the other component consists of the Chiefs of Staff of each of the Services who command and control all the Services assets – warlike, logistic, training, personnel management and regimental. The fourth arm of the military institution, the US Marine Corps, under its own Commandant, is administratively controlled at its apex level by the Chief of Naval Operations while operational control vests with the Joint Chiefs of Staff. The Chiefs of Staff are also the fountainhead for service-specific doctrinal, strategic and force-structuring aspects. Lastly, except for actual war, when tri-service plus Marine force structure in various theatres are grouped under the 'Joint Forces Commander(s)-in-Chief', the Service Chiefs of Staff superintend the combat formations and units through their subordinate 'Component Force Commanders' down to the last unit.

b) Operational Chain of Command. In the US military, war-time operational command devolves from the Commander-in-Chief

(President) to the Joint Forces Commanders-in-Chief of various theatres of war which cover nearly the entire globe. In performing his role in political direction of war, the President is assisted by the Secretary of Defence while the Chairman, Joint Chiefs of Staff, advises the President in approval of operational plans, spells out the military aim, allocates war resources, and monitors the conduct of operations.

c) Defence Acquisition Programming and Budgeting System. This is a specialist-intensive System with due technical, operational and fiscal expertise. Guided in it pursuits by the Chairman, Joint Chiefs of Staff through 'Joint Strategic Plans', 'Defence Planning Guidances' and 'Presidential Directives' as considered relevant from time to time, the role of this system in securing optimal military value against expenditure from public exchequer is commendable (2).

Inheritors of astute strategic vision, the US military institution itself remains, at all times, engaged in search of professional excellences through engagement with in-house as well as independent think-tanks which are subscribed to by veteran members of the fraternity. The US military is also more willing to experiment and implement new ideas as compared to other orthodox militaries that are either unenthusiastic or suspicious of change. To illustrate, the 'Presidential Policy Directive' of 2009, promulgated at the time of engagement in the Middle East, was followed up by the 'Strategic Planning Guidance' in 2013 at the time of disengagement, in which it was unambiguously declared that, "...military influence will help shape the global environment ... to respond quickly around the world ... that advances US national security and contributes to global peace and stability ...". Then, at the time of debate over part-sequestering of military assets, came the issuance of the 'Quadrennial Defence Review' of 2014. This document focused on 'rebalancing' – reduction actually – of the defence commitments in response to fiscal constraints. Corresponding to lower political goals, this Review motivated the military leadership to scale down the forces while retaining the ability to regain at short notice (3).

These are the formal policy promulgations of the American state that orients its entire defence sector towards its desired direction in terms of:

a) Future force planning and administration of reserve forces;
b) Professional military advise to the President, the National Security Council and the Secretary of Defence;

c) Assignment of precise responsibilities for military preparedness and achievement of military objectives to the Specified and Unified Military Commands respectively;
d) Integration of national intelligence capabilities into military planning and operational preparedness;
e) National level management of military logistics;
f) Focus of defence research, military industrial targets and arms sales;
g) System of defence procurements, defence budgeting and investments on hardware development; and,
h) Management of human resources and welfare of veterans.

However, it must be qualified here that in the American dispensation, military factor is intrinsic to political articulations, and therefore the governing system of the state is highly conducive to dynamic changes in its force-structuring and management processes without dither or delay – sequestering and re-mobilising for example. That is a flexibility that permits the US Government to reconcile its military objectives with fiscal prudence.

In conformity to the above mentioned policy promulgations, the current missions for the US Armed Forces are set out as follows:

a) Counter-insurgency operations, irregular warfare and counter-terrorism;
b) To deter and defeat aggression, and maintain effective nuclear deterrent;
c) To counter weapons of mass destruction;
d) Defence of the homeland and provision of support to civil authorities;
e) Projection of power despite Anti-Access/Area Denial Challenges;
f) To operate effectively in space and cyberspace;
g) To provide a 'Stabilising Presence'; and,
h) Conduct of humanitarian assistance, disaster relief and other operations.

In accordance with the above, the US military institution sets out its vision, broadly as follows:

a) Prevent, Shape and Win as part of the Joint Force;
b) Interoperability with allied forces;
c) Expeditionary capability; and
d) Build 'Future Forces' in the shape of:
   - Regionally Aligned Forces;

- Mission Tailored Forces;
- Space and cyberspace forces;
- Training and leader development programme; and
- Schemes and timing for modernisation with due prioritisation.

Indeed, there may not be a more efficient example of political management of military power than what the American system follows. Notably, besides dynamic rightsizing of the military forces in conformity to the government's changing priorities, the best dividends reaped from that system are reflected in:

a) One, profitable assimilation of military industry into the nation's economy; and,
b) Two, attracting the necessary numbers and quality of manpower to uphold the

'Stars and Eagle' banner, even against the citizens' usual disinclination to enlist.

Be that as it may, we may confine our focus to the process of defence policy formulation in the US government and, as stated before, not delve into the policies actually adopted because our concerns and capacities are in fundamental contrast. However, the matters to be taken note of in the context of US military administration are:

a) There is deliberate effort to avoid mismatch between political direction, military strategy and resources allocated to purpose. This effort is translated by means of issuance of 'Quadrennial Defence Reviews' at regular intervals since 1997. These Reviews are further amplified by the promulgations of 'Defence Planning Guidance' and 'Programme Objective Memoranda', whenever considered necessary.
b) The remarkable dynamics of defence budgeting while sustaining military capability. This dynamics is observable when allocations fell after the Gulf War, drastically rose by 77 per cent after the 9/11 attack, and then had to be capped by the 'Budget Control Act' of 2011. Presently, a 'sequestering policy' has been promulgated under which by 2020 the allocation would be reduced by 17 per cent, while the matter remains in debate.
c) Creation of a 'Defence Logistics Agency' under the Department of Defence while the Army, Navy and Air Force have logistic commands of their own.

In February, 2015, the US, through a Presidential proclamation, enunciated its latest 'National Security Strategy' thus elaborating upon a wide spectrum of national security endeavours. The key military features of this Strategy are: to maintain a national military establishment that is, to quote, "the best trained, equipped, and led force in the world", to be ready to be used as an instrument of power, to provide security to American citizens within the homeland and abroad, to keep the world safe by dealing with terrorism and nuclear threat, to strengthen global alliances and partnerships in maintaining global peace and stability, and so on – each role thereof having many faceted elaborations. In June 2016, the DoD announced, as one more step towards its 'Force of the Future' initiative by modernising the rules and regulations that govern recruitment, development and retention of its service members and civilian employees – all aimed at flexibility in gaining the best out of the nation's human resources and their specific skills.

Russia

In the aftermath of the break-up of Union of Soviet Socialist Republics (USSR), the once mighty Red Army was starved to such a pathetic state that Russia had to accept a state of stalemate in the First Chechen War (1994-96) – the province becoming more or less independent. In the Second Chechen War (1999), a part of the Russian Armed Forces were resuscitated by internal 'milking' and thus the rebellion was crushed, albeit tenuously.

As economy started showing signs of recovery at the turn of a decade, the political leadership was quick to set its new military goals in anticipation. This led to streamlining and activation of a revised system of defence policy-making at the level of the 'Russian Federation Security Council' in conjunction with the Ministries of Defence and Foreign Affairs. At the next stage, promulgation of new defence policies had been undertaken through different branches of the Government. Accordingly, matters related to defence infrastructure and management of the combat forces are dealt with by the Ministry of Defence and its military-manned General Staff, while other ministries are required to shoulder their part of national defence responsibilities in mutual coordination.

The system of management of national defence in the Russian Federation has the Security Council and the Supreme High command headed by the President at its apex while the Minister of Defence is the functional head. The next tier is made up of the tri-service 'General Staff' headed by the Chief of General Staff, which more or less retains its past composition made up of operations, intelligence, logistics and armament departments. Executive command and control over all aspects of management of the forces vests upon the three Service Chiefs. In war-time, theatre or regional commands assume the operational control of the forces placed at their disposal by the General Staff (4).

The process of deliberate defence policy formulation in the new Russian Federation commenced with issuance of the Presidential Decree of 1997, followed by the 'National Security Concept' in the same year. These directives called for a long-term process of reform and re-structuring of the system of defence management as well as the military force-structure, while relying upon nuclear forces to cover the deficiencies in conventional military power. These led to the formalisation of the 'Military Doctrine 2000' and the 'Foreign Policy Concept', which in turn led to the 'Military Re-structuring Plan, 2005'.

Meanwhile, a Defence White Paper, titled 'Urgent Tasks for Development of Armed Forces of Russian Federation' was promulgated in 2003, and that was followed up by the 'State Weapons Programme 2015', for the defence planners to be ready with plans in conformity with the political dictates. In 2007, and updated in 2010, a new 'Draft Military Doctrine' amplified the desired direction for the defence policy-makers to proceed with a view to 'reform' the defence structure, 'modernise' the armed forces and promote defence industry. As the 'Presidential Decree, 2010' called for, the purpose was to ensure "Russia's security and prestige". Thus guided by astute political directives, the Russian military as well as the defence establishment were mandated according to the following policies:

a) 'Instability on Southern Border', 'Radical Religionism', 'Separatist Movements' and 'Trans-national Crime and Terrorism' are to be targeted as the 'national threats'.
b) Modernisation of the forces is to be effected by: One, upgrade of existing weaponry and equipment; two, raising the quality of intake and training of military personnel; and three, manpower cuts in units and reduction in number of officers.
c) Armed forces are reduced to 1.1 million, with professional rather than conscript soldiery.
d) External and internal threats are to be viewed as one composite challenge.
e) Creation of 'National Counter Terrorism Committee', 'Federal Security Force' and a 'Peace Keeping Brigade', each with its dedicated role.

f) Thrust on 'space' rather than terrestrial systems as the medium for application of net-centricity in warfare.
g) Dependence on nuclear 'triad' to cover conventional weakness till a 'proportionality of power' is achieved, by 2020.

Remarkably, the enunciated defence policies cover the entire gamut of Russia's defence preparedness with key roles assigned to the defence establishments and defence industry. Further, the military force-structure having become imbalanced to the level of ineffectiveness, equipment modernisation and corresponding transformation of the military structure were identified as priority tasks facing the Russian defence planners, the priority concerns being in the aspects of aerospace defence, re-armament, quality of troops and their training, pay, and housing. The Russian Government has undertaken to secure the abovementioned objectives by means of a two-pronged approach, as follows:

a) 'Structural Reforms', to shift to a structure that is "more suited to 21st Century warfare and tuned to local and regional conflicts". Thus a three-tiered organisational structure for the military institution with the brigade as the basic formation, unified strategic commands, cutting down on officers, and doing away with conscription in favour of a professional army are the recourses adopted. These reforms aim at better operational coordination, improved mobility, and full combat-readiness of the military forces.
b) 'Material Reforms', to equip the armed forces with state-of-the-art weaponry and to address personnel management issues such as education, training, pay and housing for the armed forces personnel.

Under implementation since 2008, it is reported that most of the Structural Reforms have already been implemented while the Material Reforms, which are necessary to ensure that the structural reforms deliver, are progressing well. The 'State Armaments Programme 2020' (SAP-2020) is the first component of the Material Reforms; with the state of arms and equipment falling to abysmal levels, the SAP was devised to restore Russia's military power. It is a ten-year armament programme which is expected to modernise 70 per cent of Russia's weapons by 2020. The Russian defence industry has a key role to play in the implementation of the armament programme by responding to the defence procurement orders. To this purpose, the Government has committed to revitalising the defence industry and improve production of military hardware. Another area of focus is the defence research and development wherein the level of investments has been considerably enhanced.

Notably, it was a fallout of the 2008 Reforms, that the 'modular' brigade was adopted as the basic fighting formation with restructuring into 85 such brigades of 4500-5000 combatants each and a commitment to reequip the forces with latest weaponry and hardware by 2025. Shift to the system of Joint Regional Command was also a part of that Reform. In similar vein, the number of military personnel was reduced from 1.2 million to 1 million men, staff in the Ministry of Defence reduced from 11000 to 5000 personnel, and the officer-heavy General Staff cut down from 10500 to 3500.

The second component of 'Material Reforms', that is, improving the quality of the soldiery and their upkeep and training, has been found to be a vexed socio-economic issue, and the progress has been slow but resolute.

Russia's defence policies have been updated in 2014 in response to the Crimea-Ukraine crisis. Thus was promulgated a fourth version, in past two decades, of its military doctrine. This is a heavily loaded version, the added aspects of the policy being as follows:

a) NATO's military capabilities are considered as the main threats to national security.
b) External threats to Russia's interests are cited as: One, growth in deployment of strategic missile defence systems; two, propagation of the 'global strike' doctrine; three, placement of weapons in space; and four, targeting by high-precision conventional weapons systems.
c) Main internal threats are identified as: One, activities aimed at destabilising the country; two, terrorist activities against sovereignty and territorial integrity of Russia; and three, anti-Russian and 'anti-patriotic' propaganda.
d) The main objectives for the armed forces and rest of the defence establishment now include "the protection of national interests of the Russian Federation in the Arctic."

No doubt that guided by issuance of clear cut policy directives at the political level, all organs of the state are well focused in exerting towards Russia's defence build-up. By the 2020's, therefore, resurgence of Russian military power is well on the cards (5).

Even if the defence commitments are rather divergent, Russia's case is somewhat closer to the Indian situation, to the extent that both are concerned of their dated and debilitated defence capabilities. In that, the alacrity with which clear-cut defence policies are enunciated and then updated regularly, and the focused approach adopted to the implementation of these, are notable features of the Russian system of management of national defence.

United Kingdom (UK)

As its successor government, India's defence bureaucracy remains beholden to the system of defence policy-making in the British system as it had obtained at the time of independence. The problem, however, is that being bereft of deeper insight for astute management of national defence, seven decades down the line, India's defence bureaucracy and its superfluously advised political leadership seem to remain frozen in that time wrap. That conceptual inertness indeed is the core cause of the ills that afflict the political management of defence in India. Meanwhile, in tune with their contemporary challenges and strategic commitments, the British have switched over to a completely revamped system.

Tailoring her defence establishment in tune with the rise and fall of British Empire, defence policy-making in Britain has been a dynamic process since the early 20th Century. It is so that in December 1945 itself, just after the World War II, a committee of three experienced military experts was appointed to set up a Ministry of Defence (MoD) which could be designated to formulate "unified defence policy for all three Services". Subsequently, the entire defence structure was gradually revamped through the following initiatives at the political level:

a) The 'Duncan Sandys (Minister of Defence) Reforms of 1958', to streamline the 'Central Organisation of Defence'.
b) The 'Mountbatten (Chief of Defence Staff) Reforms of 1960', to reorganise the military force-structure and promote unified system of command. In 1964, at Prime Minister Macmillan's initiative, these changes were further fine-tuned by Lords Ismay and Jacob. The result was the establishment of a unified MoD to coordinate the inter-service matters and enunciate policy issues.
c) Quantum revamp of the roles, structure and procedures in respect of: One, the MoD in 1967; two, personnel and logistics management system in 1969; three, management of defence procurements in 1970; and four, management of defence finance in 1977.
d) Another round of reforms, necessitated by practical difficulties of implementation of the new defence policies, was undertaken

through the 'Lewin (Chief of Defence Staff) and Nott (Secretary of State for Defence) Reforms of 1980'. Next followed the 'Heseltine (Secretary of the State) Review of 1984', which formalised the hierarchy of defence policy-making.

Notably, revisions in defence policies had been vigorously contested at each stage by imperialist as well as military hardliners, and resisted at each stage by vicious inter-service rivalry. Success of that endeavour was however in evidence in the Falkland War (1982) and the Gulf War I (1991) when the nucleus of war time force-structure could be quickly expanded and comprehensibly empowered in a short time, with commendable results. Finally, in scaling its defence establishment within the two key parameters of the 'Cold War' and economic viability, Britain's political leadership was able to reconcile the entire system with the contemporary national priorities.

In the post-Cold War dispensation, in 1998, the British Government undertook a professionally objective 'Strategic Defence Review', followed by issuance, in 2003, of a 'Defence White Paper'. Thus was enunciated the following doctrinal and functional policy directives from the political leadership to the military institution as well as the larger defence establishment:

a) Structuring of 'Joint Force 2000' – consisting of Joint Defence Doctrine Centre, Joint Helicopter Command, Joint Ground Based Air Defence, and Joint Nuclear, Chemical and Biological Defence – headed by a four-star officer, who is designated as the 'Chief of Joint Operations'.
b) The entire gamut of defence logistics – including industry, production, capital acquisition and maintenance of military hardware, and operation of the defence supply chain, storage and distribution, movement and transportation, medical support etc. – was delinked from the combat hierarchy and brought under an autonomous organisation headed by another four-star officer from the combat support arms (Engineers), and designated as the 'Chief of Defence Material', of status equivalent to the Vice Chief of Defence Staff to function under the aegis of a 'Defence Logistic Board'. The Defence Logistic Organisation and the Defence Procurement Agency were thus combined under the Chief of Defence Materials, under whom functions the 'Chiefs of Materials' for each Service.

The above mentioned policy directives were the result of deep and deliberate studies, confabulations, debates and experimentations among the nation's top military and civilian experts. Indeed, it was the nation's political leadership that displayed the wisdom to initiate that process and guide it through its course. To this purpose, the political leadership was wise to call upon highly regarded military intellectuals and civilian experts in the field of defence industry to work out the right mechanisms in dealing with the contemporary challenges to national defence. Thus by 2008, fresh reviews of the apex level defence structure and management could be followed up with improving the measures to make these operationally more effective and administratively efficient.

Notably, British government's revised defence policies have been instrumental in fostering autonomous distinction of defence logistics, industry and fiscal management from operational combat forces, the idea being to delink long term, multi-sector and quasi-military ventures from the dynamics of force-structuring for war. But more importantly, these unambiguous policy directions have made it possible for the military leadership to focus on meeting the political mandate within the resources demanded and allocated. It is so that the following strategic concepts have been found ripe for implementation:

a) Structuring of a 'Joint Rapid Reaction Force' having expeditionary capabilities to operate in conjunction with the American Forces;
b) Projection of power through carrier-borne forces;
c) Emphasis on littoral, brown water – rather than blue water – operational capabilities;
d) The Air Force is geared up to undertake air-lift and stand-off operations;
e) Reductions in heavy armour, infantry, land-based aircraft and anti-submarine ships;
f) Restructuring the Army into two light, three medium and two heavy brigades;
g) Grouping of the legendry Special Air Service, the Special Boat Service and the newly raised Special Reconnaissance Regiments into a 'Special Forces Group';
h) For homeland security, a Para-military 'Civil Contingency Reaction Force' was raised to operate under the Home Office.

The latest initiative of British government in tuning the nation's defence forces finds expression through the promulgation of 'Strategic Defence and

Security Review of 2010'. This was a policy review over military force-structuring with its focus on "the Armed Forces which the UK will need over the next decade and beyond to meet the most likely future threats". Discard of the aircraft carrier project and some smaller ones and nearly one-fourth reduction in the establishments of defence headquarters and estate management office were the outcome of this Review. It is expected that more cuts to unaffordable ventures may be due yet in the next review. However, realising that policy-making was one thing but its implementation was quite another and that the latter was contingent upon reconditioning of the entire system, the British government simultaneously went ahead with the constitution of a committee headed by Lord Levene and entrusted it with the task of carrying out a "full and fundamental review of the way national defence was being managed". Thus was finalised a comprehensive report on 'Defence Reforms', covering the structure and higher management of national defence and measures to make these operationally as well as administratively more cost-efficient (6).

The Levene Report made 53 recommendations, remarkable among these being integration of policy-making, right balance between centralisation and decentralisation, operational and logistic jointness, and strengthening the professional relationships between the Prime Minister, Defence Minister (Secretary of State) and the Service Chiefs. It went on further to delineate the responsibilities between the defence cadre civilian bureaucracy and the military staff, the former having heavier representation in defence logistics, industry and fiscal management while the latter retaining predominance in operational policy-making. Another remarkable recommendation was to reconvene a monitoring committee on annual basis to report progress on implementation of the policies to the Parliament through the Secretary of State. Notably, it was a result of these landmark political initiatives that a 'Top Office Group' consisting of the highest civil and military officials was convened to oversee the nation's defence preparedness vis-à-vis the political mandate ascribed to the armed forces as well as the rest of the defence establishment and industry. Curiously, in their corporatised instincts, the forces were described as the 'User Process Owner' while the material managers were designated as the 'Service Provider Process Owner'.

No doubt, the frequent and far-reaching changes in the Britain's higher defence management and military force-structure were a direct result of disintegration of the British Empire which caused her strategic commitments to undergo vast down-scaling. Consequently, the process of formulation of the national defence policy is guided by the directives of 'Defence and

Overseas Policy Sub-Committee' of the British Cabinet headed by the Prime Minister, and promulgated by the 'Defence Council'. The last named is the apex policy-making body on matters of national defence, and consists of the Secretary of State for Defence, the Chief of Defence Staff, Permanent Under Secretary of State, the three Service Chiefs, Chief of Defence Procurements, and few other professionals.

In the present British system, the Department of Defence is also the Headquarters of the Chief of Defence Staff as well that of the three Services. Within the MoD, headed by the Secretary of State for Defence, management of the defence sector is carried out by the 'Top Office Group' which consists of the Chief of Defence Staff and the Permanent Under Secretary of State; the former managing the military institution and the latter the other components of defence establishment like finance, procurement, research and development, estates, move, maintenance, etc. The next rung of the military institution is composed of the three Service Chiefs, a Chief of Joint Operations and a Chief of Defence Material. Thus, in war time, command and control of joint Services forces vests upon the Chief of Joint Operations. The Chief of Defence Material is a semi-autonomous organisation headed by another four star officer and charged with the entire gamut of military logistics starting from projections, production, procurement and supply to the three Services through dedicated Chiefs of Materials or Directors Generals of Logistics for each of the services.

There are remarkable features to note in respect of the British government's management of the nation's military power within affordable fiscal commitments. These may be summarised as follows:

a) One feature is that the contemporary political leadership, bereft as it is of much of military-strategic insight, is wise in calling upon military intellectuals to lead the systemic review committees.
b) The second feature is that while the higher management of defence is entrusted to civilian and military experts in the ratio of 3:1, that ratio is reversed at the policy-making level, thus making it military predominant.
c) The third feature is that control as well as accountability of the military-centric, combat dedicated armed forces and their operational logistics has been segregated from that of the base defence logistics and industrial sectors. By implication, defence establishments are made accountable for the maintenance of the military institution.

These measures have allowed the British government to:

a) Keep the armed forces lean, young, professionally focused and flexible to mobilise at short notice, and demobilise, as necessary;
b) Harness the professional expertise of senior and experienced military officers in the process of precise defence policy-making; and,
c) Marshal competent civilian experts and a permanently dedicated defence bureaucracy to push a vast defence industry towards best productivity.

Another feature of the British initiative is that there is strict monitoring of implementation of the policies. Inheritors of strong strategic vision, Britain is thus able to articulate her military power much in excess of her rather small armed forces and thus extract maximum advantages of its optimal investment on military institution.

Australia

Tormented by growing disquiet in the Pacific Region in the recent years, the Australian government has committed to a very astute exercise of defence policy-making that is focused on maritime surveillance, littoral warfare and stand-off operations to protect its vast shores. Their defence policies are therefore aimed at maintaining a compact but potent armed force to retain their relevancy in the Western Block and to provide for expansion should the course of global politics so demand.

Australia's Defence White Paper, released by the Prime Minister himself in February 2016, is aimed at achievement of "full alignment of national strategy, capability and resources to make the Australian Defence Force more capable, agile and potent". Australia thus commits to increase defence spending over the next decade, and through a 10-year 'Integrated Investment Program and Defence Industry Policy Statement', invest on new weaponry, military infrastructure and science and technology skills to promote naval shipbuilding, intelligence, surveillance and reconnaissance, space, electronic warfare and cyber capabilities. The White Paper further commits to advanced training, modern equipment, better health care and efficient logistics systems for the Australian Defence Force. Lastly, Australia's national defence policy aims at harnessing native innovation and expertise to extend advantages of its defence industrial base to the rest of the economy, creating jobs and encouraging regional businesses and export potential. In a situation not unlike India, Australia's defence policies are worth taking note of by our defence planners.

France

Inheritors of great military traditions, France offers a good example of deliberate curtailment of defence expenditure to take clever advantage of their membership of NATO while doing one better by keeping her defence industry in profitable trade. Sedated by decades of peace and societal softening under a far-liberal democracy, the French government had been jolted by the sloth mobilisation and professional dilutions seen during the coalition operations in the Gulf War I. The Government then sought to resuscitate its defence structure through articulation, in 1996, of its 'Modernisation Model 2015', to be implement through a series of five year 'Defence Programme Laws'. Updated and amplified at regular intervals, the last one being in 2013, the basic features enunciated in these 'Laws' may be summarised as follows :

a) Ability to project military power worldwide;
b) Dependence on strategic sea-lift rather than air-lift;
c) Interoperability with allied forces;
d) Priorities of capability build up are spelt out as: satellite based net-centricity, mobility, tactical deployability, precision deep-strike and protection of troops from weapons of mass destruction;
e) The force is re-structured into nine 'flexible brigades' made up of fifty one 'manoeuvre regiments', including Special Forces units.
f) Overall strength of troops is reduced from 2,50,000 to 1,35,000 professionals of high quality.

According to the latest Defence White Paper of 2013, France enunciates a new armed forces model based on a 'principle' that is defined by the term 'Operational Contract', and which is promulgated by no less than the Head of State. This principle requires the French military institution to be enabled in conduct of a broad spectrum of engagements that include intervention missions. For comprehensive guidance of the managers of national defence, the 'Operational Contract' is further translated into specifics of the capacities which the military institution must possess. In terms of military force-structure and operational tasking, the specifics are as follows:

a) Capability to deploy approximately 66,000 land forces composed of seven joint, two combat, three multi-purpose and two light brigades, 200 heavy and 250 medium tanks, 115 utility helicopters, 140 reconnaissance and attack helicopters and some 30 tactical drones, besides the support and logistic back up forces;

b) The Naval forces are built around a 'Strategic Oceanic Force' with four nuclear-powered ballistic missile submarines for high-intensity combat operations, and a 'Crisis Management Missions Force' consisting of an aircraft carrier, six nuclear-powered attack submarines, three combined support and command vessels and 15 frontline multi-mission frigates. Besides, 15 patrol boats, six surveillance frigates, and required numbers of naval patrol aircraft, mine-laying capability and support vessels are specified for the protection of France's maritime spaces;

c) The Air Force is tasked to deploy in deterrence missions, followed by preliminary, deep-penetration and ground manoeuvre support operations on the one hand; and on the other hand to conduct crisis management missions or missions to protect national air space. Besides, air transport, surveillance and intelligence capabilities are to be upgraded. To this end, the inventory shall be composed of 225 air and naval fighter aircraft, 50 odd tactical transport aircraft, 12 multi-role refuelling aircraft, 12 theatre surveillance drones, seven detection and aerial surveillance aircraft and a fleet of light surveillance aircrafts.

The specifics are further elaborated by the flowing key directives:

a) To undertake 'deterrence missions' in protection of territory and population over land, sea and sea approaches, the force-structure would confirm to the capability of fielding up to 10,000 troops at the level of an army brigade or equivalent, together with the relevant resources of naval and air forces;

b) To engage, where necessary, in international crisis management across three geographical theatres, with resources consisting of up to 7,000 troops, naval units including a combined support and command vessel group, and approximately 12 fighter aircraft;

c) To engage in major coercive operations involving the special forces of up to two combat brigades, representing approximately 15,000 land troops, 45 fighter aircraft and naval aviation;

d) Priority development of land, sea, air and space based intelligence with commitment of modern human and technical resources;

e) Development of military cyber defence capabilities as part of intelligence and operational planning;

f) Upgrade of Special Forces of the 'Special Operations Command' in terms of personnel, command and intelligence capabilities.

Finally, in keeping with the traditional French policy, the White Paper goes on recognise the defence industry as an essential component of France's strategic autonomy, which, with over 4,000 companies and hundreds of thousands of jobs, is viewed as an export oriented pillar of French economy.

Germany

Chary of reviving her past Bismarckian posture, Germany maintains a very precise defence establishment that barely meets the NATO's military stipulations. Accordingly, she has enunciated her political directions to her armed forces through promulgation of 'Defence White Paper, 1994', 'Blue Ribbon Commission, 2000', 'Defence Policy Guidelines, 2003', 'Defence White Paper, 2006' and its subsequent amplifications like the 'Defence Policy Guidelines 2011'. Germany's defence policies are thus indicated by the adoption of the following measures:-

a) Six areas of modernisation are specified in conformity to alliance commitments;
b) The strength is reduced from 3,40,000 to 2,50,000. Conscription is to continue, mainly to foster social discipline;
c) The erstwhile 'Crisis Reaction Force' (50,000) and the rest of the 'Main Defence Force' are restructured into:
    i) Intervention Forces (35,000) for 'high intelligence tasks';
    ii) Stabilisation Forces (70,000) for medium or low intensity operations;
    iii) Support Forces (1,47,000) for 'stabilisation' operations and homeland defence;
    iv) A 'Special Forces Command' has been raised with two each of special operations divisions and air-borne brigades;
    v) Notably, the civil transportation sector has been earmarked for strategic air and sea-lift purposes.

Point to note is that even if varying in nomenclature and finer details, all the three nations – Australia, France and Germany – have Ministers of Defence and Chiefs of Defence Staff at the apex of the system of defence management, followed by three Service Chiefs, small bureaucracies to attend to matters of general administration and semi-autonomous departments of logistics, armaments and procurements (7).

Defence Policy in Some Other Nations

Interestingly, there are also some unique examples of defence policy-making. For example, Saudi Arabia has opted for state-of-the-art military capabilities in intelligence machinery and conventional warfare to protect her royal regime against its growing list of fanatical detractors. In a converse example, Pakistan government's defence policy-making is dictated by her military doctrine – rather than the other way round. This is a doctrine that propagates 'offensive-defence', proxy-war, nuclear proliferation, 'jihadi terrorism' and subversive intelligence operations – a combination made most dangerous by her access to modern American military thinking, funding from Islamic nations and obsessive anti-Indian affliction. Here, military doctrine seems to dictate politics – a situation not usually envisaged elsewhere (8).

China's Defence Policy and Military Modernisation

In the scheme of People's Republic of China (PRC), military power is a fundamental plank of statehood, which in turn is the preserve of the Communist Party of China (CPC). Therefore, national policy-making in PRC is indistinguishable with that of the Party's, just as the civilian and military policy makers are but one body, more or less. Thus the Politburo of the Communist Party and its core military authority, the Party's 'Central Military Commission' (CMC), are mirrored in the government in the form of 'State Council' and its 'National Military Commission' respectively. Conversely, the Ministry of National Defence functions notionally under the National Military Commission and confined its control to defence industry, military diplomacy and higher management of the People's Armed Police Forces (PAPF). This system permits China's military institution to have its policy directives clearly spelt out by the CMC, and marshal all the other state institutions to further the People's Liberation Army's (PLA) objectives.

Till recently, when the latest set of modernisation at the apex level was promulgated and slated to be completed by 2020, the PLA had been controlled through its General Headquarters under the guidance of the CMC. The PLA General Headquarters functioned through four Departments, namely, the 'General Staff', 'General Logistics', 'General Armament' and the General Political' Departments, each headed by senior four star officer. Thus the CMC and the head of the General Staff acted in the manner of a defence council consisting of experienced military officers. The next tier consisted of Military Area Commands (MAC), seven of these, which controlled all forces, including the PAPF located in their respective Military Regions (MR). Both, the PLA General Headquarters and Headquarters MAC had tri-service composition, though representation of the PLA Army had been overwhelming. The third tier consisted of static Military Districts (MD) and combat formations in the form of Group Armies, varying numbers of which the MACs exercised control over.

Further, under the concept of 'War Zone Campaign' (WZC), a specially constituted Joint Forces Headquarters, taking its directions directly from the CMC, had been designated to be planted on the MAC through whose region the doctrine of 'informationalised warfare with Chinese characteristics' was intended to be applied against the chosen adversary. Notably, most of the so described system remains valid even in the new dispensation which came into force in the final months of 2015, wherein many informal changes introduced over the past decade or so in the organisation of the PLA General Headquarters have been formalised; besides, there are certain synergic improvements at the top, as highlighted in the last paragraph (9).

When the PRC set its course towards 'Four Modernisations' in early 1980's, its leadership had the wisdom to slot 'Military Modernisation' at the fourth place. Meanwhile, having been jolted by its tardy performance in the war with Vietnam in 1979 and the display of the campaigning might of the 'Revolution in Military Affairs' (RMA) in Gulf War I, the purpose sought by the PLA was to harness the rest of the modernised state institutions in boosting its operational strengths and so gear up to fulfil the national dream of achieving a super-power status in the contemporary world order.

Promulgated under the 'National Military Strategy Guidelines for the New Period' of 1993 vintage and its updated series of 'Defence White Papers' that enunciate the purpose as 'Fighting Local Wars Under Conditions of Informationisation', China's 'military modernisation' has been a well-articulated and deliberate initiative. Towards that goal, the defence policy challenges have been indicatively spelt out as:

a) Integration of Taiwan;
b) Containment of America's role in Asia and dealing with Japan's military challenge;
c) Maintenance of national integrity and internal security in the peripheral territories, particularly in Xizang (Tibet) and Xinjiang;
d) Enable national growth through protection of overseas assets and lines of transportation, and engagement in economic schemes in remote areas.

Implicit in the CMC's defence policy is the preservation of Communist rule and China's hegemonic predominance in the neighbourhood. PRC's defence policies are promulgated, implemented and revisited accordingly. It is that singularity of purpose that has enjoined the PLA to develop its doctrine of 'Integrated Joint Warfare' and formalise its execution under the concept of 'War Zone Campaign' – all under the overarching ambit of a war-waging concept of 'infromationaisation with Chinese characteristics' and 'innovation of asymmetric strategies'.

In restructuring its military establishment, PRC's defence policies are aimed at the following end results:

a) Upgrade of military-industry through indigenous technological research and development, import of dual-use technologies and transfer of military technology from Russia and Israel.
b) Expansion of military as well as quasi-military industrial base to cover the entire range of technologies – nuclear, aviation, missile, space, ship-building, communication, engineering, down to small arms and other wherewithal of war.
c) Structuring of the Ministry of National Defence in tune with the CMC Departments, and upgrade of the 'People's Armed Police Force' (PAPF) as another arm to maintain internal stability and control internal rebellions.
d) Restructure of the joint 'Military Regions', and reorganisation of field formations into 'combined corps', divisions and brigades, the last being accepted as the basic fighting formation. Upgrade of the 'Second Artillery Corps' which operates nuclear and missile forces into a more autonomous entity is a part of that initiative.
e) Reduction of manpower from 2.3 million to 1.7 million by transfer of the massive ranks of non-combat employees and rationalisation of combat units. Besides modernisation of weaponry and equipment, this reduction is also sought to be compensated through qualitative 'professionalisation' of the soldiery, their scientific education and empowerment of the 'cutting edge' – the Non-Commissioned Officers.
f) Centralised control over Information Warfare (IW) resources – reconnaissance, navigation, unmanned aerial vehicles, etc. – and development of cyber-war, space-war, and the 'Three Warfares' – psychological, media and 'legal' warfare, to wit – capabilities.

g) Initiation of high-technology space and counter-space programmes with thrust on development of reconnaissance, navigation and communication satellites and satellite interception capability.
h) Infusion of strategic capabilities into the PLA Navy and PLA Air Force for longer ranges of operation, precision strike capability and multi-dimensional deployment of marine and air-borne corps.
j) Nomination and capability enhancement of 'Rapid Reaction Forces' and 'Special Operation Forces', into 'Packets of Excellence'.
k) Development of 'Integrated Logistic System' to support intra and inter-service operations.
l) Sustained allocation of defence budget with an average annual growth of around 12 per cent, to facilitate focused and long-term planning (10).

Strategic wisdom in China's defence policy-making is further reflected in her promulgation of transformational timelines, as follows:

a) Full activation of the modernised systemic order by 2020;
b) Course correction and implementation of informationalised military capabilities by 2030;
c) Completion of full range of modernisation by 2050.

Presently, The CMC has announced the commencement of its next step of PLA modernisation. The four main Departments and 11 subordinate Offices and Cells which formed the PLA General Headquarters are thus formally reconfigured into 15 parts consisting of seven joint-services 'Departments', three 'Commissions' and five 'Offices', all functioning within the CMC. At the next level, the seven MAC are to be consolidated into five joint-services 'War Zone or Theatre Commands'. Alongside, the overall strength of PLA is to be reduced by three lakh redundant and non-combatant personnel, and the Second Artillery Corps is reorganised into a full-fledged service – namely, the 'PLA Rocket Forces' – to operate the entire triad of nuclear and conventional missiles in an integrated manner. No doubt thus, once firmly established and experienced in what may be termed as the 'new way', China would be benefitted by a highly efficient mechanism for the management of her military power.

Notably, a discussion on China's defence policy-making would remain incomplete without the mention of the salient role that the CMC has assigned to military-diplomacy. In clear perception of its international standing, PRC has stepped up on its defence exchanges, joint exercises, United Nations

(UN) missions, arms exports and disaster relief. Indeed, astute defence policy-making is the motivator as well as sustainer of the PLA leadership's propagation of what is described as the concept of 'War-fighting in the New Period' (11).

Defence Policy Making: Overview of Universal Trends

It will be seen that the universal concept of RMA and similarity of politico-military challenges are well reflected in the common features of defence policies adopted by the advanced nations. These commonalities of political challenges are motivated by: Firstly, rise of international competitions for resources to satiate the growing clamour for development from empowered citizens; and secondly, globalisation of security concerns in light of the spread of organised sub-conventional and hybrid warfare. These conditions compel the forging of military as well as civil-sector alliances among the nations to protect their common interests. Such alliances – or its more amenable synonym of 'alignments' to flavour the favoured term of 'strategic partnership', so to say – permit nations to decide as to what kind of military leverage they would exercise in furthering their political agenda. A corresponding sweep of more or less similarly construed 'Defence Reforms' undertaken in most countries across the globe is a natural corollary of this situation. Therefore, it may be interesting to understand as to the considerations under which such defence policies are incubated, and compare these with what prevails in the Indian system of national defence. These considerations are listed as follows:

a) Recourse to warfare being an indeterminate excursion, no governing system wants to fiddle with the existing – 'time tested', to wit – order, if that can be helped. Defence policies are therefore revisited and revised only when goaded into action by economic, political and strategic demands, in that order. Indeed, the Indian state has reached that stage.
b) Revamp of the nation's defence structure has invariably initiated at the behest of political leadership. Articulation of government's defence policies, however, has in each case, been mentored by military intellectuals, duly assisted by civilian experts having intimate experience in management of defence establishment. Neither such military mentors nor such experienced civilian experts are marshalled by the Indian system, run as it is through superfluous acquaintance rather than expertise on issues of military administration, and ruled

as it is by invocation of easy expediencies rather than insightful engagements as a way out of policy predicaments.

c) To meet military-specific requirements, defence policies invariably permit, formally and informally, special dispensations from various procedural restrictions that are otherwise applicable to the civil sector. These relaxations permit the defence sector to enjoy priorities with regard to procedural clearances, fiscal flexibilities, personnel management, information access and legal sanctions. As evidenced by stagnating trans-border projects, slippages in defence procurement, de-motivating personnel management policies and inadequate response of the defence establishment towards the needs of the military institution, this condition is seldom met in the present Indian system, pious proclamations notwithstanding.

d) Unstated but clearly discernible, there are many instances of nations scaling down their political goals to bring these within what might be attainable with the military power that they can afford to sustain. If the modest level of military deterrence preferred by India against her adversaries is a result of mismatch between her political aspirations and fiscal capabilities, then there is wisdom in finding a rational equation between these two determinants of military preparedness.

e) By investing in nuclear weapons and missiles to deter military aggression, nations have sought to scale down their investment on conventional military capabilities in times of peace. A robust defence industry and procedural flexibility to build-up forces in quick-time when necessary, enables them to make that choice. However, leaned upon by hostile nuclear neighbours from two flanks who await the opportunity to dismember her, and when her ability to meet force by force is dependent on imported weaponry and weak indigenous military industry, India's situation is different. India cannot follow this trend to lay store on missile warfare while allowing her conventional forces to stagnate, though many pseudo-strategists in the governing establishment are inclined to think so. Missiles and nuclear weapons are no substitutes for conventional military power.

f) Export of military hardware is increasingly finding acceptance as a bona fide sector of global trade and an economically profitable venture. Having repudiated that option under misplaced sense of 'non-violence', India had allowed her early investments on defence industry to regress. However in the recent years, that notion has been got rid of. Even then, the wait would be long because defence industry needs a long gestation period to be profitable.

g) Visionary governments have all opted to distinguish their systems of defence management into 'combat', 'logistic', and 'procurement' streams. The Indian system too is crystallising towards such an arrangement.

h) Under the combat stream, force-structure is based purely on military appreciation of the need for standing military formations under unified, functional and specified commands. Provision has also been made to build up the force levels from designated military reserves within a specified time. No such concept is formalised yet in the Indian system.

j) The logistic stream is an autonomous joint-service entity headed by military experts and staffed by dedicated military and civilian personnel. There is no such competent and empowered logistic stream in the Indian system of national defence.

k) Under the procurement stream, the dedicated defence requirement assessment and acquisition system is manned by long experienced civilian bureaucrats, scientists and qualified cadre of military officers. Here again, the Indian military acquisition system is run by part-time officials.

l) A customised defence budgeting system regulates the fiscal aspects of maintenance and modernisation of the defence establishment. Defence budgeting in India is an exercise of 'thumb rule' dispensation.

m) The Higher Defence Management structure is created based on studies and recommendations made by noted military experts, and based on military advice, periodically modified to suit policy-making and implementation. This apex level defence management body functions with defence-dedicated civilian bureaucracy, politically appointed domain experts and experienced military professionals, with majority of the top echelon being manned by the latter two categories. In contrast mired in anomalies, defence management in India functions haltingly, not necessarily according to the desired priorities.

n) Defence policy-making has ever been afflicted with resistance to change and parochial turf protection. The progress is therefore slow, which in a way is not that bad because it gives time to adjust, correct and assimilate. To that extent, India's strategic concerns may not cause despair; there is time to improve and modernise.

In this context, it would also be worthwhile to list out certain revolutionary features of the military doctrines the world over; highly advantageous features which could only have been brought about by landmark policy promulgations. These are:

a) Structuring of rapidly deployable, all-arm, inter-service forces.
b) Strategic transportation by civilian and military sea and air-lift assets, all-terrain ground mobility and flexibility in tactical manoeuvre .
c) Shaping battlefields with precision and stand-off firepower.
d) High technology Command, Control, Communication, Computer, Intelligence, Integration, Surveillance and Reconnaissance (C4I2SR) capabilities, reinforced with Space assets.
e) Empowerment of Special Forces to undertake unconventional military operations and to act as point elements of conventional forces.
f) Smaller construct of modular units manned by highly trained troops who are organised to undertake all the 'four generations' of warfare.
g) Synergy among political, military and civilian organs of the state, particularly in peace-keeping and 'stabilisation' tasks.

Indeed, nations have adopted different policies to secure their military objectives as it suits their political agenda. One common thread running among these policies, however, is the high honour and recognition reserved for the soldiery to keep their motivation high against the most excruciating 'call' of national service, maximum provisioning for their safety and welfare, and high compensation in terms of their rights and material benefits. It would therefore be in order to conclude the survey here with the observation that enunciation of clear and comprehensive defence policy provides the foundation for a meaningful defence establishment to evolve.

Having had an overview of the reforms in the process of defence policy-making as well as the resultant defence policy initiatives adopted by major military powers, we may now turn homewards to see as to what might have been our cause in this regard.

END NOTES AND SELECT REFERENCES

(1) The culture of 'citizen-soldiery' still prevails in the USA. Besides, as a super power, use of military force to further state strategies has become a declared policy of the US. The political and bureaucratic cadres are therefore well versed with matters of military management. This understanding is best depicted in the following documents:

a) 'Quadrennial Defence Reviews' of 1997, 2004, 2009 and 2014 as undertaken by the US Department of Defence, Washington.
b) 'Strategy Planning Guidance, 2013', issued by the US Department of Army, Washington.
c) Col Rajesh Singh, "US Reforms to its Higher Defence Organisation: Lessons for India", IDSA, New Delhi, Jul 2014.

(2) With an ever powerful political-industrial-military lobby perpetually lurking for 'profit at any cost' in a highly competitive arms industry, securing the interests of the fighting forces is a no mean achievement for the US military acquisition system.

(3) Astute management of the military institution is best depicted in the manner the US military, when called upon to do so after the Vietnam War, and again after the Gulf War, downsized itself in conformity to moderated political goals and down-scaled budgetary provisions, while yet continuing to nurture its intrinsic combat potentials, and re-raise, without fuss, its forces when the political mandate was expanded.

(4) Of late, this post has gone to civilian politicians, and that has led to the Chief of General Staff assuming larger professional authority. Some of the relevant commentaries in this context are available as follows:
a) Dmitry Gorenburg, "Russian Military Reform Moves Beyond Soviet Legacy", 2013.
b) "Russia's Defence Industry Tries to Keep Up with Growing Demand," Russia & India Report, 2012.
c) SIPRI Database, 2015.
d) Report, "Military Reform: Toward the New Look of the Russian Army", 2013.
e) "New Arms Program to Change Russia by 2020", Ria Novosti, 2013.

(5) Indicated by its muscle-flexing in Central and West Asia, the Russian military institution is fast regaining its past glory. Its military industry, through massive sales of arms, has played a central role in bankrolling that resurgence.

(6) Col Rajesh Singh, "British Reforms to its Higher Defence Organisation: Lessons for India", IDSA, New Delhi, Jul 2014.

(7) In France, the Defence Minister is the Commander-in-Chief, with the Chief of Defence Forces and the Secretary of General Administration, who heads the defence bureaucracy, functioning under him. Similar is the case with Germany, where in war time the Chancellor takes over as the Chief of Federal Armed Forces Command.

(8) Anti-India centric political obsession, sponsored by extremist theocracy is the plank for Pakistan's survival, as well as oxygen for the Pakistan Army and the sinews of its supreme political grip. Notably, Pakistan's defence policies have paid excellent dividends to her rulers. Besides enriching them and keeping the masses in stupor, these policies have elevated a smaller and weaker Pakistan to a superior India's equivalent stature, drawing concessions and liberties even while remaining a cause of global instability.

(9) Gautam Banerjee, "China's Defence White Paper-2013", Vivek, Vivekananda International Foundation, New Delhi, 2013, www.en.wikipidia.org, www.china

vitae.com, www.indiandefencereview.com/spotlights/the-challenges-posed-by-China's-military-posture-in-tibet/3.

(10) Gautam Banerjee, "PLA: Thrust on Integrated Joint War-Fighting", Indian Defence Review, New Delhi, Dec 2011. www.china-defence-mashup.com, www.global security.org, www.chinatimes.com.

(11) Relevant inputs are also available from the following publications:
   a) 'Annual Report-2014', Shanghai Institute of International Studies;
   b) 'China's White Paper on Defence-2014', 'China's Military Strategy White Paper-2015', China Military Online;
   c) http:/www.stratfor.com/weekly;
   d) Xinhua/People's Daily Online/Press Releases.

*

CHAPTER 3

EVOLUTION OF DEFENCE POLICY MAKING IN INDIA

"One sided pursuit of peace and disarmament is a powerful incentive to the adversary to intensify its own pursuit of war."

– **Luttwak**

Overview

Independence in 1947 brought a new responsibility upon the nation's political leadership – that of the management of the state's military institution. So far, over the many centuries past, the indigenous aristocracy had been kept away from that responsibility, exceptions being few and far between. Later, the British rulers capped any prospect of any Indian rising above the level of sub-unit command barring a couple of exceptions during the World War II. As a result, most Indians came to visualise the military institution as little more than groups of gallant and heavily armed 'Rambos' living in exiting isolation from the native society, while India's new political leaders could hardly appreciate the benefits of the latent, intrinsic power of the military institution. Thus bereft of exposure to strategic thinking and experience in political articulation of military power, and self-deceived by the notion of gaining international stature through peaceful rhetoric, the post-Independence governing establishment stood readily tinted by a culture of ignorance, motivated antipathy and misplaced innuendoes against the nation's military institution. As a result, the entire system of defence policy-making in independent India had been afflicted with disorientation, even blunders.

To appreciate the shortcomings in India's present system of defence policy-making, it is obligatory to recount the manner in which the process has evolved under the post-independence dispensation. This is the matter of discussion in this chapter. The course of discussion starts from an appraisal of the political aspects of defence policy-making before the landmark changes in the system, including the trends of fiscal planning, are reviewed.

Political Aspects of Defence Policy-Making

Any discussion on defence policy-making must begin with an invocation of the practice in which governments promulgate well considered 'political directives' that the nation's military institution is mandated to fulfil. Indeed, application of military force to seek political ends is the most crucial – exacting, risk-prone and irreversibly decisive – event among a nation's endeavours'. Obviously therefore, unlike other acts of governance, this particular mandate is to be exercised only as the last resort for the preservation of nationhood against its ultimate nemesis. As a corollary, that mandate must emerge from deep and deliberate political considerations by the wisest among the nation's statesmen, and once promulgated, no sacrifice or cost may be spared in its fulfilment.

Contrarily, since strategic application of military force and its tactical articulation in combat require exclusive professionalism in the art and science of warfare, these roles have to be assigned to what must be a purely military pursuit. That 'call' therefore has to be responded to by those who are 'commissioned', trained and equipped by the state for that purpose – men and women of extraordinary character, unyielding commitment, high standards of training and honed experience of the entire gamut of warfare. In other words, even if framing of political direction and its military application have to be undertaken in exclusive domains – the former by a strategically astute political leadership and the latter by professional military hierarchy – the two functions are intrinsically inter-wined and convergent. Thus at the point of delivery, it is impossible to separate the process of defence policy-making from the state of military preparedness. The purpose of reiterating this obvious dictum is to point out that this understanding is not heeded in the system that prevails in India; here there is inadequate congruence between the two (1).

In principle, the larger obligation of defence policy-making rests upon the nation's political leadership for them to respond to the following responsibilities:

a) One, as mentioned above, the promulgation of an appropriate 'political directive' that is in tune with national goals, for the military institution to orient its strategic discourse accordingly.
b) Two, to orient the rest of the defence establishment to conform to their assigned roles in the nation's defence preparedness. Indeed, these roles have to be in tune with the strategic doctrines and tactical concepts by which the military institution commits itself to the furtherance of the political directive. Stimulation of true convergence among the various sectors of defence establishment towards their military-specific purpose is therefore a crucial part of the political leadership's charter, just as it is with the participation of a robust civilian sector in the promotion of national defence (2).
c) Three, framing policies to marshal the nation's resources and so to provide for the war wherewithal for the military institution in terms of men, military hardware and logistic back up for prosecution of war plans, thereby enabling it to structure its forces in accordance with the political directive.
d) Four, to spell out the desired political 'end-state' while planning for military engagements. For it to be a beacon for the military leadership to plan appropriate strategies of force-application, that 'end state' cannot but has to be defined only through a conjoined civil-military deliberation.

Obviously therefore, in terms of variety and quantum of activities, defence policy-making at the political level has more to do with foresighted build-up of defence manpower, infrastructure and arms industry. That such build up have to be contrived in tune with a diverse range of operations of war, sciences and technologies, and long gestation for manufacturing industries, all of which call for high fiscal investments, renders the matter of political management of defence a responsibility of deliberate farsightedness. Indeed, defence policy-making requires the nation's political leadership to display due strategic understanding of the characteristics of warfare and its various contemporary forms, and pre-empt the looming friction-points and weaknesses (3). Bedsides, understanding of the extra-ordinary cerebral make-up of the soldiery and upholding the hoary covenant of state-soldier relationship are equally important responsibilities for the nation's helmsmen.

Let us see as to how has independent India fared in this regard.

Post-Independence Disorientation

As the British left, they structured a mechanism for the management of national defence in independent India. That mechanism consisted of a 'Defence Committee of the Cabinet' for promulgation of political directions at the apex level, while a 'Defence Minister's Committee' with Service Chiefs and Defence Secretary as its members attended to the routine policy-issues at the Ministry level. Then there was a Tri-Service 'Chiefs of Staff's Committee' to respond to Cabinet confabulations and at the same time, guide the conduct of inter-services matters. Integrated approach to defence management was promoted through the committees for 'Joint Intelligence', 'Joint Planning' and 'Joint Training'. Besides, there were expert groups for optimal management of military logistics and development of wanted technology. Finally, each Service Headquarters had its own mechanism for focused policy-making, and had the advantage of exercise of full control over the in-service executive mechanisms. Catering to a parallel aspect, there was the 'Defence Coordination and Implementation Committee' chaired by the Defence Secretary to synergise defence research, development, finance, production and acquisitions (4).

This World War II dispensed system of synergic policy-making applied to all the departments and appendages of the Ministry of Defence – viz, Defence Production, Research and Development, Ex-Servicemen Welfare, Finance, Defence Estates etc. – and the distinction made in the present discussion between military institution and defence establishment had no cause to exist at that time. Notably, with their representation in the Defence Minister's Committee and other Joint Committees, and in continuation of the World War II dispensation, the Service Headquarters had been an intrinsic part of the ministerial as well as tri-service policy-making system.

Of course, in the immediate aftermath of the Independence, there was little enthusiasm among the new political leaders in delving into India's military inheritance, whatever be its glory. But the misplaced idea of delinking national defence from nation building had somewhat been checked, if temporarily, by the military's acclaimed role in controlling the mayhem of Partition, and retrieving for India a larger part of Jammu and Kashmir from Pakistan's grab. The mechanism therefore functioned well during the following few years when the Committees met regularly even if for the purposes gradually rendered mundane under the new dispensation. But soon enough, a dispensation of post-independence romanticism over sublime peace, liberty, progress, equality and India's much touted stakes at global stage diluted the seriousness of that defence policy-making mechanism. With the very military institution, not just military power, excluded from that dream sequence of the nation's peaceful progress, the defence policy-making mechanism was perniciously allowed to atrophy thus.

The 1950s thus saw the advent of a new post-independence era that was characterised by the following developments:

a) An era of illusionary peace-rhetoric gained ground among the Indian leadership even if there was nothing in the international power-politics to encourage such ideas. All the peaceniks of the nation's top leadership – the Prime Minister, his successive Defence Ministers and trusted advisors – made themselves believe that independent India needed no recourse to military security; conversely, they even considered the military institution as a threat to Indian democracy. They however, brought themselves to maintaining, under piqued reluctance, a defence force that was designated just to check Pakistan's occasional, limited armed forays, till, as it was believed, that adversary came to terms with itself. In strategic innocence, that belief-turned-policy translated into neglect of the military institution and fiddling with its cerebral fibre – no military could remain stoic when assailed as to its very necessity, by its own beneficiaries, and vilified on presumptions of its insinuated intentions regarding power capture. It was not unusual that the celebrated Indian military institution slid into decline mode (5).
b) Regular functions of military management, rather than nurturing the forces, became mired in negativity. First, apportioning among the three services, of the institution of Commander-in-Chief and its re-designation as 'Chiefs of Staff' was contrived to their being, in practice, disfranchised from the apex policy-making bodies. The Committees of the Cabinet and the Defence Minister ceased, more or less, to function while the intended authority of the Chief of Staff's Committee was undermined by the myopic Service Headquarters themselves, much to the satisfaction of the bureaucracy – the situation was not helped by a politically obsessed and innately destructive Defence Minister.
c) Soon enough, the Service Headquarters, in their short-sighted urge, disowned the Joint Committees and subverted the authority of the Chiefs of Staff Committee, thus rendering these as mere embellishments and little more. This was a haughty self-infliction

on the part of the military institution, the most telling effect of which being the loss of its lien upon the nation's joint intelligence set up and the defence establishment at-large. Unable to consolidate the authority of the joint services Chiefs of Staff Committee, the Service Headquarters pushed even themselves out from the policy-making high table!

d) It was then the turn of the Service Headquarters to be done-in. Placid in the peace-rhetoric, the services were left out of the Government's priority contention, and the Service Headquarters were formally assigned to the status of 'Attached Offices', and so obliged to put up with marginalisation from defence policy-making process. The Defence Ministry, manned by bureaucrats coming from any and all departments, and therefore being nonplussed of the matters military but for their assumed 'administrative acumen', sought to down play the services related issues, deferring to misinformed assumptions from pseudo visionaries and disregarding the glaring signs of approaching security crises. Deep systemic aberrations thus found home in India's system of defence management wherein subjectivities of professional policies were put to scrutiny by novices pretending as 'know-alls' (6).

By the mid-1950s, growing belligerence in the neighbourhood caused the Indian military to be asked to prepare to dissuade Pakistan's military adventurism – a sort of deterrence by denial. But China did not figure in that scheme. This policy led to expansion of the Army to form 12 divisions equivalent to nearly 18 and the Air Force from seven to 21 squadrons. This was followed with the acquisition of key weapons like the Centurion tank and Hunter, Mystere, Canberra, Gnat and MiG aircrafts, along with the requisite industrial base to carry out licensed manufacture and maintenance. No doubt, these measures made it possible for India to thwart Pakistan's attempt to grab Kashmir in 1965, but as stated, could find no part in dissuading China from attacking and mauling India in 1962.

By far the most damaging stance adopted by the government at this time was to propagate, under the overall ambit of its Industrial Policy of 1956, its supercilious policies regarding the defence industry. National leaders in power made themselves believe that independent India's World War II inheritance of a fairly well established indigenous defence industry was needed to be maintained, but only at the minimalist level. This thesis had its roots in the Government's conclusion that whereas it would be difficult to find arms suppliers under its non-aligned dispensation, the defence industry was needed to be kept in business, but only to the extent of just about keeping a placid defence force kitted with back-generation wherewithal, that would be 'adequate' to ward off Pakistan's military pin-pricks – and nothing more. Thus even as the country's Second Five Year Plan saw the ordnance factories and research, development and manufacturing industry being infused with limited upgrades towards achievement of 'self-reliance in defence manufacture', functioning of these sectors remained conditioned by modest targets and languid work culture – bits of profiteering and kickbacks being a part of the game. Mainly, these terms were as follows:

a) Replacement of existing military equipment, with limited product improvement to cater for technological and economic practicalities – and not specifically to meet the purpose of periodic military upgrades – was to be the goal. The very thought of regular technological modernisation of weapons and equipment, leave alone innovations in military technology, was considered as unnecessary.
b) Export of arms and military hardware to earn what was viewed as 'blood money' was considered to be utterly devilish, and piously forbidden. The industry was kept straight-jacketed into the public sector while the private enterprise was shooed away; the latter in any case found that there was little to profit from investing in producing dated equipment in limited scales for a stagnant sector.

These two impositions prevented the growth of research, development and production of defence hardware in India. That sealed off a source of diplomatic clout and export earnings. More than anything else, that prevented India from achieving defence self-sufficiency against galloping militarisation of the antagonistic neighbours. Indeed, that policy disorientation continues to haunt India's strategic resurgence even today – as indeed it would continue to for the coming future (7).

Even when dependence on military power to protect national interests is not considered to be compelling, wise nations do not falter in preserving the seeds of their military resurgence. Thus, they take care to keep building the competence of their defence establishment and carefully nurture the 'core' of their military force-structure, so as to keep alive the spirit, ethos and skills of their military institution. As the subsequent events proved, the newly anointed rulers of independent India were not up to that wisdom (8).

Post-1962 Orientation

Events – a political blunder and a farcical military confrontation but for the blood spilled by spirited but destitute Indian soldiery – leading to the 1962 debacle are too well known to be recounted here. Aftermath of that crippling blow to Indian nationhood saw the downslide of the military institution being arrested in right earnest. The grave emergency led to defence funding and acquisitions of weaponry and equipment being boosted and deliberate policies regarding sanctioned levels of force-structure, equipment profile, manpower establishment, training and administration being promulgated. The defence budget went up from around two per cent of the Gross Domestic Product to over four per cent. For the Army, 11 mountain warfare divisions and corresponding corps and command headquarters were raised, weapons and equipment profile was upgraded, training standards were notched up, due orientation was given towards mountain and guerrilla warfare and behind-the-line operations, and manpower ceiling was raised from nearly five to over eight lakh. Similar upgrades were instituted in the Air Force, the sanctioned squadron strength being raised to 39 plus. The Navy was, similarly but to a proportionally lesser scale, was strengthened with two carrier based fleets and modestly enhanced mix of surface, underwater, air and logistic combatants. The intelligence set up, mauled by the Intelligence Bureau's faux pas vis-à-vis the Chinese build up, too saw some restructuring. With the US led Western Powers linking the supply of defence equipment to politically uneasy conditions, the former Union of Soviet Socialist Republics (USSR) came forward to be the sole source of Indian military armament.

More importantly, while internal management of the military institution had always been left to in-house deliberations and barring exceptions politics had no role in matters of high level promotions and postings, after the debacle that tradition of non-interference became unexceptionally inviolable. These steps imparted to the Service Headquarters a good degree of authority in defence policy-making, while the Indo-Pakistan War of 1965 forged a new paradigm of inter-service jointness. And that sunshine lasted, occasional hiccups notwithstanding, till the late-1980s. Thus gradually, over a period, developments as described in the following paragraphs, took place.

Following the experiences of the 1965 War, build-up of fighting formations and compatible capabilities in terms of fire support, mobility, communications, field fortifications, operational axes and logistic installations continued. Later, the aftermath of the eminently successful 1971 War saw the emergence of concepts of obstacle based defences. The war strategy revolved around defensive and reactive operations across India's Western plains, involving penetration and manoeuvre warfare to destroy enemy forces and capture territories. Finally, 'strike corps' offensives deep into the enemy's guts were envisaged. Needless to state, Pakistan, rather deservedly, was that enemy, China having veiled her innate belligerence to be busy with her 'four modernisations'. Indeed, by the early 1980s, the Indian armed forces was a fairly modern military institution that could deter China from escalating the border incidents in Sikkim and Tawang, force Pakistan to discard conventional aggression to invest in proxy war and nuclearisation, and encourage other neighbours to look up to Indian help in emergencies.

Advancements in terms of modern and high-skill intensive equipment, battle procedures, experiences and expertise, however, had one adverse fall-out. It caused the three services to adopt specifically designated paths of tactical and technical progression. That divergence however, instead of being confined to the functional level, went on to subsume the military leadership's strategic vision, thus dividing the three services into disparate entities even at the apex level. The inherent jointness among the three services, a legacy of World War II, was thus overtaken by autonomous ambitions, and a sense of competition, marred by 'gamesmanship', ensued between the services. As each service went its own way more or less in exclusion of the others, the Joint Committees turned disjointed. The purpose of joint training was negated by each service preferring their exclusive and specialised training institutes even if to cover similar syllabi, and the concept of joint logistics was stymied by the absence of serious efforts to combine even the routine revenue and maintenance schemes of similar nature. With each Services Headquarters finding full time engagement in fostering internal, in-service professional excellence, and competing among themselves for resources, their chair in the apex defence policy-making bodies lost significance. This fracture, exacerbated by growing complexities of military management which could no more be regulated just through weekly meetings of a few heads, started to point at the inadequacy of the Defence Minister's, and even the other Committees. Issues had to be moved on files and the need for deeper and wider confabulations added to the complexities of policy-making, naturally so.

Meanwhile, intense domestic political tumult of the late 1970s led to the 1950s generation of political leaders coming to power, who, with their intense occupation in domestic politicking, allowed the politician-military disconnect to grow. That left the other elements of defence policy-making

– the defence bureaucracy, intelligence, finance and scientific, for example – to take the centre stage in management of national defence by default. Gradually, the sanctity of what was an arrangement for participation, if informal, of Service Headquarters in defence decision making, got diluted.

Defence Planning in 1980s

In spite of the above listed distractions, intermittent glimpses of astute intent among military leaders and defence bureaucracy had also been in evidence in the past. That was so when the MoD created a 'Defence Planning Cell' with which it could couple defence planning to the Government's 'Five Year Plans', the first one covering the period 1964-69. However, in absence of long-term defence planning and assurance of fiscal support, this Cell could not make the expected mark. In 1977, a high power 'Committee for Defence Planning' was convened under the Cabinet Secretariat, but even this recourse was found inadequate to strike the right coordination between the military institution and the research, development and production arms of the defence establishment. Then, in 1986, under a farsighted political initiative, an 'Integrated Defence Planning Staff' was constituted. However, its good work was done-in by concerted impairment from the Service Headquarters and the defence bureaucracy who found it to be an aberration to their superior authority. Soon enough, afflicted by inter-service diversities and bureaucratic apprehensions of its growing stature in matters of national defence, the set up was consigned into irrelevance; political complacency over national defence, borne out of a still strong military institution, accelerated that process. Resultantly, the most debilitating effect of incongruous defence planning was that the governments of the day could not optimise the process of defence preparedness. Neither could it garner the maximum out of its investments on national defence nor could it stimulate the defence establishment to meet the military necessities, as enunciated by military professionals, as indeed it must be.

Notably, the imbalances in the system of defence policy-making had not become apparent during the military build-up period of the mid-1960s and early-1970s, when professional military advice had to be sought and accommodated. Then, a decade plus of relative peace that followed the outstanding military victory of 1971 caused the defence policy-makers to rest in smug satisfaction. In the second half of the 1980s, as India's role in regional security architecture gained the centre stage by the expression of her military power, much of the orthodox political class was discomfited by the government's extra-territorial military involvements. Thus even if undertaken in mutual consent, India's military involvements in regional politics and diplomacy – in Sri Lanka, Maldives, Bangladesh, Nepal, Bhutan and Myanmar for example – was not viewed favourably by a governing class that was still afflicted with the 1950s mind-set. There were arguments in favour of a 'reverse military diplomacy' policy, so to say, from a strong lobby of pacifist political analysts who saw India's 'military activism' as rather undesirable. This preference was actually a part of native political dynamics, which the defence policy-makers – that is, the defence bureaucracy exercising a virtual 'power of attorney' on behalf of political leadership – in their superfluous understanding, translated to grousing and dithering over committing to even routine upkeep and regular modernisation measures for the nation's military institution, much in contravention of the principles of good defence management. The culture of dismissing the military institution was back in business thus (9).

During that period, the military institution prepared itself based on what was known as a 'Directive' spelt out by the Defence Minister. This 'Directive' enjoined the maintenance of certain war waging capabilities, leaving it upon the professionals to decide regarding the kinds war to wage, grand strategies to adopt and political as well as military end-states to achieve. Thus in late-1970s and early 1980s, the concept of the "K-Day Scenario" was propounded by the military hierarchy. Subsequently, as the military capability developed, a "Pro-active" or "D-Day Strategy" was developed, which was translated from time to time to various forms of operational concepts. Conversely, as official reports indicated, notwithstanding its sanctity, the government failed to equip the military institution to be in position to fulfil the provisions of its own Directive, and the forces were faced by mounting shortfall in weaponry, ammunition, military hardware, even junior leadership and quality of soldiery.

In effect therefore, the system of policy-making in the Defence Ministry was such that while the Directive to the military institution had been broadly spelt out, it had neither involved itself in the formulation of robust and affordable military strategies nor did it provide to the services the wherewithal to do so. Meanwhile, oblivious of gradual marginalisation from defence policy-making, each Service Headquarters played its own factional tune, the other two watching in condescending interest while remaining intent on exercise of internal autonomy, exclusive expertise and strategic self-centrality – all of them soliciting the defence bureaucracy to further their cause. Only the rise of emergent situations could impel right jointmanship;

the rest of the time was spent in partisan self-actuation, sometimes even at the other service's expense. All this while, domestic politics so engaged the polity's attention that national policy-makers found no expediency in arresting the growing military debility. By the early 1990s, the distance between the national leadership and the military institution had become stark while the military institution was being 'hollowed' by shortages of every kind.

1990s: Relapse to Policy Disorientation

As the decade of 1990s began, budgetary provisions for the military institution had to be relegated in favour of the nation's economic survival. Such is but a common occurrence even among the most powerful countries, and that condition is well negotiated by the sagacity of a government-military combine, the latter ensuring that the cerebral and professional competencies of the military institution are not allowed to be atrophied. In fact, the military fraternities in those countries view budget-cuts as opportunities to discard the old baggage and trim their organisational fat.

In case of India, however, the economic crunch led to the government's virtual abandonment of its responsibilities over the nation's military affairs. Thus started a competition within the bureaucracy to undermine the military institution – even the smallest but crucial schemes needed by the services were either deflected into a 'black holes' or subjected to dilution, freeze and eventual dismissal. The 'Bofors scandal', perpetrated by politicians and bureaucrats, was found as an excuse to deny the soldier his due wherewithal of survival and success! The standard stance adopted in dismissing almost every demand, even the routine revenue expenditures on ammunition and weapon spares, was that 'India's economic survival took priority, and that there shall be no war in the foreseeable future'. The military hierarchy, which would have cushioned the government's policy to squeeze defence allocations through deft adjustments and balancing acts, had been, in traditional innocence, left out of the scheme. In short, strategically naïve managers of national defence decided that it was good economics to let the military institution atrophy! As it should have happened – and actually does in most mature countries – adverse fallouts of these disorientations in the practices and procedures of nation's military management through the 1990s should have been controlled by the elected managers of national defence. In this instance, no attempt, however, was made to address the permeation of systemic inadequacies; rather than that it was allowed to fester.

The military leadership did try to manage the poverty by protecting the core military competencies, but the results of that rear-guard rescue were mixed at the best. Impeded by fiscal and technological limitations, its resolve to build up the force-structure in accordance with contemporary call of defence preparedness in any case had by now turned into a disjointed exercise. To accommodate, as far as possible, the political mandate, the military institution then took to commit what limited resources it was provided with, to attend to, through prioritisation, just some of the cutting edge systems in its combat arms. Having to jettison the force-multiplying accessories of such newly inducted combat-arm systems, compromises were also made by settling for lower quality and quantity of combat-support elements and reconciling to insufficient logistic stockpiles. Indeed, these were the compromises which were liable to turn dangerous and costly in war. That then was the situation that prevailed over the past quarter of a century, unavoidable upgrades being incorporated intermittently and incrementally, more in materialistic rather than conceptual sense of wholesome military modernisation (10).

At this juncture, in 1998, the Government decided to opt for nuclear weaponisation and enhanced missile capabilities, basically to deal with the recessed threat from China and the covert nuclearisation of Pakistan. It was a sensible step, the purpose being to prevent China and Pakistan to indulge in nuclear bullying to add to their ever-looming conventional military threat. That it was a purely deterrent measure and a political signal, nothing more, was clearly enunciated to the world at large through the issuance, in 1999, of a draft nuclear doctrine, 'minimum or credible nuclear deterrence', 'no first use' and 'massive retaliation designed to Inflict unacceptable damage' being its key features. India's nuclearisation, however, gave wrong impetus to an ill-conceived notion among the defence mandarins who took nuclear tipped missiles, operated by scientists and controlled by bureaucrats, both doubling up as nuclear strategists, to be an alternative to conventional military deterrence. The draft nuclear doctrine was formalised in January 2003, but in keeping with India's abhorrence of nuclear weapon use, the nuclear weapon set up was kept at low key and bare stage. Illusion of arm-chair strategists, who ruled the roost, towards the health of the nation's military institution, however, continued to remain perverse. The decade thus saw the military institution debilitated by material deficiencies perpetrated and structural voids unaddressed, till a crippling 'hollowness' percolated deep and profound into its structure. The nation's war waging capacity, and as a corollary, its projection of military deterrence touched a nadir thus (11).

That was the situation to invite Pakistan to inflict the 'Kargil War' on India, when almost the entire all-India military resources had to be pooled to fend off what was just a local military challenge. The same military debility encouraged Pakistan's imposition of terror war and China's growing assertiveness in dealing with India. The three decade-long quietetude among the inimical neighbours that had followed in the wake of the show of India's military prowess in 1971, ended thus (12).

Set-in of Systemic Morbidity

As the 1971 War-induced cohesion within the Defence Ministry, the services and the rest of the defence establishment faded with time, the Chiefs of Staff Committee, intended to jointly administer the military institution, turned into a social meeting of little significance, its insignificance exacerbated by short tenures of its transitory Chairmanship. With the military hierarchy failing to devise by themselves or to motivate the Government on institution of a competent system of policy-making, and the political leadership remaining innocent to that purpose of statesmanship, modern practices in management of national defence, with due representation from the services and all others of the defence establishment, failed to materialise. Bureaucracy, as always prevailing over the eyes, ears and hands of their political masters, became the virtual policymaker on national defence, filling up for the originally intended role of the Chiefs of Staff Committee and the Service Chiefs, and invoking their purported 'wisdom' over the entire range of military matters to do so. What began in the aftermath of independence as a matter of conscious, if faulty, policy of minimalist upkeep of the nation's military institution in favour of socio-economic freedom and progress, later turned into a policy of marginalisation and starvation of that institution under a regime controlled by an unconcerned political establishment and its handymen bureaucracy.

By the early 1990s, role of Service Headquarters in policy-making system was reduced from being the principal participant to that of a recommendatory body – that too only if and when 'invited', not for confabulations, but just to register their response to an issue. Even the sanctified option of Chairman of the Chiefs of Staff Committee and the Service Chiefs in exercising their exclusive access to the Prime Minister and the President became practically defunct. Unable to appreciate the intangibilities and complexities of military matters and yet not willing to exchange their 'generalist' privileges to earn due experience in defence management, the defence bureaucracy took to disposing of the issues raised by the Service Headquarters through the old tactics of seeking pointless consensus from all and sundry departments and advisory bodies. This vain process of 'wider examination' actually translated into freezing or killing the issue, much to an ever-pacifist Ministry's silent relief. The pristine concept of 'military necessity' was buried once more, as it had been before the 1962 debacle (13).

More crucially, through innocuously incremental amendments to the rules of functional control and provisions for answerability to their military users, gates were opened up for the smart-operators of the various military-dedicated defence establishments to assume autonomous control over their 'fiefdoms' and gradually relieve themselves from accountability to military supervision. Organisations meant to serve national defence thus turned policymakers using self-serving intuitions and handy expediencies in place of hard professional achievements to perform that role. Over the following decades, scientists came to decide as to what weapons, ammunition and equipment would best 'serve' the military, while the defence finance decided as to what scale of entitlements of these wherewithal would be 'adequate' for warfare. Similarly, Ordnance Factories and Defence Public Sector Undertakings decided the time lines, quality and costs of hardware to be provided to the military, the Defence Estates devised land managerial practices in exclusion of military accountability, and politicians, deterred by the enormity of the responsibilities associated with national defence, decided to let the bureaucrats handle the complex burden as best – or worst – as they could.

An equally worrisome aspect that remained dormant in public discourses barring occasional expose's was the prevalence of deep-seated archaism in conceptual, systemic and procedural management of national defence, which the bureaucracies, in the Ministry as well as Service Headquarters, were not enthused in modernising – familiarity, control and immunity from accountability being their motivations to perpetuate the passé. At the political level, short-sighted expediencies led to disown any military threat even when Pakistan's proxy war was at its peak, and so enthused, an unaccountable cabal of bureaucracy contrived, behind the facade of procedures, to retard rather than facilitate the upkeep of the forces. The lowest priority accorded to defence preparedness translated into random rejection of even basic military necessities in the name of cost-cutting. This was done by: One, keeping the military hierarchy at an arm's length from defence policy-making;

two, by setting free the military-dedicated defence establishments from military oversight; three, through repudiation of the concept of 'military necessity'; and four, by triggering a rush for unscrupulous trade manipulations among the indigenous and foreign defence industry.

Not surprisingly, as a result, the standing armed forces were starved of even mandatory replacements of weapons, equipment and training consumables. Ammunition, tactical missiles and mine stocks plummeted, necessitating imposition of severe restrictions on training and use of life-expired lots, and with even routine spares like lubricants, tyres and batteries going out of stock, maintenance and overhaul of weapons and equipment turned exasperatingly inefficient and over-delayed. Shortage of officers of battle leadership level, training and meterage restrictions, shrinking of firing ranges, and even neglect of cantonments administration and military works, added to the emasculation. Gradually over the next few years, the military institution was so debilitated by mounting deficiencies and voids in its composition and structure that it was practically impossible to recoup in a practically admissible time frame (14).

Marginalisation of the military hierarchy in defence policy-making was complete, except when the defence policy-making body – one or two politicians and few top Defence Ministry bureaucrats, but no military professionals – felt the urgency to call for military opinions to be submitted to their judgment. Moreover, even when that call was occasionally made, the three services offered divergent responses thus causing exasperation among the policy makers. A stage thus came when it was not considered necessary to consult the military hierarchy on India's stance on usage of nuclear, biological and chemical weapons, or while rewriting a new Cantonment Act, or while acceding to scientists' authority in blocking indefinitely the procurement of a weapon system, or the auditors' authority to decide upon the scale of bullet-proof jackets, or the defence estate managers to dole out military land to encroachers – remaining free of accountability all the while (15)!

The Kargil Shake-up

Having first 'invited' Pakistan to add to her proxy war in Kashmir by opening another game of war in Kargil, and then preventing any major loss of territory at excruciating costs of men and money, India's defence policy-makers finally woke up to address the imbalances in the nation's defence structure. In 1999, a 'Kargil Review Committee' made several landmark recommendations, which was followed by constitution of a 'Group of Ministers' and four 'Task Forces' to vet the recommendations. Finally, in 2001, the Group of Ministers came out with a report titled 'Reforming the National Security System' to pave the way for Cabinet level approval and implementation of various far-reaching measures. Revamp and creation of many structures was initiated thus, the major issues being as follows:

a) Integration of Service Headquarters within the Ministry of Defence;
b) Creation of Headquarters Integrated Defence Staff (IDS), the Andaman & Nicobar Command, and the Strategic Forces Command;
c) Restructure of the Joint Intelligence Committee, the tri-service Defence Intelligence Agency, and the National Technical Research Organisation, and establishment of formal linkage with the Ministry of Foreign Affairs;
d) Revamp of the National Security Council and its associated advisory groups;
e) Creation of the institution of a Chief of Defence Staff (CDS) to ensure single point military advice and inter-service jointness in planning and execution of operations;
f) Streamlining of Defence Planning Guidelines, which further led to:
    i) Revamp of Defence Procurement Procedure through the Defence Acquisition Council (DAC) and Defence Procurement and the Defence Technology Boards;
    ii) Drawing up of 'Long Term Integrated Perspective Plan', and its sub-sets in the form of Defence Five Year Plan, the Services Capital Acquisition Plans and Annual Acquisition Plans;
g) Devolution of financial powers.

Inter alia, the initiative also contributed in streamlining, to much extent, the culture of management and accountability of various departments of the defence establishment, besides bringing about an awakening among the citizenry to the liabilities of national defence. Also streamlined were the processes of fiscal control and defence acquisitions. However, when it came to the system of defence policy-making at the apex level and issuance of formal political directives to the military institution, the endeavour fizzled out, just as it did in case of many other substantial issues of modern defence management. Failure to truly incorporate military staff in the ministerial bureaucracy, continuation of the anarchy of professional military projections being subjected to duplicated and mutually exclusive layers of 'scrutiny', by inexpert bureaucrats, scientists and auditors, stagnation over the institution of an empowered 'Chief of Defence Staff', and dilution of military institution's 'user control' over defence research, development and production are some such issues which continue to prevent the accrual of full advantages of the streamlining initiatives of the above mentioned Report. In the final analysis, the improvements remained modest in real terms – frozen mind-sets, misplaced fears, turf one-upmanship and plain political indecision closing the doors to wisdom (16).

Post-Operation 'Parakram' Initiatives

In the aftermath of the 2001 mobilisation and military posturing against Pakistan – referred to as 'Operation Prarakram' – the military hierarchy became more intent on propagation of a war doctrine which would cover, besides the concepts and guidelines for application of military force, the equally salient aspects of deterrence and power posturing.

With Pakistan intent upon using her nuclearisation to immune herself from India's conventional military retaliation, and so continue with her 'proxy war' in Kashmir with impunity, this was also the time when the innovative doctrine of 'Cold Start' operations or the 'Proactive Offensive Doctrine' was developed. Even if somewhat trimmed up later, this doctrine put Pakistan's habitual marauders into so much fear as to hold out obviously bombastic threats of brinkmanship and then opt for the self-destructive idea of using tactical nuclear weapons against India's supposed aggression. Soon enough, each of the three services proceeded to propagate their doctrines. Having made a rather cursory attempt at propagating an army doctrine in 1998 in the form of a document titled 'Fundamentals, Doctrine and Concepts', the Army published a better focused 'Indian Army Doctrine' in 2004, following it up with issuance of its 'Sub-Conventional Warfare Doctrine' in 2006. The Navy, taking off from their past versions of operational and development strategies, published its doctrine in 2004, and followed it up in 2009 with an 'Indian Maritime Doctrine'. Similarly, the Air Force, having been the first one to propagate its Gulf War I-influenced doctrine in 1996, propagated its revised version in 2007, and followed it up in 2012 with a 'Basic Doctrine'. All of these doctrinal excursions purportedly have confidential parts, which deal with more specific nuances of war-fighting.

In 2007, the Mod, in answer to a query, stated that the national security strategy, its corollary, national military strategy and its further corollary, national military objectives had been translated into a 'Long Term Integrated Procurement Plan' (LTIPP) to equip the defence forces. No doubt, there are regular confabulations in the MoD to prepare such plans, but such interactions do not qualify to fulfil the purpose of a formal and sacrosanct National Security Strategy, least of all a national military strategy or objective. To that extent, the claim seemed to be rather tenuous. In any case, the doctrinal propagation of indigenous military theology appears to have been devoted, in form, to incremental equipment modernisation rather than propagation of comprehensive directives in matters of warfare under India-specific conditions. These convey little more than military aspirations which, even if perceived professionally, had been dominated by partisan service-centricity. The enterprise therefore failed to provoke the development of ingenuous joint warfare strategies over the entire spectrum of warfare in the context of India's military challenges. Moreover, in absence of formal endorsement from the political leadership and commitment of support from other state-institutions, implementation of the proffered propositions were destined to remain in half-cock.

Between 2006 and 2008, the IDS, after due inter-service consultations and accommodation of self-perpetuating afflictions, issued its 'Joint Forces Doctrine', a 'Joint Special Forces Doctrine' and a 'Joint Amphibious Operations Doctrine'. The 'Raksha Mantri's Directive' too was reportedly updated. Following up, the services too conducted elaborate studies aimed at modernisation of their organisational structures and the operational capabilities of their combat formations in tune with the imperatives of modern warfare and native strategic challenges. These initiatives were indicative of the fact that over the past decade, the military institution had consciously graduated from informal propositions of their war strategies to formal enunciation of doctrinal ideas. It also indicated that under a dispensation that was prevailed upon by lack of political and bureaucratic attention, and sustained by the proviso of consensus on self-centrality among the three services, transformation of the military institution into a truly modern, efficient and cost-effective national asset had started to attract serious professional thought.

However, being devoid of political participation and the government's formal endorsement, such initiatives failed make reckonable headway. After all, these could be workable only when the political 'end-state' was specified, fiscal provisions made and the entire defence sector aligned in terms of intelligence, mobilisation, transportation, deployment, industrial surge-production, etc. Even the effectiveness of the doctrine on Sub-Conventional

Warfare would have to be contingent upon the Army's primacy in unified command, integrated intelligence, civic actions by other state-institutions and kick-start of political process. Conversely, being beyond the military institution's preview, the aforesaid conditions were difficult to be met in absence of complementary and clear cut political directives. Translation of military doctrines into restructure and modernisation, therefore, remained unfulfilled pending a revamp of the placid structure of management of national defence and the system of defence policy-making (17).

Another Attempt at Defence Reforms

Arguably, implementation of the noble intents of the post-Kagil War and the post-Operation Parakram initiatives to streamline the management of national defence could not make the intended headway because while devising the action plans, common systemic inertia against fundamental changes in defence policy making system could not be overcome. Resultantly, the intended improvements, basic ones at that, continued to remain in limbo. Thus faltered the mission aimed at upgrade and restructure of various formation headquarters, units, and logistic installations, covering the voids in weaponry and equipment, modernisation of the forces through indigenous or import procurements, and restructure of the overall military force-structure. Many times, when some of such proposals did fructify after many years in systemic orbit, optimal fruition of the schemes had been prevented by arbitrary truncation of full-capability features of the organisational upgrades as well as the acquired weapons and equipment – due to ill-informed impositions of the bureaucrat-scientist-auditor combine and their ambivalence over the corresponding restructure of military organisation and manpower. In similar vein, many times the scheme were consigned to stagnation till these were overtaken by technological advancements, fiscal reprioritisation or political distractions. Thus presided over by an inert MoD, technical upgrade of even regularly scaled weapons and equipment, acquisition of modern artillery guns, communication and surveillance systems, combat aircraft and naval armaments – any of the crucial modernisation schemes, in fact – suffered the ignominy of neglect while the nation's military capability turned weaker – and more. It was immaterial whether this dereliction was an act of deliberate policy or actually a real incapability to work the system (18).

After a decade long procrastination, in 2011, the Government, more to deflect the rising clamour of concern among the strategic community than aiming at substantial progress, convened another 'Task Force on National Security Reforms', also referred to as the Naresh Chandra Committee. However, all that this Task Force could do besides tentative tinkering with some of the Kargil Committee and Group of Minister Recommendations was to suggest dilution of the proposed institution of the Chief of Defence Staff into an acceptable façade of 'Permanent Chairman' of Chiefs of Staff Committee, who would be a figurehead of certain loose tri-service commands and an 'equal' among his peer Service Chiefs, and would remain divested of coordinating and overriding authority. Other recommendations of this Task Force were:

a) Creation of three tri-service, Special Operations, Aerospace and Cyber Commands;
b) Establishment of a political-military-foreign affairs policy advisory bureau;
c) Setting up of an agency to oversee project implementations; and
d) Liberalisation of joint private and foreign investment in defence industry (19).

The dawn of the second decade of the new millennium thus found the class of defence managers absolving themselves from the imperative of professional military participation in policy-making and opting to be oblivious of the principle of military necessity. More fatuously, they identified preservation of military power to be a contradiction to economic progress, and thus caused the nation's military institution to atrophy. Even if the political concern towards national defence planning has improved in the past few years and the matter of defence modernisation, preparedness and fiscal planning has attracted serious attention of the Government, it will take a decade, if not more – and if the thrust on resuscitation of the nation's defence capability is not allowed to be diverted – to restore the damage inflicted upon the nation's military institution. The diagnosis of that ill is clear: One, disinterest of the political class to rid the military institution of obsolescent organisations and equipment, to purge inefficient procurement processes, and to rationalise manpower management policies; two, assumption of the politician's role in management of national defence by the bureaucracy, much to the latent relief of the political class; and three, reticence among the Service Headquarters in firmly and conjointly articulating their concerns. Presently however, there are hints of better counsel gaining ground, though reckonable improvements in the nation's defence planning will take some years to make mark – if not derailed by distracting events.

We may now proceed to examine another key feature of the nation's defence – planning and funding for military preparedness.

Trends of Defence Planning and Financing

It has ever been a practice for the national governments to regulate budgetary support to their military institutions in order to articulate the desired military power in fulfilment of their political goals. Defence budgetary planning is a process which is built upon geo-strategic appreciations, threat assessment, military strategy to protect own interests and force-structuring for that purpose; it is not a matter of bureaucratic book-keeping or an indulgence of political expediency. Indeed, it is a sanctimonious exercise to deal with adversaries with whom one is obliged to live and over whose deleterious machinations one has no control. In case of India, the policy-makers being estranged from military perceptive, the salience of competent defence planning is even more demanding. It was so that one of the corrective steps taken after the debacle of 1962 was that the system of 'Five-Year Defence Plans' – replaced by 'Roll-On Plans' during the most of the 1970s years before being reverted back – was devised to maintain the desired level of defence preparedness.

These Five-Year Plans, and the fund allocation under these Plans, were meant to be a joy-stick for the government to regulate its military preparedness in tune with its political goals. Taking the step further, during the Sixth Defence Plan period of 1980-85, the military institution made an attempt to find long term continuity and stability in the nation's defence planning through the recourse to '15-Year Perspective Plans'. But even then, the Perspective Plans remained captive to each service, and therefore the overall planning was confined to bureaucratic, rather than professional compilation of schemes, in most cases separately rather than conjointly sponsored by the three services. Finally, in the 1990s, fiscal limitations and fluctuations of economic burden scotched the prospects of long-term planning. The system fell into disuse, till it was revived in 2001 by the newly formed Headquarters IDS.

The points to note are that all this while:

a) Firstly, the military institution remained denied of a comprehensive and unambiguous political mandate for it to devise the right strategies and force-structure in fulfilment of that mandate. It was left to the military institution to gather what political hints it could and devise its strategies as well as force-structures. Accordingly, each

Service found its own goal-definition and action plan, albeit with fair degree of mutual consultations, but well short of the desired depth of inter-service integration.

b) Secondly, mission statements enunciated in the Five-Year Defence Plans were rhetorical rather than being strategic beacons for the military institution to align itself. Each Service therefore chose its path of progress according to its own perceptions and priorities. Inter-Service integrated planning being less than obligatory thus, it was natural for some redundancies and incongruences slipping into the overall military force-structure, training and logistics. Fiscal capacity being limited, this caused the Defence Ministry bureaucracy to practically assume the role of mediator, coordinator, arbitrator and approver of Defence Plans. This 'mediator' being bereft of military insight, the arrangement naturally led to reconciliatory indulgences among the individual services and the bureaucracy in the spirit of 'give and take' at the cost of inter-service integration and operational jointness.

c) Thirdly, in many instances – during the 7th, 8th, 10th and 11th Plans – Defence Plans could either be approved very late or not approved at all due to fiscal diversions to meet political priorities or the sprouting of contradictory strategic appreciations among the policy makers. Even when approved 'in principle' by the Government, the schemes could not be duly coupled with allocation of corresponding funds, thus allowing expediency and concoction to overtake the deliberately considered priorities.

d) Lastly, even if Plans were approved and funds allocated, there was no certainty that the planned schemes would find fruition – defence scientists, auditors, vain politicians, greedy vendors and even the rival services playing detracting roles.

As stated, in 2001, a new Headquarters IDS, was created to further the cause of inter-service jointness, and pending the appointment of a Chief of Defence Staff, was made responsible to the Chiefs of Staff Committee. With this the practice of tri-service long-term planning was revived in 2001 and after many revisions, a 'Long-Term Integrated Perspective Plan, 2012-27' was finalised in 2012-13. The purpose of this Plan was for it to be translated into three 'Short-Term (Five-Year) Plans' – the 12th, 13th and 14th Defence Plans – which in turn would be divided into 'Annual Acquisition Plans'. Further, this Plan was translated into an open source 'Technology Perspective

Capability Roadmap' for the defence industry to take a cue from and to develop military-industrial capability accordingly (20).

However, its implementation in building up a military capability that is commensurate to the challenges of India's security remains constrained due to the following inconsistencies:

a) Formulation of the Perspective as well as Five-Year Plans, undoubtedly have to be the preserve of each of the three services. However, in a dispensation wherein each service plans to fight according to its own designs of warfare and with its own desired weaponry while just about accommodating the causes of the other two services as best as it can without compromising on its own priorities, true integration of the nation's overall war-fighting capabilities are liable to become a matter of default. Thus there are redundancies, duplications and overlaps which could be better integrated into a wholesome war-machine.

b) Long-Term, Short-Term and Annual Plans have no committed or indicative funding to support. The current Long-Term Integrated Perspective Plan 2012-27 as well as the 12th Defence Plan are in fact approved by the DAC, which under a farcical notion of indicating 'progress' is a body biased to capital procurements. That leaves revenue procurements to a lower priority, which is a dangerous trend as it causes 'hollowness' in modern armed forces' combat capabilities, and gives false confidence to the custodians of national defence. Besides, the DAC has but only informal control over the DRDO and Public Sector Undertakings (PSU), while even less lien over the Private Sector. The Government's approval therefore falls short of the stamp of endorsement of the apex defence policy-making body – the Cabinet Committee on Security (CCS). Further, with the assignment, through an act of Parliament, of the national exchequer's accountability in exercising control over fiscal deficit, there is no certainty that the approval of the DAC might find budgetary sustenance unless the CCS plays its part.

c) A Long-Term Integrated Perspective Plan should dictate the formulation of Five-Year Plans which in turn should be broken down into Annual Plans. Due to different rates of progress among these three links as well as the fast pace of defence technological developments and changes in geo-political scenarios, long term plans have to be put through periodic course corrections. These course corrections can only be realised by having a regular system of monitoring and then having these endorsed every time through government approvals and budgetary adjustments. The Indian system of defence management does not lend itself to that call; it has to be made responsive to deal with such action-implementation-correction loop – on time.

d) Plans are focused at capital schemes whereas the revenue commitments play equally crucial role in the matter of military preparedness. The system of nurturing military preparedness therefore has to be more comprehensive and integrated than what the Defence Procurement Procedure or the DAC can offer.

e) The government tends to view military preparedness through the prism of prevalent geo-political situation and the immediate 'aggressive' intents of its adversaries. Besides, burdened by ever growing demands for higher fiscal commitments from the civil sector, it is obliged to retard the pace of military modernisation at frequent interludes. These conditions create gaps between the security demands and affordable fiscal capability. Contrarily, military force-structure is a matter which needs sustained long-term and assured fiscal commitment more than intermittent flood of funds; in order to sustain a stable level of preparedness and training, military expenditure cannot be a matter to be revised frequently. Due to these two contradictions, built up of military institution is a complex exercise of fine-balancing acts, interim compromises, reconciliations and innovative substitutions. This challenge is easier appreciated than met.

In sum, there is no sanctified process that binds managers of national defence to articulate their military security concerns through duly deliberated allocation of defence budgets; or to accord the right fiscal support to approved revenue and capital schemes; or to more or less adhere to time-lines of various schemes. It is not even certain if the intended level of military preparedness is in synchrony with the political goals, neither is there evidence that the government's defence plans meet the criteria of optimum cost-effective military preparedness.

Lately, conscious of looming military threats and prodded by loud cries from the strategic community, signs of a new coming are apparent. But for the coming of a new dispensation of defence management, one imperative must be to ensure the right balance between the undertakings of military upkeep and modernisation, and the exchequer's term-linked fiscal capacity to support that. The matter however, cannot be resolved by modern fiscal management practices alone.

A glance through the military acquisition plans would reveal that there is only limited compatibility between the expenditures on various aspects of intra as well as inter-services operational capabilities. Due to fiscal limitations, the bias of investments are invariably in favour of some of the visible elements – sophisticated weapons mainly – while the rest of the equally important but latent elements – like accessories and support systems – get relegated to atrophy. For example, Army may have to apportion its acquisitions in favour of its infantry and armoured forces, leaving out the support elements – engineer or air defence capability, for example – to stagnate. Similarly, among the commitments of air superiority, air defence, air-lift and close support, the Air Force may have to commit higher expenditure to its own pressing concerns, while the Navy may find it expedient to bias its investments in favour of either sea-control, or maritime security, or amphibious mission capabilities. Warfare being but the perfect orchestration of 'all' elements, these are compulsions which leave the overall force-capability in various states of imbalance and thus injects serious debilities in prosecution of war. The very purpose of incurring expenditure on defence gets negated thus.

Inadequate fiscal allocation – a fact of life ever – therefore have to be managed through integrated approach to force-structuring and rationalisation of overall operational capabilities. The root of imbalance and the resultant fiscal drain is however attributable to the inability of the nation's defence planners to set realistic strategic objectives that are fiscally sustainable by the national exchequer. For true advantages of efficient fiscal management to accrue therefore, India's managers of national defence may do well to set their strategic goals in proportion to their capacity to spend on defence. In similar vein, military strategists have to innovate strategic insights that would find compatibility between the operational objectives and funds committed to the right balance in force-structures.

Overall Inferences

The point to note therefore is that in the Indian system of defence management, a substantial political directive that would provoke strategic vision and lend to formulation of a realistic military doctrine, is yet to be promulgated. It is not the case that the India's defence management had been groping directionless all these years, but what is meant is that the governments of the day have depended on informal and tentative understandings between the MoD, the military institution and the defence establishment to manage national defence. Defence preparedness being a long term commitment, such tentative policy understandings are invariably compromised with each change of guard, and that afflicts the nation's military institution with tentative upkeep, disjointed modernisation schemes and fluctuating fiscal support. Crystallisation of indigenous military theology has thus been stymied, and that in turn has caused imbalances in the military force-structure. The result is that returns from the nation's investments on military security remains below par. In the contemporary period of geo-political and economic trends, that is a debility serious enough to raise alarm.

To Summarise

a) In absence of a formally promulgated National Defence Strategy – as sub set of National Security Strategy – and specific provisions to prepare themselves accordingly, each of the three services are left with no choice but to make unilateral assumptions over their political mandate, guess-estimate the political end states of military force-application and then devise their individual doctrines to meet that mandate. Accordingly, they propagate their own brand of military strategies and seek to structure, equip and train their forces in separation rather than doing so in a regime of jointness, and whereas the political leadership, bureaucracy and even the sister services remain but casual participants in that excursion. With such cursory linkages between political intent and conjoined force-capabilities, it is but natural that all of such efforts are liable to turn imbalanced in practice and defocused in performance.

b) While the Defence Minister's and various other Committees, including the Chiefs of Staff Committee, have limited lien over the system of defence policy-making, institutionalisation of the Chief of Defence Staff, to restitute the defence management system, remains blocked. In fact there are strong efforts made to dilute the roles of that institution.

c) Regular feedbacks rendered to the government regarding growing deficiencies in all the three services against their duly sanctioned scales of operational weapons, munitions and equipment have not made substantial headway in arresting the downslide in the nation's military capability. Warnings from the strategic community regarding the dangers of debilitating military capabilities have not

> been able to activate the government in pushing through even the planned and funded hardware productions and procurements to fill the 'hollowness' of military wherewithal, whereas entangled in procrastinating rituals, even duly 'approved' modernisation schemes remain mired in excruciating time and technological slippages.

That is the where the situation stands in the Year 2016. No doubt, the self-defeating designation of Service Headquarters as 'attached offices', exclusion of services' representation from government's higher defence policy-making mechanism and release of the rest of the defence establishment from direct accountability to the military institution are but the manifestation of a systemic incongruity in India's defence management. The cause is simple and straight forward: political indifference, and professional acquiescence to it.

To reiterate even at the cost of repetition, the Indian government, burdened by political and economic pulls, has been unable to sustain a level of defence preparedness that it mandates upon its military institution. The process of defence policy-making is afflicted with superficiality and ambivalence, so much so that there is perpetual mismatch between the commitments of regular force-upkeep and periodic modernisation measures, and actual resources allocated to that purpose. Past managers of national defence did not seem to be intent on priming and empowering the military institution to devise its native military doctrine that would have met the political mandate within an affordable fiscal regime. Ambivalence in policy-making thus churned out pedestrian policies, while tardy implementation of the plans raised the cost of national defence without the due enhancement of defence capability. Thus while defence expenditure mounts, military capability stagnates (21).

That is not how a developing country, burdened with serious deficiencies in almost all aspects of developmental indices, and subjected to severe external and internal security threats, should manage its ultimate bastion of sovereign nationhood – the military institution. To escape from that systemic trap, a better structured system of defence policy-making have to be devised that would facilitate enunciation of the political leadership's formal policies and guidelines to its military leadership. That in turn would trigger within the military institution, an urge to devise more efficient and innovative application of military power to achieve the intended political goals. With issuance of corresponding political directives to improve the performance of the defence establishment in its response to the service users, it would then be possible to make the best purchase out of a tight but appropriate defence budget and so achieve a regime of focused, cost-efficient management of national defence.

Era of Strategic Awakening?

Presently, the Indian state and its apparatus for national defence management appear to be professing a departure from its past strategic estrangement. Prodded on the one hand by incessant hammering from a hostile neighbourhood, and rising demands of geo-politicking on the other, the government seems to be intent on breaking free of its inheritance of a stagnant military institution. But the debility is deep-set; it will take decades to change track from the politics of military pacifism to assume such military power that would protect the nation's sovereign principles from the instabilities provoked by inimical powers. Towards that end, many initiatives have been taken at hand, some of the key ones being: Fine tuning of the 'Defence Procurement Procedure'; making forward movement in some of the import dependent modernisation schemes; opening private sector participation and Foreign Direct Investment in defence industry; call to the DRDO, DPSU and OFs to tighten belt and deliver; and most of all, indications of committed participation of the MoD in management of the military institution. No doubt, it will take time for the military hierarchy to be infused with due confidence upon the defence management system in the MoD; it will take longer before the military atrophy is finally reversed, but eventually, true fruition of a new strategic wisdom would be contingent upon reformation of the system of defence policy-making – without disruption, diversion or let up (22).

Having taken stock of the default mutation of an amateurish, informal and defocused system of defence policy-making that prevails in the arena of India's national defence, the stage is set to examine as to how can the that system be made more responsive to the call of the day. The following chapter is devoted to that end.

END NOTES AND SELECT REFERENCES

(1) Indian defence managers do not seem to be intent on following their own policies, as depicted by the policy of maintaining large defence forces and yet keeping them in a state of 'hollowness'. The result is that her deterrence against military aggression is effective only partially – and wearing thin over time.

(2) To reiterate the covenant stated in the beginning of the discussion, the term 'defence establishment' here consists of the bureaucracy, scientific research and development, quality assurance, defence estates, defence industry both public and private, the railways, and even the service providers like the departments of energy, education and human resource. Needless to state, all of the defence establishment must be dedicated to the needs of their sole 'user', that is the military institution, rather than propagating partisan interpretations of their own self-promoting inclinations.

(3) "A certain grasp of military affairs is vital for those in charge of general policy", – Clausewitz.

(4) Having been through the experiences of the World War II, significant advantages of that system were that: One, jointness was inherent in the services' mind frame; and two, opinion of Service Headquarters was taken rather seriously at the political plane. The disadvantage was that the novice political class was wary of the military institution while being helplessly dependent on the bureaucracy; the latter, on its own accord, being intent on capturing the centre stage of authority in the ruling regime.

(5) K Subramanyam, "Nehru's Concept of Indian Defence", Strategic Analysis, IDSA, Nov 2008. There are various versions of what the Prime Minister of the newly independent India told the then British Commander-in-Chief of Indian Armed Forces. Those days, political discourse was largely in the form of thematic conversations and expressed opinions rather than by issuance of formal policy pronouncements, and therefore the versions shape up based on individual quotes. The purport was unambiguous though: there was no need for an army in a nation which championed the cause of global peace, and therefore the police was adequate to administer the nation. Later, he asked his Indian Commander-in-Chief to confine to the containment of Pakistan's belligerency, and leave the matter of dealing with China to his diplomacy. Accordingly, certain major weapon acquisitions and force expansion were effected to counter Pakistan's military build-up by her western power treaty allies; and these steps did prove worthy during the 1965 War. But China never figured in that calculation. Further down the years, when many newly independent nations went under military rule, there was a fear of military coup in India. As it turned out, this fear was contrived rather than being any close to reality, with the advantages of that subterfuge going to an empowered bureaucracy – and China, of course.

(6) Uninitiated as they were in political instrumentality of military power, the political and bureaucratic classes found it inconceivable to view the military institution as anything more than a somewhat better armed Central force that was to undertake police actions gone out of control, nothing more.

(7) Air Vice Marshal Samir K Sen, "Military Technology and Defence Industrialisation", Manas Publications, Delhi, 2000. Such simplistic, if not foolish, ideas dominated a process of informal, if not casual, policy-making in a false-ideology regime that was seeped in what is known as 'Nehruvian' views. Thus the basic economics of defence industry was discarded in myopic innocence – there was no sane counsel, no protest.

(8) Military ethos and traditions, in many ways being in contravention of natural human instincts, take decades to build up, while strategic culture takes generations to be imbibed. Similarly, competency in military science and technology requires long term investments, cognitive as well as tangible. That indeed is the reason that prompts even an ever neutral nation like the Switzerland to maintain a competent military institution.

(9) This was the period when India was sucked into, not unwillingly of course, a sequence of regional military interventions – blocking Chinese intrusion at Samdorong Chu, interventions in Sri Lanka and Maldives, and joint operations with Bhutan, Nepal and Myanmar. That brought some prominence to the military institution and raised concern among the defence power brokers – bureaucrats, financial controllers and defence industrial kingpins – who closed ranks, if informally, to keep themselves from being arrested by military impositions.

(10) At this stage, many misplaced inter-service clash of interests had been invented and vigorously pursued. Thus the issues of ground-air support, maritime operations, heavy lift aircraft, helicopters, air defence system, maritime reconnaissance, common-use weapon acquisitions etc. were raked up in which defence bureaucracy happily found its place in arbitration.

(11) There is no doubt that economic survivability must have the highest priority amongst all national endeavours. In fact, military preparedness is a condition rather than a contradiction to that priority. In this instance, failure to appreciate the wisdom of maintaining complimentary balance between economy and defence led to episodes like the Kargil War and China's assertive behaviour soon after, cost of managing these episodes touching high against what the government might have saved by starving its military institution. Ironically, during the same period when the military institution was starving, the politico-military situation called for graduation of the nation's military strategy from reactive to proactive category. The disconnect between politics and defence was complete, no doubt.

(12) The last quarter of a century since 1990 saw a steady weakening of the foundations over which any military institution retains its vibrancy even when its competencies have to be temporarily sheathed. It was afflicted with growing deficiencies in basic arms, ammunition, spares, clothing and routine revenue supplies and services, while the opportunity to take advantage of the RMA and so to take a quantum leap into modernisation at relatively modest investments was allowed to pass by. Moreover, its singular success in pinning down secessionist insurgents notwithstanding, the government grew dismissive of the institutional concerns of the military hierarchy. Arguably, the instances of moral delinquencies among the military hierarchy which broke out at this time could be a fallout of the widespread dismay over the persistent operational hollowness at one end and the government's callousness over observance of the hoary state-soldier covenant, to keep the soldiery in good morale, on the other. Thus what should have been a conscious policy to freeze, but not undermine the military institution on the pretext of economic uplift, turned out to be a gross strategic loss in terms of what limited security related fiscal investments had been made during this period.

(13) Universally, the concept of 'military necessity' is the driving force for military preparedness, the best example of which is apparent in the process of China's military modernisation. Indeed, it had been so in India too but for a new found, if misplaced, enthusiasm among the polity in applying civilian yardsticks to the imperatives of national defence. Thus in the name of environment, this distraction forced compromises on training in fields and ranges, led to diminution of stocks of field fortification material like timber and camouflage fabric, and stalled strategic road construction. Similarly, the process of personnel management and acquisition of weapons and equipment for the forces came to be subjected to the traditionally languid civil terms, conditions and restrictions.

(14) By now, the purpose of defence research, defence estates, fiscal allocation for production of ammunitions and key war materials, military transportation – in fact all the key elements of military logistics – came to be defined largely by their in-house managers rather than their military end users. Virtual exclusion of the servicemen from such policy-making mechanism and self-assumption of autonomous authority by in-house cadres having vested interest in self-perpetuation finally led to the military institution becoming 'hollow' from within to the extent that its war waging potential was severely curtailed.

(15) It was so that the attempts were made, with near success, to marginalise the armed forces from nuclear policy-making and administration of cantonments. Similarly, the forces' demands for quality weaponry and equipment – weapon locating radars, tanks and guns, aircraft and spares, naval armaments etc., the list is long – were dismissed based on the defence scientists' never fulfilled assurances of producing these indigenously, while the auditors wondered as to why should every soldier have his rifle and bullet proof jacket when only some of them would actually engage in fire-fight!

(16) A partisan defence bureaucracy – made up of central civil and allied services, even revenue and railway officials – prevented reform of the archaic defence policy-making system in fear of losing its unchallengeable, unaccountable grip over state power. Politicians, on their part, chose to remain oblivious of the nuances of military administration and felt satiated with their captivity to bureaucratic advisors – advisors who had little, if any, appreciation of military issues – to proxy against their constitutional responsibility. Abetted by the vainness of an equally partisan military hierarchy, that was the reason that some of the salient recommendations of the Kargil Review Committee were stalled, nipped in fact. Failure to create the institution of 'Chief of Defence Staff' was one of those recommendations; no one seemed to suggest that if the railways, finance commission, Reserve Bank and various regulatory authorities could be found to be competent in controlling important aspects of governance, there could be no reason to believe that the institution of 'Chief of Defence Staff' would cause any upset in management of the military institution. In this context, the following publications are relevant:

a) B D Jayal, "India's Military Modernisation", India's National Security, 2003.
b) R Venkatraman, "Integration of Ministry of Defence and Defence Planning", Air Power Journal, Summer 2010.

c) Admiral Arun Prakash, "National Security Reform: Ten Years after the Kargil Committee Report", USI Journal, Oct-Dec 2012.

d) Lt Gen Satish Nambiar, "Restructuring and Integration of the MoD with Three Services Headquarters", USI Journal, Jan-Mar 2013.

(17) During the Operation Parakram, the Indian Army realised that it needed a long time to mobilise against Pakistan from its hinterland base areas, thus allowing the latter adequate time to prepare and react. The 'Cold Start' Doctrine was therefore innovated with some of the highly lethal mobile formations, 'battle groups' so to say, being grouped under the local formation headquarters and located close to the border. The purpose was to unleashed these battle groups at minimal notice to take Pakistan by surprise, before she could gear up to resist, while the rest of the main forces located in the hinterland caught up some hours or days later to maintain the momentum of attack. A brilliant innovation that shook the Pakistan military hierarchy, its efficacy, however, remained uncertain due to a rather inadequate association of the back-up establishments of the state – like those needed for transportation, war mobilisation, operational logistics and defence production – and somewhat tentative endorsement from the other two services. In any case, as the history of warfare points out, achievement of strategic surprise of that magnitude, successfully at that, is rarely achievable even for the militarily active states – and India is not one of them. The other development was the stitching together of a Joint Services Doctrine which, devoted to a broad rhetoric while keeping away from delving into individual services' domains, and contained little of substance in terms of common structures, joint planning, training and preparation and joint war-fighting.

(18) Contrived justifications apart, it is an irony that the military dedicated establishments like the DRDO, DDE, DPSUs and the Ordnance Factories have been more or less freed from military oversight, and so have many times found their interests in clash with that of their sole purpose of existence – the military institution! Likewise, the state seems to have chosen the military institution – it not having fallen to the growing practice of democratic intransigence – to introduce societal and fiscal experimentations – like keeping redundant ordnance and stationary depots, de-notification of training and firing areas, diluting standards just to commission women, permitting near-permanent depletion of war reserves to cover fiscal deficits, and to control political-bureaucratic-industrial corruption in the process of defence acquisition. The soldier is thus burdened with, apart from defending the nation, propagation of probity among the defence managers!

(19) The attempt was to make the proposal more acceptable to the fierce turf warriors – in the form of the service bureaucracies presided over by the three Service Chiefs, and the actual wielders of unquestioned authority, the defence bureaucracy – all of them remaining comfortable with piggy-back riding on certain genuine systemic hurdles and so perpetuating the status quo. This Permanent Chairman of Chiefs of Staff Committee was therefore designated to exercise authority only upon the Strategic Forces Command, the Andaman and Nicobar Command, Cyber Command, the National Defence University etc., with no authority to arbitrate or

override on inter-services differences. Actually, this arrangement could turn into a farce considering that the first two Commands are beholden to the services for the smallest of military resources while the last two float yet in the realm of notions, nothing more. In effect, the Permanent Chairman would not be different that the rotational one, with the added injury if being a lame functionary.

(20) These issues are well discussed in the following publications authored by Amiya K Ghosh and published by KW Publications, New Delhi.

a) "India's Defence Budget and Expenditure Management in a Wider Context";

b) "Resource Allocation and Management in Defence: Need for a Frame work";

c) "Defence Planning in India at Cross-Roads".

(21) The constitutional mechanism to evaluate the performance of the defence establishment in implementation of defence policies and its commitments to the revenue and capital plans – that is, the 'Parliamentary Committee on Defence' – does not enjoy the status it should, given its sensitive charter. This Committee is but an advisory body and its Annual Reports are accorded the least cognisance.

(22) Some of the modernisation schemes which have started stirring out of frozen files are: procurement of modern trainer, multi-role fighter and air-borne surveillance and control aircraft, ultra-light howitzers and self-propelled guns, air defence systems, helicopters, naval armaments, tactical missiles and many of the much needed weapon and performance enhancing accessories. Alongside proceed the cases of creation of Special Operations Command, construction of naval warships and submarines, fielding of tactical command, control and communication systems, resuscitation of ammunition stocks, and quantum upgrade of logistic infrastructure along the border belt. There are many more cases in hand. But since the salience of the proverbial 'hob nail' in successful prosecution of warfare is as crucial as a tank or machine gun, there are even more cases which need to be progressed in order to seamlessly link up all aspects of military operations, before a comprehensive war waging capability, across the entire spectrum of contemporary warfare, is achieved.

*

CHAPTER 4

REFORM OF APEX LEVEL DEFENCE MANAGEMENT STRUCTURE–1

"When the pace of change accelerates, the militaries that change and adapt are likely to gain massive advantage over potential enemies who are less agile."

– **Prof Scott Stephenson**

Enunciation of the Purpose

Major changes have occurred in India's geo-political posture since the last couple of decades. Thus while she is confronted by emergence of increasingly ominous threats from her inimical neighbours – one habitually condescending and militarily assertive and another instinctively inimical by ideological compellence – the spectrum and nature of warfare itself that she has to fight in future have undergone revolutionary changes. Besides, management of national defence is a dynamic process that evolves in tune with the rest of the national discourse in terms of social, scientific and economic developments, and as a corollary, a dynamic coalescence of political aspirations. This principle is particularly applicable to India as she charts her course towards breakthrough economic development, societal progress and rising stakes in regional as well as global dispensations. Inexorably, these aspects of aspirational discourse lead to emergence of new implications for national defence and therefore have to be tackled by deliberate revisit of the existing system of defence management as well as the policies and practices that emanate from it.

In the post-Kargil Conflict era and following the strategic stand-off with Pakistan during 'Operation Parakram', the knowledgeable Indian citizenry of today is more aware of India's state of defence preparedness with regard to imposition of military deterrence, power articulation, defence diplomacy and defence industrial capability. Therefore, while management of the nation's security challenges have become more complex as well as sensitive to the cause of Indian nationhood, scrutiny from the informed citizens, of the manner these challenges are handled, have assumed higher salience in India's democratic discourse. Indeed, striking the right balance between diplomacy, military power and fiscal affordability on one end, and meeting the empowered citizen's nationalist aptitude on the other, would be imperative in that context.

The twin conditions as mentioned above call for review of the entire gamut of management of national defence, the purpose being to reform the entire system according to contemporary conditions. But for such wider and deeper review to succeed, the first step must be to modernise the national defence management structure itself and reform its system of defence policy-making. The fundamentals corrected thus, adoption of sensible courses in efficient management of national defence according to contemporary conditions would be facilitated.

The system of national defence being a matter of centralised control and more or less outside deep public scrutiny, its reformation must flow out from within the government's internal policy-making structure – somewhat like a self-actualising mission. This mission, no doubt, is a tedious call in the maze of conflicting political and economic priorities, fiscal limitations, lack of strategic experience and bureaucratic – civil as well as military – resistance, much of these being quite understandable, if exasperating, and impossible to dismiss. The goals defined for defence reforms therefore must be able to reconcile such contradictions. Indeed, with geo-politics, technology and social behaviour turning new leafs, the right time to postulate, adopt and implement reformation in the construct of the nation's defence management has arrived; few years down the line it might become more complex and costly. And as discussed earlier, the start, before anything else, must be made from revamp of the national defence management structure and its system of defence policy-making.

As discussed in the previous chapter, there had been many attempts to reform the structure of defence management in India to bring it in tune with the challenges of the contemporary strategic dispensation. Notably, most such attempts have had to be triggered by adverse fallouts of catastrophic security situations like the debacle of 1962 and mess up in Kargil Confrontation; rationalisation of the nation's defence management and policy-making apparatus to keep in pace with the call of the times has seldom been politically pre-empted (1). Within the military institution, however, there have been many instances of foresighted build-up of operational capability to keep ahead of looming military threats or at the least to keep pace with the emerging strategic situations, but in the absence of corresponding update of defence policy-making system at the political level, these initiatives could not fulfil the right promise. Resultantly, the improvements brought about have been little more than patchwork of incremental upgrades aimed at the redress of past shortcomings; and even then, these initiatives have petered out before reaching the intended objectives (2).

In order to obviate repetition of the past failures, it would be prudent to consider, within the overall ambit of defence reforms, the three inter-related aspects of apex level national defence management structure, as follows:

a) The system of defence policy-making;
b) Policy implementation, monitoring and performance evaluation; and,
c) Course corrections, rationalisation of imbalances and feedback.

To reform the national defence management structure, the first matter to home on to is to the kind of policies that are needed to emanate from it and as to what do these policies have to accomplish. Next, the purpose being to enhance alacrity in defence policy-making, the management structure must be rooted at native conditions and therefore naturally imbibed, thus guarding against in-congruencies. Indeed, these two considerations are to be valued if we wish to make the venture succeed – unlike the past attempts which have failed to achieve the intended purpose.

But before proceeding further, we may recapitulate the definitions as highlighted in the Preamble itself, that is:

a) Challenges of national security are managed through the invocation of 'National Security Strategy/Policy'.
b) National defence is one, albeit the exclusive one, part of national security. National defence is built-up according to a 'National Defence Policy' which governs the military institution as well as

the defence establishment, the former as the sword arm of military security and the latter as a foundation of national power.

c) Finally, military security is one part of national defence, and it is achieved through application of appropriate 'Military Strategies'.

Indeed, promulgation of National Security Strategy which encompasses a corresponding National Defence Policy as its sub-set, promotes the innovation of right Military Strategies, application of which offers military security to the nation.

Reforms at the Apex Level

The fundamental purpose of organising national defence is to take recourse to military force-application when more civilised methods of preserving national integrity and guarding national interests – such interests that are contingent upon exercise of 'sovereign will' and 'freedom of choice' – fail to work. To that extent, the cause of national defence managers must be to be able to field adequate military forces, prepare and maintain these in fighting fettle, institute efficient procedure for mobilisation and marshal these either for imposition of deterrence or prosecution of war; creation of requisite defence logistic infrastructure and estates to maintain, train and deploy forces, all within an appropriate and affordable fiscal commitment, must be a part of that reformation. Further, that cause must encompass the recourse to defence research, development and production of military hardware to sustain own forces, to promote defence exports and to engage in military-to-military ties. At the delivery end, the objective must be to evolve the nation's geo-strategic as well as military perspective with the purposes of deterring military aggression from external adversaries and anti-national militias, and nurturing military-diplomacy as well as defence-economic cooperation at the international level.

In this chapter, the first issue to address in the context of reform of apex level defence management must be aimed at modernising its structure. Next, with the goals of the reforms defined, specific propositions related to systemic reforms in policy-making could be discussed. The final step would be to delve into certain key propositions that could flow out of astute policy-making, so as to bring the benefits of reforms to the military institution, the defence establishment, and finally, to the national cause. To achieve the abovementioned purpose therefore, the start would be made by briefly touching upon the existing apparatus for managing national security – it would be seen that at the apex political level this apparatus is a competent one.

The National Security Policy Making Apparatus

Formal constitution of an apex level political body, duly counselled by competent professionals to deliberate upon the task of national security is a universally adopted practice. Promulgation of the appropriate mandate for the nation's military institution to organise itself accordingly, duly supported with allocation of the due structural and fiscal provisions, flows out of that constitutional body. In the Indian system, there is the 'Cabinet Committee for Security' (CCS) to fulfil that role. It is a committee of decision making politicians having the counsel of professionals who are competent in nuances of national security. Indeed, in past occasions, the political leadership has shown strategic maturity in handling the 1965 and 1971 Wars, the Sri Lanka, Kargil and 2001-02 'Parakram' Operations, and the process of nuclear weaponisation, notwithstanding the debates in hindsight regarding the end states achieved.

Presently, to advise and guide the nation's political rulers, there is a formally constituted and empowered body of grand strategists – referred to in many countries as the 'National Security Council' (NSC). In the Indian system, there is the NSC with its Secretariat which assists and advises the CCS, a 'National Security Advisor' (NSA) and the consultative bodies in the form of the 'National Security Advisory Board' (NSAB) and the 'Strategy Policy Group' (SPG). The national level intelligence work is attended to by the 'Intelligence Coordinating Group', which is responsible for tasking and coordination among various intelligence agencies like the Intelligence Bureau (IB), Research and Analysis Wing (RAW), National Technical Research Organisation (NTRO) and Defence Intelligence Agency (DIA), and further assisted by the Technical Coordination Group (TCG) and the National Information Board (NIB), each having their many satellite expert groups. Management of the nuclear force is organised under the overall control of a 'National Command Authority' (NCA) which has its stand-by or alternate set up and is supported by its dedicated Strategy Programme Staff. The NCA is made up of a 'Political Council' and an 'Executive Council' to operate the intended nuclear posture, the former composed similarly as the CCS and the latter having the National Security Advisor, Service Chiefs, Commander-in-Chief of Strategic Forces Command and heads of the DRDO and Department of Atomic Energy (DAE) as its members. Matters of national security at the political level are therefore reasonably well taken care of.

At the next level, an empowered policy-making body is needed to translate the political mandate – that may be enunciated through a National

Security Strategy – into an efficient mechanism for national defence. This body prepares the military institution to find a right balance of organisational architecture, force-composition, equipment profile and professionally trained and motivated personnel. Similarly, it guides the defence establishment to be truly responsive to the requirements of the military institution. As discussed in Chapter 2 above, in advanced countries, this purpose is fulfilled by their Departments of Defence through promulgation of formal national security strategies, regular undertakings of Strategic Defence Reviews and issuance of Strategic Guidelines for the military leadership as well as the defence bureaucracy to follow. Needless to state, formal and lead participation of military professionals in these functions of the Departments of Defence is mandatory.

In India, the Ministry of Defence (MoD), manned by a bureaucracy and headed by a Defence Minister or Raksha Mantri (RM), attends to that responsibility. Curiously, neither possesses the necessary strategic expertise and experience of military functions, nor do they appreciate the benefits of integrated military participation in policy-making. In theory, the CCS, the rest of the security apparatus and the MoD, all have the option of inviting professional military advice, but in absence of formal membership of military professionals in the policy-making bodies, the decision itself to exercise that option remains in the hands of those who might not always appreciate the necessity. In any case, in matters of national defence, professional advise 'invited' from 'visiting fellows' cannot be expected to do justice to the complex cause. Absence of formal military participation at the policy-making level further adds to in-optimal harness of the nation's intelligence assets for the formulation of military-specific intelligence task-tables and processing of strategic information at the MoD level.

As a result of this anomaly, the MoD, at its best, performs merely as a post office to attend to the staff work associated with projections made by the services on various capital, revenue and personnel management schemes. At its worst, the MoD invokes the process of scrutiny to deflect or dilute professionally adjudged projections, cost saving and latent one-upmanship being the usual motives. It is so that there are left gaps in strategic formulations at the level of the MoD and the Ministry of External Affairs (MEA) which have to be filled up through ad hoc mechanisms that are cobbled up from situation to situation. In other words, the matters of national defence at the ministerial level are attended to in an unstructured and situation-specific consultative mechanism. Presently, the provision of in-built military advice in the national security set up and structured integration of duly appointed military staff, with due decision making authority, into the MoD remains hostage to archaic, military-wary anxieties which captivate the system. That, in fact, is the reason behind many of the deficiencies in India's management of national defence, starting with the inability to promulgate a formal national security strategy and ending at perpetuation of a disjointed military force-structure (3).

Policy-articulation and implementation mechanism at the third level, within the distinct domains of three branches of the defence services, each having its dedicated intelligence, finance and such paraphernalia, as well as the defence procurement agency, various defence-dedicated establishments and the defence industrial sector, are undertaken 'in-house' more or less. Thus there are the Service Headquarters of the military institution and various Departments and Directorate Generals of defence establishments to attend to the functions of executive level policy-articulation and implementation in isolation. Competent by themselves, however there is the express need for reform of these hierarchies in tune with the modern conditions and necessities. For the military institution, the reform would be aimed at fostering a culture of joint-force centric rather than just arm and weapon centric modernisation, adoption of comprehensive rather than just incremental force-restructure, and reconciliation of the disconcert between military strategy, military force-structure and financial, technological and industrial resources committed to national defence. Similarly, for the defence establishment, the purpose would be to render credible the undertakings of defence acquisitions, development and production of war-quality hardware, better maintenance of expendable stocks of war materials, management of defence estates and execution of construction works – not just for organisational self-perpetuation, but for the benefit of its military user.

The inference is clear: while the matter of national security at the political level is adequately attended to, albeit sans integral military advice, at the next level, that is the policy-making MoD level, its translation into national defence policies suffers from structural and procedural, and therefore qualitative, deficiencies. Lastly, at the third tier of management, the three services of the military institution on the one hand and the various domains of the defence establishment on the other, exercise excessive inner autonomy, bordering on self-centrality, to conduct their business in the manner that their aspirations, rather than the overall cause of national defence, require. Appropriately therefore, the first step of defence reforms would be to restructure, firstly, the MoD at the policy-making level, and secondly, the three services and various department of the defence establishment at the executive levels.

Ultimately, the thrust at all the above mentioned three levels has to be directed at finding answers to technological and fiscal challenges that confront the innovation of native military strategies and efficient management of military personnel, forces and hardware. Strengthening the bureaucracy's stakes in defence management, incentivising defence research and industry to bring relief from import-dependence, and offer of special provisions for development of defence infrastructure – all under the spirit of 'military necessity' – have to be intrinsic to that effort.

Goal Definition: Reform of National Defence Management Structure

Indeed, it would be prudent to define an appropriate goal to focus upon before setting out to discuss reform of the national defence management structure and its system of defence policy-making. Obviously, that goal would be contingent upon the threats emanating from the neighbourhood, mainly China and Pakistan but not the least from the rest when they are often misguided and enticed into India-baiting – as it has been in the case of intermittent pin-pricking from Sri Lanka, Nepal and Maldives. Besides, defence policy-making has also to account for the latent threats which might emanate from super power sanctions, and various denial regimes and adverse impositions if and when these suit their interests – the US cushioning the injurious fallouts of her involvements in Afghanistan and West Asia, or power wrangling between US and China in South-East Asia, for example (4).

Taking cue from the observable trends, it is realistic to postulate that a political direction for the Indian military institution could be outlined as:

a) One, to dissuade China from attempting to secure her territorial claims by military means; and,
b) Two, to defeat Pakistan's never-ending military campaign – proxy, subversive or regular war – and deter her from indulging in military adventurism in the future.

Added to these directions could be the commitments to:

a) Suppress insurgencies gone out-of-hand;
b) Participation in UN and allied operations; and
c) Response to calls for disaster relief.

This way, formal enunciation a plausible political direction, that could guide the adoption of appropriate military doctrine and corresponding strategies for application of military power to the furtherance of the political purpose, may be set as one of the goals of reforms in national defence management structure. In other words, reforms in the system of defence policy-making must lead to political promulgation of a 'national security strategy or policy' that balances national aspirations with the nation's fiscal, technological and industrial resources, its leak-proof implementation and its periodic review from professional considerations.

Next, to deal with the challenges of national defence there is the MoD which is responsible to ensure that the armed forces have the training, equipment and institutional back-up that is necessary to fulfil their mandate within an affordable budget. As for management of external threats, the MEA assumes the role of the 'lead agency', more or less, just as the Ministry of Home Affairs (MHA) pitches in when the nation's integrity is threatened by externally aided insurgency – justifiably so. These ministries of the Government of India function with the back-up from over a dozen internal agencies and interact with various strategic partner nations, the aim being to protect, in the realm of international power-play, the security, independence and interests of the country. Deliberate and collaborative function between the three Ministries – and the fourth if the key role played by the Finance Ministry is considered – however, is limited to occasional interactions at the apex level when the discussion is dominated by political considerations and diplomatic restraint. Hard evaluation of the capacity of the military institution and productivity of the defence establishment to meet the political aim do not figure in such confabulations. In effect therefore, confabulations over the nation's the nations' military capability – and its corollary, military options – stand conditional to four separate, virtually autonomous and often disjointed, even anomalous factors, that is: One, as to what external threat the MEA may envisage from its own angle; two, what resources the MoD may find for its military institution; three, as to what intelligence, police and other civil support may the MHA provide; and four, as to what fiscal support may be forthcoming from the Finance Ministry. Thus while the purpose of conjoined government level strategising and organising for national defence remains uncertain, even at the CCS level, the decision as to what military requirements need to be acceded to remains but contingent on bureaucratic interpretations from professionally diverse hierarchies. The result is that India's huge defence sector is afflicted with as many voids as there are redundancies that breed operational hollowness for war, besides weakening the prospects of military diplomacy and arms trade in peace.

Accepting that in the post-1990 era, India has not been disposed towards using military power to ameliorate its geo-political concerns, but just to keep her border territories secure against threats of forced usurpation, even that purpose would still be dictated by growing militarisation and sovereignty defying machinations of geo-politics on the one hand, and build-up of indigenous economic strength and defence-industrial capacity on the other. The second goal of reforms in the system of defence policy-making therefore must be to institutionalise an intimate mechanism for long term inter-ministerial strategic decision making, as discussed above.

Further, in the contemporary dispensation, national security must be built upon the twin pillars of national defence policy and internal security policy. This is so because warfare by various alternate means has emerged as an enticing trend, and consequently, orthodox segregation between external and internal threats to national security is neither always practical nor is it synergic in effort. The purpose of protecting the nation's integrity would therefore be contingent upon maintaining internal stability against export of insurgency or proxy war, demographic infiltration, rise of radical inclinations, people's revolt and lawless mobocracy. Conversely, in the Indian system, these two pillars of national security stand tilting away from each other, joining up but exceptionally to deal with exigencies and then reverting to their own cocoon of status quo. Of late, in handling the various classes of threats to national integrity, there have been certain formal assignments of roles to the Central Intelligence Agencies and the Central Armed Police Forces (CAPF), but yet, comprehensive synergy of effort is yet to be achieved. For example, while the Border Security Force (BSF), the Indo Tibet Border Police (ITBP), and the Central Reserve Police Force (CRPF) have defined roles to perform, operational level unification of their capabilities with the nation's military forces has got diluted over the decades of post-1971 distractions in favour of departmental autonomy. Even the management of intelligence queries of the CAPF are met more due to their cadre affinity rather than a structured mechanism.

As a result of autonomous, self-fulfilling existence of the CAPF, the nation's internal security mechanism remains at half-cock. It is so that various security organisations remain short of optimal synergy, compartmented undertaking of operations remains inconclusive and threats continue to simmer even when recessed – Counter-Maoist operations being a glaring example. At the other end, military operations are planned and conducted in superfluous assimilation, many times even total exclusion, of the CAPF. Ultimately, the exchequer lands up paying the cost of all such deficiencies; indeed, the contrast with the synergic system of regular, reserve, militia and police forces that is operative in US, UK, Russia and China, is glaring. Formal and firm linkage between national defence and internal security, and inter alia, effective assimilation of the CAPF into military operational duties, as had been the case earlier, would bring the nation better dividends in terms of military deterrence, posturing and war – humouring the autonomous aspirations of the CAPF cadres need not dictate state policies. Indeed, that purpose of synergic association of the CAPF with the military institution must be met through the national defence management structure and its system of defence policy-making. That would be the third goal of the proposed defence reform (5).

The fourth goal of reform of the national defence management structure would be to further the cause of optimal modernisation of the military institution in tune with its contemporary responsibilities and rational commitment of national resources to that purpose. For a country of high reckoning in global economy as well as regional politics while still engaged in developing mode, there is bound to exist a capability and resource gap between what responsibilities the Indian military institution has to attend to and as to what resources are made available to it. Flexible force-structuring of the military institution with an optimal balance between regular, special and reserve forces for achievement of the overall military strategic objectives rather than tactical service-centric goals, and deployability of these in judiciously scaled response timings are the imperatives to close that gap. Indeed, the system of defence policy-making must be conducive for the military institution to catch up with the long stymied joint doctrinal innovations, right force-structuring to include reserve forces and the Territorial Army, modernisation of organisations and equipment coupled with discard of the redundant and obsolescent, inter-service jointmanship, qualitative upgrade of personnel and modernisation of their training, and synergic harness of intelligence capabilities – all being aimed at the nation extracting the best dividends from its military institution in terms of security, peace and stability – and affordability.

In similar vein, the system of defence policy-making should promote a similar transformation in the defence establishment for them to go a step more intimate in their contribution, according to their domain expertise, in building up the nation's defence capabilities. Astute policy-making on defence research and development, defence industry, defence estates, build-up of military logistics, adequate budgetary provisions and fiscal management, and finally, defence procurements and acquisitions, may therefore be the fifth goal of reform of the national defence management structure.

In the backdrop of the discussion so far, it would be in order to discuss the proposition for a more competent national defence management structure along two distinct lines, as follows:

a) One, structure for policy-making on purely military matters, that is, policies aimed at the military institution, including its more robust linkages with the national intelligence set up;
b) Two, a stronger policy-making structure to manage all constituents of the nation's defence establishment.

Higher Policy-Making Structure for the Military Institution

Taking advantage of the discussion on universal trends of defence policy-making and the requirements in the Indian context, it is now possible to propose a more effective architecture for higher defence policy-making in India. However, taking note of the hurdles and failures experienced in reforming the system of defence management in the past, the matter to be careful in this effort are that: one, going beyond pure organisational theories, the architecture must be customised to the Indian situation as it actually prevails; and two, the propositions should be appealing enough to break through the deep-rooted prejudices over the value of defence professionalism and recognition of exclusivity of military expertise which grip the nation's ill-qualified defence managers. Therefore, it would also be helpful to take note of the functional difficulties faced by the other countries during implementation of their desired objectives and corrective measures adopted to overcome the hurdles, resistance form rigid organisational cultures being the first one to be overcome. Indeed, the professional fortitude displayed within the defence hierarchy of advanced countries in pushing through the reforms would have to be emulated, and the tendency to succumb to cultural pulls and prejudices, to permit deviations and compromises from the professionally focused path, firmly rejected. Finally, due to the defence bureaucracy's familiarity with the British system, the experiences of the UK and to some extent, that of the USA governing establishments may be adopted as reference points in this endeavour. Then, once the proposed measures are formalised and implemented, at the next stage, many elements of these measures would have to be revisited and corrections applied based on experiences gained in implementation. The propositions for defence reforms have to cater to that requirement too.

During the course of discussion in Chapters 1 and 3, and experiences of some advanced countries as noted in Chapter 2, it is clear that in the contemporary dispensation, a nation's military power rests upon three pillars, one of which is military-predominant in character while the other two are driven by diverse fields of civilian competence. These three pillars are:

a) One, military forces composed from the three services of the military institution and which are administered through military-specific policies and military law.
b) Two, the defence establishment consisting of bureaucracy, procurement system, estates management, science and technology development facilities and military hardware production industry.
c) Three, the nation's dual-use infrastructure which provides for the fundamental plank over which defence capabilities are nurtured – like scientific institutions, law and order, transportation, telecommunication, energy, food, education, health and employment.

Notably, each of these three pillars is ruled by divergent conditions in terms of organisational goals, infrastructural requirements, core competencies, management practices and performance targets. For example, the first two are integral parts of the Defence Ministry while the third falls in multi-ministerial sectors. On the other hand, dictated by their distinct roles, cultural norms, organisational regulations and executive practices, the above mentioned first pillar is distinguished by its purely military character while the other two are more or less in civilian domain, both working towards a common goal, that is, fostering a regime of effective and affordable national defence. Therefore, to meet these diverse characteristics, it would make sense to devise the structure of nation's higher defence management into two distinct branches – or departments. As discussed in Chapter 2 above, this arrangement would be in tune with the practices successfully experimented with, and adopted by the defence ministries of the advanced nations.

The proposition begins with classification of two distinct but goal-congruent departments under the Indian Ministry of Defence (MoD). These are described as:

a) The Department of Defence Forces (DDF);
b) The Department of Defence Establishments (DDE).

Higher Direction of War: The Ministry of Defence (MoD)

Distinct roles performed by various constituent agencies of national defence in the shaping of optimal and cost-efficient military institution have been discussed in Chapter 2. Efforts made by the Indian government to modernise and upgrade the system of defence policy-making, and the rather modest results that could be garnered out of such initiatives have also been discussed in Chapter 3. Thus equipped with home grown experiences and taking advantage of conceptual studies and insightful experimentations carried out in other countries on the matter of defence management, time is ripe to devise customised propositions which may find favourable application under the Indian conditions.

We may now elaborate an outline structure of the MoD that rests upon the three pillars of competencies which are to be managed under two distinct departments as discussed above. The point to note is that while the imperatives of reforms must be sacrosanct, neither the proposed nomenclatures nor the charters need to be so; formalisation of these aspects have to be a follow-up matter of micro deliberations, implementation and adjustments based on hands-on experiences.

To begin with, the MoD is proposed to be broadly structured as indicated at Figure 1 below.

MoD (Headed by Raksha Mantri or RM)

RM's Secretariat (RMS)

Department of Defence Forces (DDF)	Department of Defence Establishments (DDE)
(Headed by Minister of State or MoS, DDF)	(Headed by Minister of State or MoS, DDE)

Figure 1: The MoD

Thus leaving out the CCS which must remain as the apex political body to mandate overall directions in the course of national security endeavours, the MoD would continue to:

a) Firstly, translate the political mandate on national defence into all round defence preparedness;
b) Secondly, exercise overarching control over the military institution as well as the defence establishment; and,

c) Thirdly, marshal and coordinate all inter-ministerial and inter-sectorial resources which go to strengthen national security in general and national defence in particular.

Accordingly, the MoD may be structured into two distinct departments, each headed by a Minister of State (MoS), with the RM presiding and in full control over all affairs of national defence. The RM's secretarial services would be performed by the Raksha Mantri's Secretariat (RMS), headed by a Principle Secretary. This Secretariat would be staffed by services professionals as well as a stream of defence-dedicated bureaucrats complementing each other's professional expertise and executive experience.

Propositions regarding the two afore-stated Departments are discussed next, in the following paragraphs.

Exercise of Strategic Control: Department of Defence Forces (DDF)

The proposition envisages a 'Department of Defence Forces' (DDF) to superintend through its functional arm – the Integrated Service Headquarters (IHQ) – all matters specific to the military forces and related to direct prosecution of war. Within the ambit of the political mandate vested upon the military institution and exercised through the RM, this Department would bear the prime responsibility of policy-making to cover all such aspects as recruitment to release of personnel, training, upkeep and modernisation of field formations as well as static institutions, equipment management, operational logistics, fiscal management and creation and maintenance of infrastructural assets that are dedicated to the direct prosecution of military operations.

Ministerial control over this Department could be exercised by MoS, while a tri-service institution of the Chief of Defence Staff (CDS), headed by the person of CDS and with the Service Chiefs as its members, would attend to the responsibilities of elaborative or secondary policy-making. The institution of the CDS would be responsible for prioritisation, implementation and monitoring of various schemes and fine tuning military management at the national level, besides providing secretarial support to the secretariat of the MoS. Accordingly, besides the institution of CDS, the IHQ will consist of the three existing Service Headquarters, and even if staffed mainly by military professionals, would have the required numbers of defence-dedicated civil servants, defence scientists, finance managers and similar experts at appropriate levels of hierarchy according to the need of domain expertise and experience.

Proposition of an Outline Organisation for DDF

An outline structure of the proposed DDF, which may form the basis of discussion and further evolution may be considered as depicted at Figure 2 below, and followed up with detailed explanation of the proposition in subsequent paragraphs.

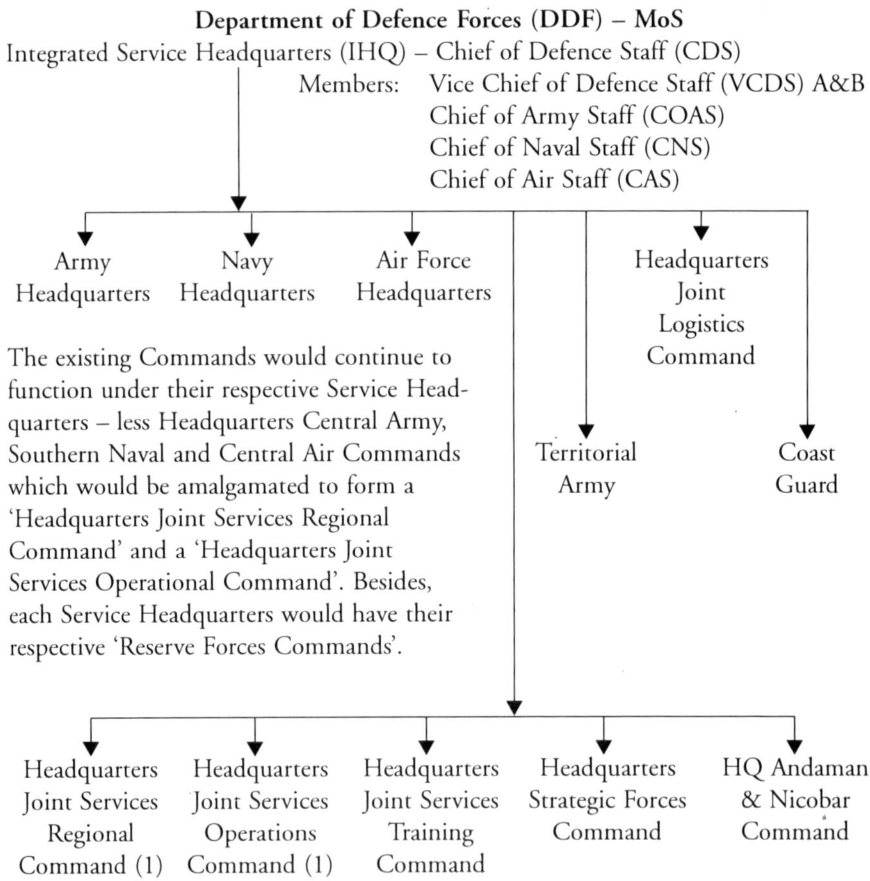

(Certain more command headquarters would have to be raised to meet the imperatives of modern warfare, for example, special forces command, IW or cyber command, space command, national defence university etc.).

Figure 2: The DDF

The outline structure depicted above is indicative of the certain keynote features, namely: One, the institution of CDS; two, operationalisation of Joint Service Command Headquarters; and three, upholding the sanctity of Service Headquarters. Let us examine these features in that sequence.

Defence Preparedness and Strategic Planning: The Institution of Chief of Defence Staff (CDS)

With the political leadership nonplussed by arguments and counter-arguments over an issue of which they have but vague ideas and no more, the time has come to break free of nearly two decades of post-Kargil log-jam and move forward in the quest of defence reforms, which cannot proceed in a cost-and-time bound manner but through the institution of CDS system. Indeed, no matter what are the reasons genuine or contrived to resist the change from comfort to unfamiliar zone, modern military institutions cannot be managed efficiently, effectively and affordably by three autonomous and self-centric services functioning in splendid autonomy. Indeed, for the possession of an efficient, modern and affordable military institution to happen, institution of the CDS system is the only course left.

Accordingly, the decade-and-a-half of confusion and resistance over the institution of CDS which is seen to be a harbinger of the concept of joint-services operational commands – that in due course it must be – and feared to lead to upsetting the established control hierarchies – that it need not be – requires to be redressed. Indeed, apprehension of a diminishing role for the Service Headquarters, and inter alia, that of the Service Chiefs who, it is feared, would be left with no operational responsibility, and that such a system would be counter-productive, remains palpable over the years. Therefore, deliberate measures need to be taken to get past this conceptual stalemate, the last word being that an astute institution of CDS, besides optimising the nation's defence capability, would release the nation from the sufferings of archaic and wasteful processes of defence planning.

The proposition envisages that the IHQ would be a tri-service institution – made up of a CDS at its head and the three Service Chiefs as its members – as the Government's apex military advisory body. Obviously, to handle the complex charter of the institution of CDS, there would have to be two Vice Chiefs of Defence Staff (VCDS), one to attend to staff functions and training and the other to oversee over-all military logistics and acquisition plans. In the military hierarchy, it is also the apex policy making body on joint services matters. These conditions cannot be diluted; diminishing the role of the institution of CDS in order to get past the systemic fear and resistance over change would be a profanity that would set the system back from the very purpose of defence reforms. Thus the salient charter of IHQ would be to carry out holistic and long-term perspective planning for defence preparedness and its prioritisation at the national platform – to encompass not just the budgetary and procurement matters but also the futuristic vision in shaping war strategies and the corresponding force-structuring, training, personnel and motivation issues (6).

Use of the term 'institution of CDS' is noteworthy as it refers to an institution in which professionals and systems of diverse experiences and purposes are forged together to function towards a singular goal. Apart from the three service Chiefs, the institution of CDS is manned by past-experienced tri-service staff at the decision-making level and by service-specific staff at the directional level. In the interest of smooth and efficient functioning, the executive level work is left for the Service Headquarters to undertake under the direction and supervision of their own decision-making and directional level hierarchies. In this arrangement therefore, joint-staff work is predominant in 'broad decision-making' and translating 'broad decisions' to 'general directions', while service and arm specific decision-making and executive directives are vested upon the Service Headquarters' charter. This kind of subtle delineation is necessary to cater to the complexities of each of the elements of modern military institutions and the domain expertise that is needed to exploit these to the maximum advantages in war. Indeed, this is a system that has been found, after many trials, workable in advanced militaries.

Joint Services Commands: Military Force Application

To address the apprehensions of what is viewed as dilution of the roles and competencies of the single Service Headquarters and their supposed loss of operational flexibility and fiscal autonomy, the facts to appreciate is that: firstly, in the contemporary political-military-fiscal dispensation, the power of effective national defence can only be afforded through joint-services approach; secondly, the institution of CDS is fundamental to the congruence between political mandate, fiscal allocation and military capability; and thirdly, for the previous two conditions to work, it is necessary to adopt the joint-services command system.

Argument against joint-services operational commands is bolstered by the logic that modern means of strategic mobility allows air power – and to a reckonable extent even naval and ground forces – to respond across the geographical segregations, and therefore, dividing these assets on regional rather than all-India basis would be wasteful for a nation that has no ambitions beyond its borders. Another factor which limits the parameters of inter-service jointness is that modern warfare requires military personnel up to a fairly high hierarchical level to acquire life-time experiences in best exploitation of the complex characteristics of the numerous war-inventories and astute tactical harness of these. Similarly, to avoid redundancies, ambiguous ownership and clash of demands in joint-services environment of war and peace, it is necessary to formulate new mechanisms, processes and procedures to regulate management and control of multi-purpose military assets like dual-use weapons and equipment, support services and logistic infrastructure. Therefore there would have to be instituted a mutuality of right balance and judicious reconciliation between nurturing single-service domain expertise on the one end, and experience of joint command, control and staff work on the other, for the joint-command to perform successfully. No doubt, these factors require serious consideration and experimentation in terms of training, posting, exposure to experience and career planning of personnel, and conjoined harness of multiple-use military wherewithal.

The arguments have merit, and the answer lies in proceeding through the reforms while taking care of the systemic and perceptive hurdles rather than stymieing the progress. There is no doubt that in a contemporary military institution, it is rather pompous to continue with the existence of as many as 17 odd autonomous service-specific command headquarters to prosecute what must be a joint-service warfare, with each of the counterparts duplicating many of each other's charters of work, while operational planning remains consigned to their autonomous rather than synergised perceptions and priorities. The cost of such disjointed management of defence is rather heavy for a nation which nurtures no military ambitions beyond keeping its territorial and sovereign integrity un-assailed and commits its priority to societal progress (7).

To get past this stalemate therefore, centrality of the three Service Headquarters needs to be assured while promoting jointness in war-fighting, gaining experiences in phased manner and applying course corrections to gradually evolve into a more efficient joint-services command structure. Induction of the three Service Chiefs as members of the institution of the

CDS, equitable distribution of roles and promulgation of a judicious charter for the joint staff to function, followed by brisk evolution towards perfection, would be the imperatives in this context (8).

New Definitions

Taking cue from universal experiences of defence reforms in devising own course for restructure into the system of joint-services command, it may be useful to define a set of nomenclature for India's military command headquarters, as follows:

a) A 'Joint Services Operational Command' (JSOC), would be a tri-service command headquarters organised for conduct of joint warfare in all dimensions; its extent of operations defined, not by fixed geographic or regional boundaries, but by the prevalence of a strategic situation. Therefore, in response to a strategic situation, the JSOC may be mandated to command and control military operations within a boundary specified to secure such military objectives that are defined at the MoD and DDF level. As a corollary, the JSOC's operational boundary may fall across any one or more of the geographic regions or Regional Command Theatres while forces from each of the three Services are placed under its command for operational employment. The allocation of forces is sanctioned by the institution of CDS while the Service Headquarters provide these forces duly organised, trained and equipped for deployment in operational role. Presently, creation of one JSOC has been suggested while two more may be raised subsequently to cater for two-front war and commitments in the Indian Ocean.

b) 'Joint Services Regional Commands' (JSRC) are theatre level regional command headquarters of joint-services composition organised to exercise command and control over all military assets, institutions and installations which may be located in their geographical jurisdiction. All forces of the three services located in a particular readjusted and redefined geographic region are to be controlled by the concerned JSRCs. Needless to state that there would be exceptions and cross-orbating (orbat = order of battle) of forces across regional boundaries due to operational tasking as well as administrative convenience. Simply put, JSRCs are the tri-service incarnation of India's existing command headquarters.

c) 'Reserve Forces Commands' (RFC) are single-service command headquarters which have under them certain fighting formations to act as strategic reserves. To keep within the ceiling of resources assigned at the disposal of the Indian military institution and yet retain flexibility of need based deployment, it would make sense to maintain a reckonable part of the forces as strategic reserves. Besides regular formations, the proposition entails institutionalisation of a system of time bound mobilisation, when necessary, of professionally skilled and periodically refreshed former servicemen who are released lately from 'colour service', to be formed into units and formations which remain sequestered at peace time.

d) Operational control over the JSOC and JSRCs is exercised directly by the institution of CDS while that over the RFC, unless specified under war situations, is exercised by single Service Headquarters. Indeed, each Service Headquarters have control as well as responsibility for the state of operational and logistic preparedness in respect of all forces and support assets belonging to their service.

Proposed Stages of Restructure to Joint Services Command

Indeed, for a smooth changeover to the joint-services system of management of the military institution, there have to be the need to limit unsavoury fallouts while negotiating through many systemic hurdles; political, bureaucratic and military fixations make this task even more challenging. To chart through these hurdles in a deliberate, gradual and controlled manner, we may begin by the adoption of a mixed approach to manage the change by:

a) One, amalgamation of Headquarters Central Army, Southern Naval and Central Air Commands, to from two command level headquarters, viz, one each of HQ JSOC and HQ JSRC to function directly under the CDS.

b) Two, as for the JSOC, assignment, if tentative or flexible, of an operational area and operational role, and orbating certain formations under one HQ JSOC for this headquarters to develop in joint-service orchestration of combat expertise and experience.

c) Three, as for the JSRC, orbating of all the existing single-service assets that are located in the geographical jurisdiction of the existing Central Army, Southern Naval and Central Air Commands under one HQ Central JSRC. Command and control over all the tri-service military assets located within a readjusted boundary would thus be vested in this joint-service headquarters. Service Headquarters may retain control over all the rest of their existing single-service geographical or regional command headquarters and their subordinate formations.

d) Four, phase wise amalgamation of rest of the single-service geographical command headquarters and restructure of these into a number of HQ JSRC – say, one each to command Northern, Eastern, Southern, Western Theatres, beside the already restructured HQ Central JSRC. It would be wise to allow the environment to condition itself over a period of five years or so, thus allowing the human resources to assimilate into new culture of command and control.

e) Five, maintaining the traditional operational sanctity of the single Service Headquarters by placing under their control the strategically decisive HQ RFC as well as the 'Reserve Liability' personnel, units, and assets.

f) Lastly, raising two more HQ JSOC, one to cater for the possibility of two-front war and another one to cater to the commitments in the Indian Ocean. Thus a total of three JSOCs are to be raised to conduct operations in mountains, plains and seas.

The first feature of this proposition is crucial. To begin with, it envisages the creation of one new HQ JSOC and one HQ JSRC through amalgamation of one command headquarters each from the three services – possibly the Central Army Command, Southern Naval Command and the Central Air Commands. The JSOC, headed by a Commander-in-Chief, would be entrusted with operational command over a sensitive or one of the 'hot' theatres which may be specified as necessary, and accordingly entrusted with command over certain orbated fighting formations from the three services – for example, one or more of the Army's strike corps or Army Headquarters reserve formations and a complementary proportion of naval and air formations. Similarly, one HQ JSRC would also be raised from the above mentioned amalgamation of three command headquarters, and assigned the operational and logistic responsibilities of the same scope as it is exercised by the existing Central Army, Navy and Air Force Command Headquarters, with its geographical extents redefined to conform to tri-service dispensation. Besides, of course, there would be the tri-service Andaman & Nicobar Command and the Strategic Forces Command, all functioning directly under the institution of the CDS. All other single-service geographical commands may to continue as these exist and continue to function under the respective Service Headquarters.

Over time, as stated, two more HQ JSOC may be raised to cater for possible multi-theatre war. Next would be the amalgamation of the rest of the single-service geographical command headquarters into joint-service HQ JSRCs, one for each theatre of operations. HQ Central JSRC, for the Central Theatre, already having been in place at the first instance, there would thus be the HQ JSRCs for Northern, Eastern, Southern and Western Theatres. Besides these, as discussed later, certain additional numbers of such headquarters would be also needed for astute management and control of multi-spectral warfare capabilities of the modern era. After a period of five years or so, as the HQ JSOCs and JSRCs find bearing, all the 17 odd top heavy and operationally semi-autonomous behemoths would get consolidated into just half the number of Command Headquarters to function under the IHQ (CDS) that are fully empowered as prosecutors of joint-strategy under the conditions of modern warfare.

Nuances of 'Integration', 'Jointness' and Domain Professionalism

No doubt, managing the reconfiguration and restructure of existing single-service regional commands without upsetting continuity and effectiveness of organisational, operational and logistic balance would be a challenge humungous. To retain balance therefore, while four or more HQ JSRC, each headed by its joint-services Commander-in-Chief, are created through amalgamation of two or more single-service regional headquarters, all the existing organisational tiers below the HQ JSRC would continue to retain their existing service-specific structures, and function under their respective Chiefs of Staff. This is a crucial stipulation to meet the imperatives force-structuring, and that enjoins us to define the military nuances of the terms 'integration' and 'jointness'.

Firstly, prosecution of warfare must be an integrated tri-service undertaking in terms of overall planning to secure military objectives. In such plans, each of the roles and tasks to be performed are to be assigned to one or more single-service component of the joint forces which are allocated to secure the objectives. To illustrate, destruction by fire power may be carried out by artillery, naval armament or air attacks either singly or jointly, and in varying proportions depending upon the ruling conditions, each exploiting its available numbers and characteristic strengths. Integrated operational plan is thus executed by joint-service orchestration of various single-service task forces. Needless to state, Integrated planning and orchestration of joint forces require special expertise to be acquired by training and exposure.

Conversely, astute exploitation of modern and highly complex military systems consisting of hardware, support accessories, logistics and fine-tuned battle procedures that evolve through long experiences require long years of service and arm specific training and practice. Obviously therefore, when it comes to the execution of integrated battle plans by joint forces, single-service land, sea and air components of the joint force-structure would continue to execute their part of the overall undertaking according to their specific battle drills, procedures, tactics and weapon-usage. Simply put, while modern warfare must be an integrated orchestration of joint-service force structure, service-specific roles in land, sea and air have still to be performed by single-service components through the expression of their service and arm specific expertise and experiences. This simple fact needs to be upheld in career management of personnel so as to maintain the salience of building up domain expertise over years of training and exercises, even while meeting the demand for adequate exposures to joint-service staff work.

Three, to avoid unmanageable degree of systemic turmoil, disruption and cross-connection, transition to joint-services structure needs to be carried out in deliberately controlled and orderly manner. To do so, it would be necessary to preserve the existing vertical hierarchies of single-service domains while horizontal inter-service linkages are established and mutual familiarity, confidence and dependability built up. In other words, while at the service and command headquarters levels the HQ JSOC and HQ JSRC may function as an 'integrated' tri-service entity, the lower combat as well as static formations and units have to continue to function in service-specific modes, much like as it is done today.

In fulfilment of the above listed stipulations within the merged and readjusted geographical regions, single-service corps and equivalent level formations would continue to operate in the manner as it had been before the restructure. The only difference here would be that each service would function under the control of respective Chiefs of Staff from that service while the apex level command authority over all of the tri-service regional command orbat vests upon one joint-services Commander-in-Chief assisted by his joint staff secretariat. In effect therefore, the existing single-service regional command headquarters, in their existing locations, would form part of a particular HQ JSRC, with the Commander-in-Chief's Office and secretariat established in any suitable location to exercise higher command over the military resources of three services as well as committal of these resources to various operations of war, through their respective Chiefs of Staff – more appropriately, the army, navy and air force commanders.

In this manner, disruption in the existing command, control, logistics, communications and even location, accommodation and infrastructural facilities would be minimal while the system evolves and stabilises. Of course, compatible infrastructure for the newly created joint-services Commander-in-Chief's office and secretariat of the restructured HQ JSRCs would need to be found in each of the geographical regions.

The Three Service Headquarters: War Worthiness, Operational Preparedness and Strategic Reserves

Next, the proposition addresses the reservations regarding the status of the Service Headquarters and the Service Chiefs. As the HQ JSRCs are established one by one over a period of time, and operational control over these shift to the CDS, the status of Service Headquarters remains protected by the retention of central reserve formations under their command, and inter alia, the major role these would play over much of the operational planning and execution. In fact, examples of advanced militaries suggest that with control over the service-specific domains – namely the aspects of turnover, training, equipping, modernisation, personnel management, logistic chains and installations, research and innovations, military technology and industrialisation, etc. – the centrality of the Service Headquarters' role cannot but remain unchallenged.

A most significant boost to the cause of national defence would accrue from the focus that the Service Headquarters would be able to direct in shaping the process of design, development and trials of sophisticated military hardware; presently, that role gets marginalised under the burden of operational priorities. The proposition would motivate the services to create a new class of tactically astute technical warriors who would be competent in devising battle-worthy and soldier-sensitive design parameters of such hardware and so enable the defence research, development, and trial and production industry in efficient production of modern military hardware. It would then be possible for the Service Headquarters to lay down formal policies regarding the performance, logistics, development period and life cycle criteria of various military weapon and equipment systems, monitor and scrutinise the projects and carry out course corrections with professional military understanding. Hiccups and heart-breaks, as observed in the case of design and development of Arjun Tanks and the Tejas Fighter Aircraft on the one extreme, and conceptual stalemate over development of 'modular' designs for tank variants and execution of Counter Surface Air Operations on the other, may then be addressed through deeper deliberations and alacrity.

Indeed, as the above listed charters – which presently remain just about superficially attended to – gain due attention in the Service Headquarters, realisation of its centrality in the matter of national defence will dawn soon enough. Membership of Service Chiefs in the institution of CDS would reinforce that centrality. The proposition in question would therefore appropriate a shift over time to the joint command system while upholding the centrality of the Service Headquarters – as it has happened in advanced nations.

Resolving Systemic Reservations and Resistance

The proposition under discussion may not be treated as either sacrosanct or rigid, and must be open to better counsel, finer innovation, flexibility, logical application and mid-course corrections. However, there may be no compromise on amalgamation of the single-service regional commands, all 17 of these, under a more appropriate numbers of HQ JSRCs, each of these amalgamating under its fold the existing service–specific command headquarters and the assets thereof. Further, there may be no compromise on prosecuting any future war or war-like application of military force under duly oriented and structured task specific HQ JSOCs. The combination of these two stipulations is at the core of the reform process and therefore qualifies to be viewed as a national cause.

Creation of joint-services commands would definitely raise hierarchical and cadre post-protection anxieties, particularly at the C-in-C rank. To get over that hurdle, due appreciation of the practical realities are needed to be appreciated within the fraternity at-large. These realities are:

a) With force-compositions, fields of expertise and experience, operational assets, infrastructure and roles of fighting formations remaining unchanged, strength and structure of the existing headquarters would necessarily have to be maintained more or less at the same level to be able to operate as functional arms of the joint-service commands, as indeed it has been the case with other advanced militaries. In fact, introduction of modern appliances of warfare would more than make up for the redundancies discarded. Therefore, career prospects would remain protected.

b) The number of existing star appointments need not be curtailed; reforms need not be bogged down by such a concern. The institution of CDS and the restructured HQ JSOC, HQ JSRC, HQ RFC, and modernisation related new raising of additional new command headquarters would take care of that (9).

Indeed, the landmark achievement of the restructure would be that the strategic concepts, planning and prosecution of war would be a joint-services and convergent effort rather than continuation of the archaic practice of committing to fight three different individual battles and patching up, when mutual agreed upon, just at certain operationally critical junctures before returning to single-service pursuits. Modern warfare does not permit prosecution of individual battles, and calls for simultaneous prosecution of different modes warfare – 'hybrid war' to wit. Therefore, notwithstanding the simplistic argument of India having no military ambitions beyond her borders, there is just no scope for disjointed war-fighting in this modern era. Besides, in the contemporary system of political control, even routine cases and concerns of the military institution would be better articulated by a joint rather than single-service approach.

Other Components of the DDF Organisation

We may now turn the discussion to the other components of the DDF as depicted in the organisational structure above. To reiterate, these components are meant to cater to joint training, logistics and maintenance of regular as well as the reserve forces by each of the three services under their respective HQ RFC. At this stage there being no higher level changes envisaged in the structure of the Strategic Forces Command, Andaman & Nicobar Command and the Coast Guard, these need not be covered in the following discussion.

Proposition on Joint Military Training

Jointness in prosecution of warfare offers the flexibility to perform most of the combat tasks – like fire attack, mobility, isolation, interdiction etc. – by more than one mean – 'interoperability' in short. Deliberate interlacing of jointness in military training therefore assumes salience in modern war, the main factors being as follows:

a) Joint warfare requires an additional tier of expertise in which wider nuances of inter-service operational interoperability are to be mastered and orthodox self-restrictions and reservations overcome. Similarly, the art of managing redundancy among the combat resources to be committed and those either to be kept in reserve or released for better use elsewhere needs to be mastered. This end is achieved by joint training in tri-service battle procedures as well as joint staff work.
b) Even within service-specific domains, modern warfare calls for deeper expertise in exploitation of complex weaponry, accessories and equipment, and higher acumen in execution of battle procedures in joint service milieu. Therefore, standards of parent service training must continue to be raised meet the true need and capability based application of operational jointness.
c) There is much scope for rationalisation of the number of training institutions which are run independently by the three services. Some of these institutions may be designating into joint training facilities and the course curricula extended to cover joint battle procedures and joint staff work.

In the existing system of service-specific control over training institutions and the curricula these follow, the standards of parent service training is commendable. However, as for the aspect of training in joint operations is concerned, that remains more or less a matter of expediency rather than serious commitment – it is mostly notional. To foster innate jointness at the functional level therefore, the answer lies in, firstly, lacing the parent service course contents with tangible upgrades of theory and practices of jointness both in operations and logistics, and secondly, conducting purely joint warfare training capsules, courses and exercises. The implication, therefore, are:

a) In order that parent service and arm-specific training standards are maintained at compatible levels of modernisation, continuation of the existing system of management of training in each service would be necessary;
b) Such course contents would have to be expanded, as appropriate, to cover the joint operational aspects of the topics addressed; and,
c) New training curricula would be needed to impart conceptual as well as hands-on training on prosecution of joint operations.

The option therefore would be to institute a joint hierarchy to superintend parent service as well as joint training curricula. The concept could be to continue to organise intra-service training through Directorate Generals of Training Branches of each of the three Service Headquarters, while the overall gamut of military training, essentially focused on joint training through purely joint as well expanded contents of parent service courses, are superintended by the Headquarters Joint Training Command. Such systemic assimilation of dual, or even multiple, control –'joint control' actually – is usual in joint-services environment; shedding past fervours and fears it is wise to understand that.

Further, to impart due expertise in joint planning and staff work at directional levels, joint-service training courses may have to be run by rationalisation of the charters of some of the top training institutions like the various war, engineering and logistic colleges. Finally, advanced and conceptual level training on integrated information, space, Special Forces and nuclear warfare would have to be conducted at a wider scale in tri-service training institutes. These tri-service institutes, besides the National Defence University, may be placed directly under the IHQ. To that extent, the traditional notion of training being a function of command gets a wider implication in the joint-service dispensation (10).

Another salient aspect of military training relates to aptitude and development of expertise among the personnel. Modern military institutions are best manned by personnel of higher education and technical skills, who would yet be in impressionable and mouldable young age-group. Contrarily, neither the modern society nor the prevalent education system are able to offer candidates for military service who meet that contrasting criteria, that is, higher education and younger age. The solution adopted by the military institution so far has been to raise the age of recruitment which, given the modern societal mores, makes it more difficult to inculcate the culture of soldierly calling. Similarly, technical training of a mostly 'non-science' stream soldiery is sought to be imparted more by rote rather than fundamental understanding of science. Therefore, to educate and train the soldiery to the level that is needed to be innovative in exploitation of modern weapons, equipment and systems, the answer may be to recruit at younger age and then put the inductees through in-house science stream education, somewhat on the lines of the Sainik School system. Alternately, education and cultural assimilation starting from secondary education level may also be organised through academic tie ups with the education industry, on the lines of what is presently done for higher technical education.

The twin objectives of mouldability into soldierly character and possession of scientific temper may be achieved by restitution of the 'Boys' ranks and educating them in military training centres and secondary school level sponsorship of recruits in civil educational institutions. Besides, it would be necessary to upgrade pure science curricula to a specified standard in the course contents of various military training institutions. This aspect may be coordinated, if necessary through contractual understandings with the academic sector, by the IHQ. The basic stipulation to be recognised is that modern, joint warfare requires the soldiery to subscribe to both, a hoary military culture and modern scientific skills (11).

Proposition on Military Logistics

Military institutions are distinguished by their dependence upon integral reservoirs of war materials that range from vast inventories of hardware, engineering backup systems and transportation system for massive loads of consumables like ammunition and supplies. Significance of this reservoir lies in ready accessibility of combat formations to the entire range of weapons, equipment and supplies in required quantities, of right quality and at right time and place. In modern times, with the necessity of vast military inventories to sustain posturing and prosecution of warfare, this imperative assumes even more salient when considered in light of the humungous investments required to be made by the state in terms of scientific research, industrial production, transportation and reserve stocking, designation of elaborate installations to perform such roles, and management of the cycle of induction, consumption, discard and replenishment of the entire range of military logistic inventories. 'Defence Logistics' has therefore emerged as a distinct sector of modern military management based on fundamentals of science, industry, production and usage under different situations, broader aspect of which are to be discussed in the next chapter.

Given that its fundamentals must be moored at empirical experiences and military foresight, Defence Logistics is a distinct field of national level persuasion, whereas 'Military or Operational Logistics' forms its core purpose. Indeed, military logistic planning is a purely military pursuit, and it has to be managed by experienced military professionals who are adept at balancing strategy and tactics with the right logistic back up. The purpose is then executed in conjunction with the technology, industry and finance professionals to achieve rationalisation and optimum exploitation of the nation's overall defence logistic capabilities. Needless to state, this balancing act is a continuous process and conforms to the stipulations of peace-time training, principles governing reserve stocking and war-time build up, surge-replenishment in war, and lastly, robust and flexible chain of sustenance of forces in combat. Accordingly, advanced nations with large militaries – US, Russia, China, for example – have created dedicated departments which are made responsible to ensure that their military logistic capability is maintained at a desired state of readiness, while at the same time the dead expenses are squeezed away. Even the smaller and smarter militaries – Britain, France, Japan and Taiwan for example – have adopted similar practices, with the understanding that while logistic capability takes decades to build and maintain, combat forces are raised in much shorter time frame that spans recruitment and training – provided the core components of military units and formations, and the requisite infrastructure for mobilisation and training are in place. Thus with their emphasis on possessing significant military logistic capability out of regulated and regular investments, advanced nations are able to retain the ability to build up their combat forces at short notice. To illustrate one example, in opting for a rather small standing combat force-structure and yet upholding her robust military traditions, Britain has delinked defence logistics from the combat hierarchy and affected its merger within the overall system of defence procurement under a 'Chief of Defence Material' of status equivalent to the Vice Chief of Defence Staff, a four star officer; most advanced nations have opted for similar systems.

Dictates of India's geographical spread and political and diplomatic concerns that requires her to maintain large military forces at a fair state of readiness, which in turn have to be sustained through complex chains of local and import based procurements, call for adoption similar practices in her defence logistics management system. This would permit her defence logistics to be optimised for cost-effectiveness while offering new vistas for the exercise of operational flexibility to the forces.

In India's MoD, defence logistics is controlled mainly between Army's Operational Logistics, Quarter Master General's and Master General of Ordnance Branches and their parallel branches in the Navy and Air Force. Besides, some of the line directorates perform logistic functions according to their specialised charters – management of stores of engineer, signals or medical origin, for example. Between these functionaries are managed the procurements, supply chains, storage, movement and distribution of consumables as well as main hardware across the country-wide grid of military bases and the operational areas served by these. Notably, in this system, there are many measures of jointness in the fields of logistic constructions and maintenance of tangible assets, supplies and medical support. The present logistic support system therefore meets the imperatives of discipline-specific technical expertise at the functional level while adapting to inter-services jointness when practical. But in the larger context of operational logistic planning, standardisation of common use items, and procurement, maintenance and provisioning of these, including transportation and stocking, there is still some scope for more of inter-service jointness.

Notably, within its boundary parameters, the record of modernisations and improvements in logistic management of the military institution has been quite significant. Better quality of rations, clothing, transportation, delivery of services, automated inventory management systems and responsive asset maintenance mechanisms are some of these which have ameliorated many of the administrative difficulties of the military institution. However, there still remains a case for India's military logistics to be freed from its appendage status in which not only its control but even its function is dictated by what is visualised by each of the services as their immediate operational necessity – this kind of operationally fixated priggishness is a typical affliction among immediate term defensive oriented military institutions. That priggish attitude stifles the development of India's military logistics to that level whence it could become capable of offering alternate avenues of operational flexibility. To illustrate, when focus is confined to anticipated operational plans and contingencies, logistic back up is most likely to be relegated to the minimalist levels – minimum placement of munitions and fuels, minimum engineering support, minimum transportation, and so on. That closes the doors against exploitation of strategic as well as tactical flexibility in terms of innovation, audacity, surprise and exploitation of fleeting opportunities. Commanders in the field are thus restricted by logistic limitations from adopting alternatives approaches to deal with fluid situations – like deployment and redeployment of alternate or additional weapons, movement over alternate axes, survivability in terrain considered to be extreme etc. – within tactically acceptable time frame (12).

Further, creation of defence logistic infrastructure being mostly within indigenous competence, upgrade of military as well as dual-use logistic capability at all-India level could compensate, to much extent, for the voids of advanced combat hardware that is caused by India's import dependence. To illustrate, larger fleets of support vessels and wider location of replenish points for the Navy, and higher density of ground support facilities for the

Air Force are within the indigenous capabilities to create, and these could offer higher purchase from the limited numbers of import dependent weaponry in terms of reach and flexibility for the forces in tactical employment. Similarly, larger fleets of high mobility tank transporters, ammunition trains, higher battle field survivability stores and longer administrative sustainability infrastructure for forces in remote field areas could act as operational force-multipliers for the Army. To that end, development of border infrastructure, for dual use, which remains but rudimentary and woefully insufficient when compared to that of India's adversary's, must be a top priority for India's national security planners, as indeed it must also be with regard to development of island based naval and air infrastructure. Indeed, creation of efficient and flexible logistic back up infrastructure from indigenous resources would go a long way in building up operational muscle – provided the short term focus of the nation's defence hierarchy is balanced out with greater appreciation of the operational potentials of military logistics.

In the same vein, within the military institution there is the need to rise above the practice prevalent, in which military logistics remains but an appendage to the anticipation of short terms operational situations and its functions limited just to support pre-conceived tactical plans. For example, resuscitation of the so far de-prioritised aspects of high-technology camouflage and deception could multiply the battle field survivability of import dependent and other key combat hardware as well as defence installations. Similarly, the grossly obsolete notion of 'cutting down the teeth-to-tail ratio' that results in long down-times for repair and overhaul of modern weapons, equipment and vehicles, is just one example when dated clichés act to the detriment of operational preparedness. Modern native military thinking must therefore graduate to the consolidation of many of the loose components of tri-service defence logistics – procurements, maintenance, stocking, roles of service installations, transportation, delivery, experimentation, audit, and finally, expense and salvage. Going beyond, the purpose should be to create a robust, modern and visionary defence logistic system that, while retaining its service-specific orientation, yet promotes jointness in tri-service domain as much as it is practical, and while remaining active in peace time, is ever ready to spring to the support of war time requirements within an acceptable warning period.

To strengthen military logistics, as indicated in the proposed outline structure of the DDF, creation of a Headquarters Joint Logistics Command

(HQ JLC), to function as an autonomous logistic policy-making body under the DDF (IHQ) may be thought of. HQ JLC would be headed by a Chief of Joint Logistics (CJL) and would exercise policy-making, joint-directive and supervisory level control over the Directorates General of Army, Navy and Air Force Logistics, the latter remaining answerable for operational logistics to their respective Service Headquarters. HQ JLC may, therefore, organise to perform according to the following charter:

a) To translate the perspective, prioritisation, inventory and budgetary policies of the DDF/IHQ, which would then be further customised and executed across the entire gamut of practical logistic management by each of the Service Headquarters, through their dedicated Directorates General of Operational Logistics, or Chiefs of Materials.
b) HQ JLC would also assist the DDE in formulation of management policies towards optimal life cycle conciliation of production, storage, usage, discard and disposal of various categories of military hardware – like the consumables, weapons, equipment and transport, new inductions and replenishment items. Codifying such policies is a complex joint undertaking for the military professionals and their industrial counterparts. Conversely, there being no comprehensive formulae to reconcile the equation between these extremely cost-intensive as well as operationally critical activities, the goal of optimum management of national defence remains a challenge exclusive. HQ JLC, in conjunction with the Directorates General of the services' logistic branches (or the Chiefs of Materials) would be expected to tackle that kind of challenges (13).
c) Unforgiving nature of war leads to situations when logistic preparedness may turn out to be over-insurance in one instance and inadequate in another. Even if this is a dilemma that is beyond full resolution ever, professional minds of HQ JLC still remain the best bet in finding near-best solutions, advantages of which are vast.

Indeed, there is much scope for the HQ JLC to cut down logistic duplications, redundancies and capability voids, and so to build up a degree of logistic efficacy that enables the combat forces to be maintained at the requisite level of operational efficiency.

Next, the JLC would play the role of military interface to the defence acquisition and procurement functions of the 'Chief of Defence Logistics' of the sister Department of Defence Establishment, as it would be detailed in the following Chapter 5. Being import-dependent for major military hardware, capital acquisitions are attended to by the 'Defence Acquisition Council' (DAC) through a 'Defence Procurement Procedure' (DPP). It is a noble process of recent origin, frequently updated, which would promote best practices and start delivering in the coming days; defence acquisitions take years to fructify after all. Meanwhile, in consequence of the past quarter century long regime of the MoD's non-performance on capital acquisitions, most of the military modernisation schemes would have to wait for rescue from oblivion. As for the defence procurements under the revenue head is concerned, though the system is robust and conducive to regular flow of replenishments, the delivery capacity is frequently stymied by indifferent production and budgetary shortfalls, and that causes the aforementioned 'hollowness' creep into India's military force-structure. Indeed, such a situation has prevailed over the past quarter of a century and as result, the extent of obsolescence as well as hollowness in the military institution has gone deep and wide. Notwithstanding the complaints over stagnation of ex-import capital acquisition schemes, that 'hollowness' in fact is a greater scourge for the Indian military institution as it gnaws at its vitals.

Then there is a separate 'Department of Defence Production' which exercises varying degree of control over the various elements of the Indian defence establishment – 39 Ordnance Factories, eight Defence Public Sector Undertakings, and 54 Defence Research & Development Labrotaries. There is also a 'Department of Defence Estates' under the MoD to manage defence lands and estates. None of these elements are accountable to their sole users – the services. This is a strange system wherein every service-providing element wields the authority to deflect the concerns of their sole users, the services, to block their requirements, demand the acceptance of whatever they manage to produce or produce not, and yet be outside the purview of user-accountability against non-performance. It is so that a substantial defence budget delivers much less in sustaining India's military power than what it actually could. The proposition for defence reforms therefore must be aimed at ameliorating that dichotomy.

In this respect, dovetailing of military logistics with the nation's overall defence logistics would be facilitated by the participation of the JLC in the following manner:

a) HQ JLC and the Directorates General of the services' logistic branches would be the interface between the user arms and services of the armed forces and the second department of the MoD, that is, the Department of Defence Establishments (DDE).

b) In its charter of interface, HQ JLC would mentor the nation's defence industry. It will therefore play the user-centric role of proposing, guiding and monitoring defence research and development, field trials of doctrine-induced innovations and standardisation. Presently, in absence of such a user-provider interface, there is a gaping void in the Indian defence management system that imposes heavy penalty on defence finances.

Lastly, going beyond the above listed charter, HQ JLC is also needed to raise defence logistics from its subaltern status and take lead in covering the fundamental disconnect between operational and logistic imperatives of India's strategic challenges. Some of effects of that disconnect are exemplified by just two illustrations:

a) Mountain warfare is obviously a major challenge for the Indian military institution – as it has been so ever since independence. The Indian mountains-specific conditions are however unmatched elsewhere, and therefore global defence industry has not found it profitable to produce military hardware that are customised for operation in such terrain. Indigenous development and production of customised military stores and equipment for such conditions would therefore have been a prudent course to adopt. Indeed, development of weapons and equipment of even basic nature – high mountain specific armaments and ammunition, customised implements to create field fortifications, means of facilitating transportation, material handling and mobility, and improvement of habitat accessories etc., – would have offered quantum operational advantages to the Indian forces over the adversaries. Conversely, till late at last, there had hardly been any effort towards such native innovations (14).

b) Management of combat inventories, particularly the munitions, for the military forces leaves much to be desired. The result is that the key weapons like tanks, guns, ships and aircraft remain under-fed even at critical junctures. Surely, an industry which sends rockets to the moon should be capable of overcoming this debility provided there is the backing of true user-guidance and synergic effort (15).

If shorn of distracting influences, rationalisation of military logistics should be the most readily achievable call today, and a most rewarding one.

It will streamline expenditure on defence procurements and so offer more 'goods' from the 'buck' while offering a wide range of flexibility to the exercise of India's military strategy.

Proposition on National Military Reserves: Reserve Forces Command (RFC)

This proposition is made in the context of 'transformation' of the Indian military institution – which, to reiterate, is a sub-set of overall defence reforms, and a larger, all-encompassing endeavour of modernisation. The purpose here is to maintain an optimum roll of standing regular forces, with their in-built reserve formations of course, at their best fettle within a rationalised level of defence expenditure, and yet retain the ability to build up the regular force level, when required, at short notice, according to the dictates of political situations and military challenges. As discussed in Chapter 2 above, most modern defence departments have adopted this approach to maintain, in best state of readiness and within a specified level of defence budgeting, comparatively smaller size of standing military forces. Integral to this step, those nations have also instituted effective procedures to call up their reservist personnel, refresh their training, equip them from pre-stocked and routinely maintained inventory of weapons and equipment, and form them up into pre-designated 'reserve' combat units and formations within a strictly specified 'mobilisation' time line. This policy of balancing regular and reserve forces permits maximisation of the dividends from the nation's investment on military power.

The strategic situation that confronts India permits only a limited space for her to adopt such a policy. But even then there is enough scope to take advantage of the concept of 'national reserves', and in so doing, overcome the unwanted contradiction of having a larger military institution that stands but 'hollowed' due to unaffordable budgetary demands. The proposition here entails raising of 'Reserve Forces Commands' (RFC) under each of the Service Headquarters, and composed, in one part, of standing battle formations – which are presently designated as 'Service Headquarters Reserves', and may be some more. In another part, the RFCs would have in their orbat the normally sequestered units and formations which, on mobilisation, are to be manned by the recalled 'reservists'. The purpose of formally placing the RFCs under respective Service Headquarters is to ensure that command, control, training and war preparedness of the standing as well as the mobilised reserve formations are accorded the full attention, for these to be committed to combat as part of overall war plans, possibly with appropriate add-on formations or units for added punch. The RFCs would thus be made up of one standing and another reservist components, and thus provide for the nation's strategic military reserves.

Intrinsic to the hoary 'Principles of War', these reserve formations are to be committed at opportune moments to force favourable decisions at strategic, operational and tactical levels, and so act as a military commander's traditional instrument of influencing the outcome of battles. In this instance, reserve formations of the RFCs are to be integrated into overall battle plans either as independent entities or as part of larger formations, and grouped as necessary under one or more HQ JSOC(s), JSRC(s) or even directly under Service Headquarters to reinforce offensive and defensive operations.

To reiterate, by reviving the concept of call for 'reserve liability' and 'mobilisation' of sequestered formations and units with weapons and equipment entering the 'fourth quarter' of life cycle, this proposition facilitates 'right sizing' of the military institution, assimilates optimum management of equipment life cycles, makes it affordable to keep regular force duly modernised, and yet tap the vast resources of trained and professionally skilled former servicemen who are released from 'colour service' at young age. Indeed, creation of RFCs is in tune with the universal trend of military force-structuring. A force of exclusive construct, this option provides flexibility in operational planning, campaigning, surprise and deception, and finally, offers additional forces when required for the achievement of strategic objectives. The proposition also permits induction of personnel having post-superannuation civil experience as well as those possessing high-technology skills who are so vital in manning the forces in modern warfare. It also conforms to the contemporary principles of defence finance and human as well as material resource management. In passing, it also addresses the reservations of the Service Headquarters regarding their operational role as well as the common concern regarding availability of higher ranks.

The Territorial Army (TA)

Based on the principle of 'citizens' army', and by its regulated term drafting of civil sector skilled employees into military service in emergency situations, imparting periodical military training to them and their need based embodiment into TA units that are maintained in skeleton form, India's Territorial Army (TA) has played a commendable role in undertaking comparatively lesser intense operational duties in wars and insurgencies. Besides, it has also played stellar role in running railways, other essential services, and production and pumping of petroleum oil during wars and major disruptions. In fact, incessant insurgencies in various parts of the country have led to assignment of near-continuous roles to the TA troops and consequently, more or less unbroken embodiment of the majority of the sanctioned TA units. Thus over time, the TA has come to occupy a significant role in the configuration of Indian military force-structure. This state of high embodiment of TA units is likely to continue till India becomes secure from her twin neighbours' never ending aggression and internal insurgencies.

Long or near-continuous embodiment of 'citizen-soldiers' has been a fallout of this situation. As a corollary, on the one hand long absence of the employees has doused the civil sector employers' enthusiasm in encouraging enrolment; on the other hand, the aspirants have started to view TA as a regular employment. The very concept of that organisation is contradicted thus, and besides difficulties in personnel management arising at a later stage, the very idea of drafting personnel possessing civil skills to military duty is defeated. For effective utilisation of the TA therefore, its cause needs to be promoted by means of binding legislation upon the employers as well as policy upgrades in matters of organisational effectiveness and personnel management.

Such amends, followed up with placement of the TA under the command and control of the CDS would pay rich dividends to the nation in terms of enhancement of operational and technical capabilities of the military institution. Besides the standard military employment, embodied TA units can also perform particularly well in the fields of static air defence, transportation in rear areas, cyber operations, trailing of terror funding and such specialist tasks at a fraction of the cost that the exchequer would have to bear otherwise. There is therefore a case to incorporate the TA organisation into the modernised force-structure through a mix of conversions from regular units to TA and vice versa. In particular, landmark advantages of possessing wider range of competencies through the TA would accrue when expert combat support operations have to be executed in the domains of space, cyber and IW (16).

Other Functions of DDF

The other aspects of the DDF's function – that is, command and control over the Strategic Forces Command and the Coast guards, as well as the new raisings of Special Forces, Space and IW Commands – need no elaboration at the proposition stage. It would be more appropriate to delve into these aspects as a wholesome package of comprehensive military transformational analyses.

Final Shape of the Proposition

Over a ten year period, we may envisage the DDF to evolve into an organisation as depicted at Figure 3.

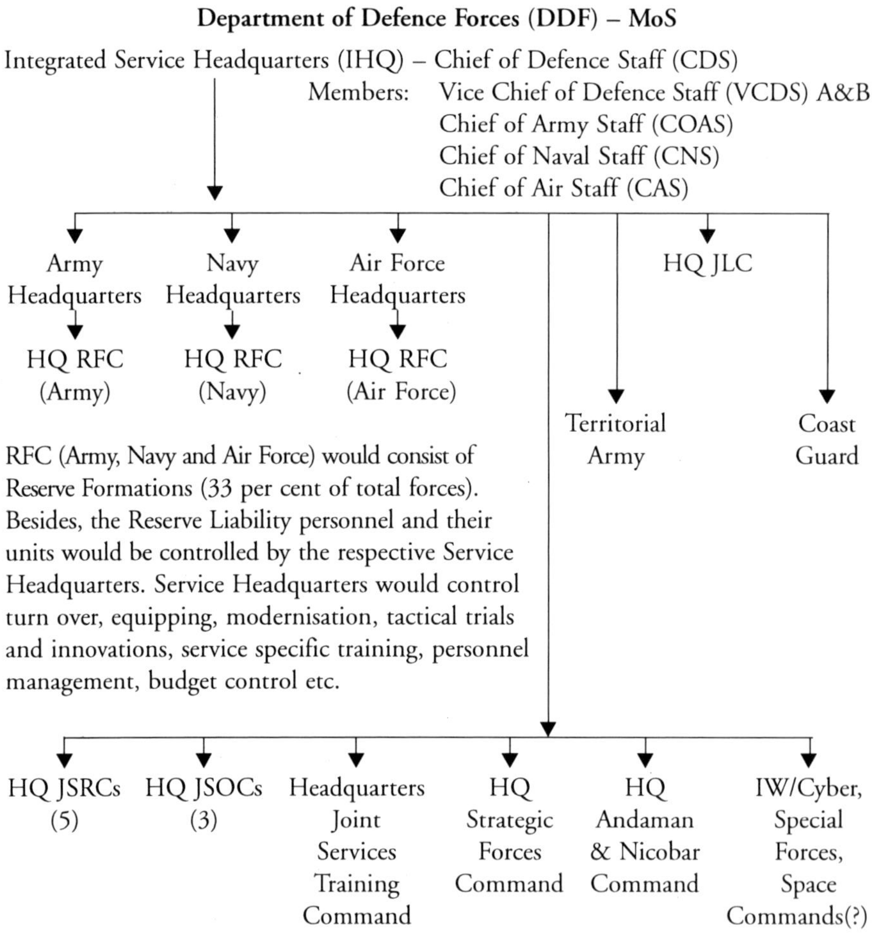

Figure 3: The Final DDF

An Alternate Model

There is another model which may be adopted to structure the DDF, the alternate being basically aimed at addressing partisan concerns. In this model, the three Services Headquarters continue to exercise control over a lesser number of amalgamated JSRCs, while prosecution of joint operations in war and war-like situations is to be directed by the IHQ (CDS) through the three JSOCs, one each of these dedicated to operations in mountains, plains and seas. Thus out of five JSRCs, two land force predominant JSRCs could function under the Army Headquarters while the rest three JSRCs could be controlled by the Naval and Air Force Headquarters respectively. Besides of course, each Service Headquarters would control their respective RFCs. However, since the JSRCs would have joint-services roles as well as composition, each of the controlling Service Headquarters would have to have fully functional sister service branches integrated into its organisation. This would be necessary for the single service headquarters to exercise effective control over their subordinate joint services commands. Such an arrangement is likely to inject the culture of jointness right into the sinews of the military institution at a faster pace.

The organisational structure in the Alternate Model would be along the lines as shown at Figure 4, and allowed to evolve further over time.

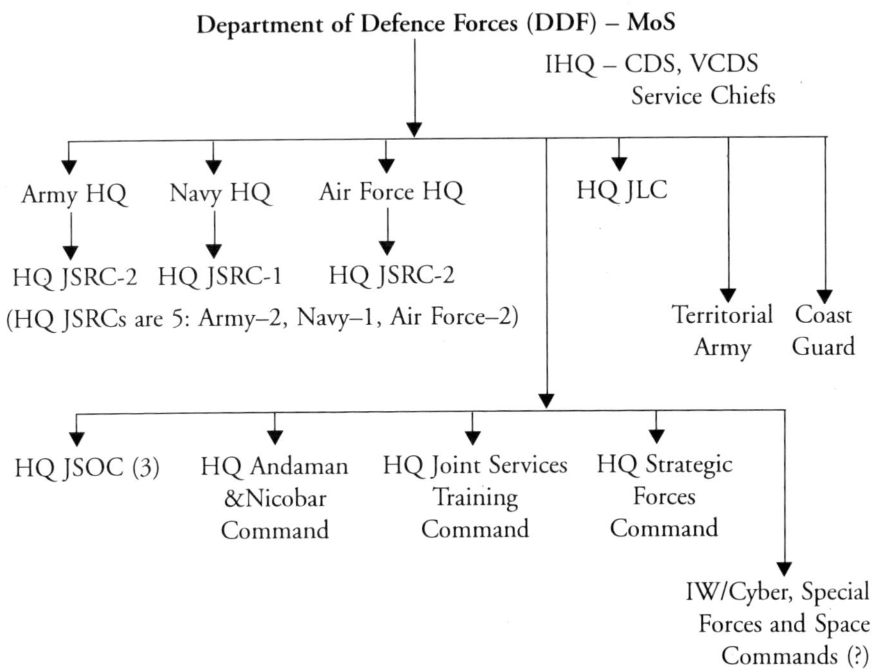

Figure 4: Alternate Model of DDF

The Second Part of the Proposition

We may now turn to the proposition regarding the second Department of the MoD, which has been described in the early part of this Chapter as the 'Department of Defence Establishments' (DDE). This part of the proposition for apex level reforms of national defence management structure is dealt with in the following Chapter.

END NOTES AND SELECT REFERENCES

(1) Actually except for the late 1970s'-early 1980s' restructure of mechanised and logistic assets of war, all defence reforms in India have been triggered by the catastrophic eruption of pre-known threats and well after the losses are suffered. That was so seen during the later phase of the Chinese aggression in 1962 when the government cried out for supply of American and British weapons and equipment, just as it was during the Kargil Conflict when it rushed out to buy weapons and ammunition – literally anything that could be found from anywhere and at any cost – at the two ends of a series of persistent strategic myopia.

(2) Indeed, most initiatives adopted by the military hierarchy could take off only under the stewardship of stronger and persistent military leaders, to be pushed through against the nation's reluctant and ever-unimpressionable defence planners. Necessitated by its varied range of deployment and narrow band of strategic options, many of such visible initiatives have originated from the Army – deployment to secure the Line of Control, the 'K-Day' and 'D-Day' offensive strategies, unique tactical procedures to counter insurgencies, the option of 'Cold Start', logistic development of border areas, and surveillance and blocking tactics against the PLA's intrusions across the Line of Actual Control, for example. Similarly, in-house, professional foresight has been displayed by the Navy in invocation of a rational set of strategic objectives and a spirit of indigenisation, just as the Air Force has focused on promoting advanced surveillance and precision engagement, transportation, command and control and flexibility in employment of air weapons. However, none of these initiatives have been ordained at the instance of the nation's defence managers; it is as if national defence is solely a burden of the military institution.

(3) It is a misplaced overconfidence borne out of strategic innocence that keeps the political leadership and their bureaucratic mandarins from appreciating the need for professional military advise. The result is that guidance from the military institution over the Chemical Warfare Convention and nuclearisation had to come through default rather than a process of deliberate professional military scrutiny. Absence of upfront military participation is also felt when terrorist attacks continue for hours unopposed while the nation's security set up struggles to cobble up some response, that is, even when forces ready at hand wait to be activated.

(4) Latent threats to India's security emanate from the regional machinations of an adversarial China. China's purpose of gaining geo-political influence around India

manifests in the form of economic and developmental enticements offered to India's small and large neighbours – Maldives, Sri Lanka, Nepal, Bangladesh and Myanmar. China also makes common cause with a fundamentally inimical Pakistan to make it difficult for India to find collateral relationships with Afghanistan and the Gulf Countries, besides stoking India's internal problems in Kashmir and probably the North Eastern States.

(5) Among many other security threats, the muddle in management of the rising threats to India's internal security has caused the Maoist rebellion to sustain and allowed settlement of illegal migration to defy the system of border management. Meanwhile partisan considerations stifle the cause of organisational efficiency in the CAPF in terms of having to bear higher cost of personnel while repudiating the advantages of drafting trained ex-servicemen, and subversion of the system of unified command and control over security operations. Military commanders, in similar vein, plan to undertake their rear area commitments with as little dependency on CAPF as possible, and that at the cost of frontline commitments. Contrast this muddle with the synergic management of integrated homeland security in US, UK, Russia and China.

(6) As it was envisaged by the Task Force on National Security Reforms or the Naresh Chandra Committee – the adverse implications of diluting the charter of CDS has been discussed in End Note 19 of the preceding Chapter.

(7) The Indian state policy is clear in its intent. It accords highest priority to socio-economic uplift of its centuries – over exploited masses while protecting its territorial inheritance, as far as possible with minimum of defence expenditure that is just enough to prevent military aggression from paying.

(8) A gradual transition of Service Headquarters from operational force-application to preparatory force-structure and force-sustainability role over a period of five or more years would allow individual consternation to dissipate and the system to reconfigure itself into modernity.

(9) This observation is substantiated by the fallouts of reforms in other nations. In UK, the number of flag ranks did reduce, but that was a result of reductions in force level. As for the number of Cs-in-C, the reduction in single-service regional command headquarters would be compensated by creation of new commands and new appointments, as indeed it has been the case in other countries. Recent reforms in China, wherein the higher PLA Headquarters was reduced by 25 per cent, higher military appointments have actually increased.

(10) Jointness at functional level is the easy familiarity and need based dependency that a rifle company or a sabre squadron develops with respect to close air support – or Counter Surface Air Operations (CASO) – or air transported operations. Similarly, it is the familiarity that air men develop with regard to the changing configurations of ground operations. At the directional level, jointness implies understanding of the intricacies of the characteristics, tactical practices and battle procedures of the sister services to a level that promotes joint planning and staff work while execution is left to the services concerned. Observable hints of jointness, albeit of limited scope, manifests in air logistic operations in Ladakh and Arunachal

Pradesh. However, the spirit and practices of real jointness seems to have faded after the 1971 War.

(11) Universally, the entry level education is conducted at military schools. For specific qualifications, the practice is to offer school, college or even university education to military candidates under sponsorship programmes. In India, this practice exists at the officers' level but has yet remained rather limited. Here entry level age in the military service for officers as well as the Other ranks have been raised under the belied impression that the candidates would gain higher educational standards and that would bring technically more qualified manpower to the military. However, the first condition is met but the second is not, what with the poor standards of basic education across the country. Thus while the pitfalls of raising the age of recruitment vis-à-vis character building persists, the danger of depending on rote-educated soldiery to deliver in joint-service environment has been added. This anomaly needs to be appreciated by the military hierarchy.

(12) Unlike operational matters, military logistics has many civil sector participants and there is much professional collaboration in matters of rations, fuels, construction and repair engineering, medical treatment etc. This interaction, and not per se the wisdom of operational controllers of military logistics – commanders and General Staff – has permitted military logisticians to effect many improvements in terms of management of inventory, stocking, transportation, supply chain, even in-house production etc. Thus over the years, substantial self-motivated improvements have been introduced by the military logisticians in terms of better quality of rations, clothing, easy transportation, fructification of demands and maintenance of assets. Amy's 'Computerised Inventory Control Project', 'Stores Monitoring and Control System' and 'Reliability Availability Delivery System', though still operating in isolation, are some examples of logistic modernisation. Examples are also the Navy's 'Integrated Logistics on Line Management System' and 'Computer-aided Acquisition and Logistics Support' which are managed through a wide-area network with an 'Integrated Logistics Support and Integrated Management Software', whereas the Air Force has in place its 'Integrated Material Management on Line System' managed through the Air Force Net. Once all networks are fully operational these would be eventually connected to the 'Armed Forces' Unified Digital Network Grid'; that would bring jointness in logistics.

(13) For example, ammunition is one costly commodity that is subject to surge expense in war and trickle consumption in peace. It therefore requires scientifically analysed approach, duly moderated by a mix of professional experience and future appreciation, to manage its life cycle relationship between the scales of production, storage, consumption and discard in a manner as to satisfy the contending parameters of fail-proof operational assurance versus economics of production and storage. That would save India from running from pillar to post to purchase ammunition as war is waged, and land up with useless lots at huge costs – as it happened in 1962 and again in Kargil.

(14) Light-weight high-strength man and heli-portable weapons and equipment, movable ammunition storage, mine layers, mountain bridges and defence stores, earth moving plants, high-head pumps, cranes, cableways, extreme climate living

accessories, etc. would raise combat capabilities – by permitting quicker deployment of weapon and equipment, faster construction of field fortifications and optimisation of combat inventory, particularly the munitions – in the mountains. This capability would impose another facet of tactical superiority over any adversary in mountain warfare.

(15) These vocations have a very high rate of knowledge stagnation and human attrition. TA therefore is an ideal organisation to engage and disengage high experts and IW 'geeks'. TA is also suitable for engagement of the wizards of shady financial transactions and arms-drug trade which combine together to sustain insurgencies and terrorism. Most advanced militaries have one way or the other followed this path to strengthen their defence mechanisms, China's PLA having emerged as the US military's co-runner in this field.

(16) Reference is also made to the following works:

a) Patrick Bratton, "The Creation of Indian Integrated Commands: Organisational Learning and the A&N Command, Strategic Analysis, IDSA, May-Jun 2012.
b) Richard Weitz, "Jointness and Desert storm – A Retrospective", Defence and Security Analysis, Jun 2004.
c) 'Military Transformation and Modern Warfare', Elinor Sloan, Fraeger Security International, Pentagon Press, New Delhi, 2008.
d) Restructuring India's Military: Out of Box Options by Rear Admiral (Retd.) A.P. Revi, Delhi: Gyan Publishing House, 2012.

*

CHAPTER 5

REFORM OF APEX LEVEL DEFENCE MANAGEMENT STRUCTURE–2

> "*What is necessary to be performed in the heat of action should constantly be practiced in the leisure of peace.*"
>
> – **Flavius Vegetius**

Recapitulation of the Proposition

In Chapter 4, besides delving into certain overarching principles and factors of management of national defence – as distinct from the larger ambit of national security – the discussion has covered the broad features of a proposition on reformed structure of the DDF. To reiterate further, the proposition envisages the DDF to control all aspects of management and command which govern the nation's military institution – that term denoting the fighting forces in military uniform, so to state.

In this Chapter, the focus of discussion shifts to the second part of the proposition on defence reforms. Here, the proposition is aimed at reformation of the management of such military dedicated, dual-use and civil infrastructure, upon which the nation's defence capability is founded upon, and which are as a group referred to in this book as the defence establishment.

To recapitulate, in first part of the proposition for apex level reforms of national defence management structure, the MoD is proposed to be broadly structured as depicted at the reproduced Figure 1 below.

MoD (Headed by Raksha Mantri or RM)

RM's Secretariat (RMS)

Department of Defence Forces (DDF) (Headed by Minister of State or MoS, DDF)

Department of Defence Establishments (DDE) (Headed by Minister of State or MoS, DDE)

Figure 1: The MoD

The Department of Defence Establishments (DDE)

Within the ambit of the nation's grand strategy and military doctrine as vested upon the MoD and exercised through the RM, the proposition envisages the DDE to superintend all defence-related as well as military-specific public and private sector ventures of the state. The DDE would therefore be the overarching managing agency for all those sectors of the national endeavour which contribute in strengthening national defence and so fall under the wider definition of 'defence establishment' as propounded in the Preamble of this book. In other words, the DDE would be a controlling and coordinating body to ensure that the military institution remains strengthened, to a level specified by the MoD, by a robust combination of human, logistic, science and technology, and industrial support. To point out once more, that is not the case at present when, firstly, the mandate promulgated to the military institution is not matched by the designated capabilities of the various enterprises of the defence establishment, and secondly, even then, the nation's defence establishment could be definitely be better geared up to meet the requirements of the military institution in terms of quality, quantity and timeliness – within an appropriate long term fiscal allocation.

Functional Propositions

Ministerial control over this Department would be exercised by the MoS (DDE), while the Defence Secretary would shoulder all functional responsibilities of control and coordination of various enterprises of the defence establishment for the common goal of strengthening the national defence. These functions of the DDE would cover the entire gamut of policy-making, institutionalisation of procedures, prioritisation of projects and fiscal management, issue of inter-ministerial clearances, management of human resources, setting output targets, and finally, monitoring progress. Notably, taking note of the experiences of defence reforms in other nations, the Department, for the proposition to be effective, would have to be staffed by a cadre of dedicated defence bureaucracy, duly reinforced with other categories of civil servants, scientists, technocrats, industry and finance experts, and of course military professionals, as necessary, to meet the needs of domain expertise and experience. Further, institutionalised integration of military professionals into research and development, defence industry, defence budgeting, and sanctified application of the concept of 'military necessity' in dealing with sanctions, approvals, funding and legal recourses would have to be instituted in to the system in the interest of retaining the focus on the imperatives of national defence, and its instrument, the military institution.

Proposition of Outline Organisational Structure of DDE

In its skeletal form, the DDE may be envisaged as depicted at Figure 5 below. In brief, the DDE would bear the prime responsibility of policy-making and coordination to cover all such ventures as:

a) Defence research and development, defence estates, the defence-industrial base for production of military hardware in public and private sectors, procurements and quality assurance of military hardware of indigenous manufacture or through import, life-cycle maintenance and replacement of scaled weapons, equipment and transport, and periodic modernisation – the entire gamut of equipping and maintaining the military forces in short.
b) Defence logistics and infrastructural platform for the military institution to perform effectively. Notably, term 'defence logistics' is distinguished from 'military logistics', which is discussed in the previous chapter as a part of the military institution. Here, the term defence logistics covers the base aspects of strategic capabilities in terms of development of roads, railways and airfields along the borders as well as in the hinterland base areas, food and fuel supply chain, war-time medical provisions etc.
c) Homeland support to military operations in terms of tasking the National Cadet Corps (NCC), CAPF and nationwide promulgation of the provisions of the 'Union War Book'.

d) Pre-recruitment as well as post-release functions of personnel management, including education, second career, resettlement and veteran's welfare in observation of the hoary state-soldier covenant.

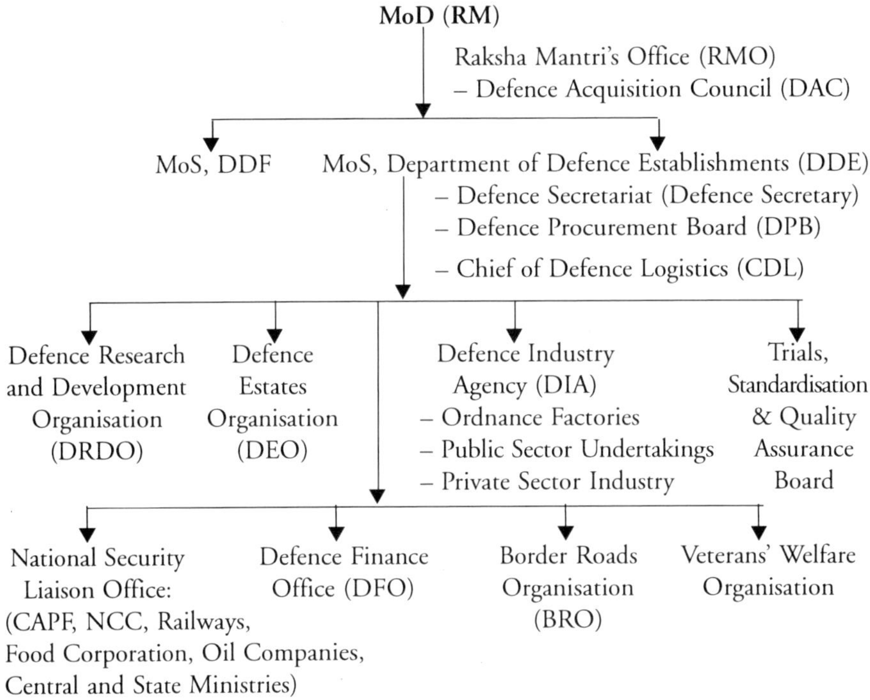

Figure 5: The DDE

At this stage it would be in order to enunciate the underlying concepts and key factors of the proposed organisational structure of the DDE, which combined together form the foundation over which the military institution is build, and inter alia, the nation's capability to defend itself. These factors are: One, the process of defence procurements; two, capacity of defence industry; three, the concept of military necessity and military lien over national assets; four, sanctity of the pristine state-soldier covenant; and five, a system of monitoring and audit of reforms. These factors are briefly discussed in the following paragraphs, the purpose being to introduce these rather than to attempt a dissection of such vast topics.

Defence Acquisitions and Procurements

As seen from the inferences drawn in Chapter 3 above, acquisition of military hardware for regular procurement to replenish scaled weapons, equipment, transport and expendable items as well as periodic force-modernisation are matters of extreme complexity. This complexity is but the result of the certain imperatives of military equipment management. These imperatives are: One, management of large inventories of diverse source items; two, extraction of best service from original and extended life cycles of hardware through refurbish or overhaul; three, control over rates of discard and expense of hardware in step with technological developments; and four, strict observance of the stipulation for cent per cent replenishment and safe levels of stocking of hardware, accessories and fast expendables, particularly the munitions. The necessity of achieving optimal balance between indigenous production, import, reserve stocking and judicious regulation of expenditure further exacerbates that complexity – a situation that the Indian defence establishment has not been able to master. There are reasons to suspect that this failure is attributable not so much to lack of ability as it is to the lack of orientation and seriousness of purpose; countries with lesser wherewithal have done better in this respect (1).

In order to comprehensively address the crucial fallouts of capital defence acquisitions and revenue procurements on the state of the nation's military preparedness, most of the modern defence departments have created dedicated organisations to deal with this aspect of defence management. These organisations are manned by top professionals having long experience in promotion of hardware designs, harness of defence technology and management of production, and have military professionals embedded to keep the right focus through in-built user participation and guidance. In India, such initiatives have remained stymied, more or less, due to the successive government's fluctuating concerns over defence preparedness, official unaccountability over defence developments and expenditures, tacit endorsement of organisational and cadre parochialism, and its condescending attitude over the principle of 'military necessity'. However, over the past decade or so, substantial efforts have been made to define and streamline a formal process to better manage the system of defence acquisitions and procurements. Presently, these processes have reached the stage of near-maturity.

In the current system of India's defence management, the task of hardware acquisitions and procurements are procedurally performed through the DAC headed by the RM, the 'Defence Procurement Board' (DPB) headed by the Defence Secretary, the ordnance and quartermaster branches of the three Services, and the line directorates in cases of arm or service-specific items. These agencies have defined charter as well as financial powers and follow the provisions of the DPP, while regulation of expenditure is undertaken by the Defence Finance. Thus at long last, after over a quarter of a century long hibernation, a substantial number of modernisation related procurements in respect of all the three Services have been cleared by the Government. However, having only recently sensitised itself on this core issue, there is much to be done at the apex level of defence management yet before these provisions start working at full effectiveness; India's past defocus and rather late entry into modern defence industry being the major deficits to cover (2).

The outline organisational structure for the DDE as proposed above envisages the following:

a) The DAC, headed by the RM, to exercise apex level control over the full gamut of capital defence acquisitions and procurements. Besides, the DAC would undertake the roles of resolution, rationalisation and arbitration over the issues of defence preparedness, as contended by the military institution through the DDF and by the defence establishment through the DDE.
b) Further, it envisages the DDE to exercise control over all fundamentals of the nation's defence preparedness, with the secretarial support and coordination among the plethora of subordinate organisations being undertaken by the Defence Secretariat, headed by the Defence Secretary. At the ministerial level, control over defence procurements would be exercised through the DPB headed by the Defence Secretary.
c) In the context of the requirements and priorities of the military institution, the process of customisation and monitoring of defence research projects, modernisation schemes and innovation of designs are to be overseen by the DDE's top military representative in the form of the 'Chief of Defence Logistics' (CDL). The CDL would also help in formalisation of policies on production scales and capacity utilisation in respect of the various constituent enterprises of the defence establishment.

The matter of defence acquisitions and procurement is by itself a multi-sector subject. Therefore further discussion, analysis and implementation of this proposition for reforms at the apex level of national defence management needs to be taken up by a group of domain experts as one of the follow-up assignments.

Build-Up of Defence Industry

One key purpose of the DDE would be to correct the severe anomaly that afflicts the nation's Defence Industrial Base (DIB). Having inherited a fairly extensive military industry, the Indian leadership had the right sense to establish a DIB in the early years after independence. However, it stymied its growth by confining that 'base' just to the replacement of dated equipment of a barely tolerated armed forces. That, and their self-righteous disdain against creation of a competent DIB which could keep up with the technological advancements through competitive export of military hardware, ensured that the defence industry never really could rise above rather modest goals and dated military technologies. India therefore not only lost out in nurturing a strong and vibrant defence industry, it also let go of an economic opportunity that has been a robust source of economic sustenance in many developed nations.

India's DIB boosts of 52 DRDO Laboratories, 39 OFs and nine DPSUs including four shipyards, all dedicated to defence, but none responsible, in real sense, either to the state, or more appropriately, to the military institution, their sole user and the cause of existence. The MoD's Department of Defence Production controls the OFs, has little authority over the DPSUs, has no control over the DRDO, and has no accountability towards the military institution. It is so that first named remains content in obliging the forces to make do with items of obsolete designs and supply even those which are not needed by forces any more, the second sustains itself through production of basic use items to captive military and civil customers, and the third seeks acclaim in farming and medicinal research while remaining stagnant on design and production of modern military hardware. The cause is not difficult to find – the practice of incorporating military professionals in such defence industrial organisations, with due authority at the conceptual, design and production levels, has given way to departmental turf-consolidation and mutual back-scratching, with the connivance of a helpful bureaucracy. The result is stark: the defence industry is yet to produce a decent rifle, and its flagship products like tanks, aircraft and guns, even the simpler ones like night sights and bullet proof jackets etc. fail to inspire combat worthy confidence among the soldiery. A key purpose of reforms in the defence establishment must be to remedy that situation.

Many steps have been taken during the recent years to remedy the situation from within the defence enterprises – the DRDO, the OFs and the DPSUs – with encouraging results. Besides, during the past couple of years, the defence sector has been opened up to indigenous industry, provisions for technology transfer have been strengthened, setting up local manufacture base has been encouraged and Foreign Direct Investment (FDI) facilitated. However, these steps are incremental rather than profound and are still held hostage to bureaucratic turf protection. Therefore, fruition of these initiatives at the ground level may be yet another decade away (3).

If the recent initiatives towards the achievement of self-sufficiency in defence production are to bear fruition, policy-makers of national defence have to orient each of the enterprises of the defence establishment to be accountable towards the military institution, and thus dedicatedly focus on strengthening the foundations national defence. In that, the goal of national self-reliance and performance accountability would be better served if the military institution is recognised as the primary, in fact the sole stakeholder, and integrated, as a 'user-partner', into the project management system right from the conception, through design and development, and up to the delivery stage. That degree of integrated approach to defence industrial development would necessitate empanelment of technically high-qualified services professionals and appointing them to the steering level appointments in each of the enterprises of the defence establishment, as well as on specified appointments in the MoD. All advanced nations assign military professionals to high-value defence projects at the apex or key levels; had that practice not been jettisoned in favour of misplaced autonomy cadre promotion, the fate of Arjun Tank, new family of small arms, Light Combat Aircraft, Unmanned Aerial Vehicles, modernisation of communications and many more such projects would have been more satisfactory.

Here, the proposition envisages the creation of a 'Defence Industry Agency' (DIA) under the DDE to perform the following, so far just about tentatively attended, roles:

a) Seamless coordination among the constituents of the DIB and monitoring of projects in terms of quality and quantity parameters, timelines, and budgetary allocations and expenditure.
b) Foster industrial and business partnership practices – joint ventures, transfers of technology, setting up manufacturing units, cross-attachment of experts etc. – to find a reckonable space in global high-technology defence industry, particularly in the field of advanced weapon systems.
c) Resolution of inter-ministerial issues between the ministries of Defence, Finance, Home, External Affairs, Heavy, Medium and

Small Industries, Environment and Forests and finally, the State Governments.

The issue of reforms in the various constituent enterprises of the nation's defence establishment is a subject by itself, and therefore best addressed by the combined wisdom of experienced professionals coming from the within as well as outside of such organisations, and then guided by the user's concerns which are best enunciated through the defence bureaucracy and professional military representation.

Synergic Application of Resources for National Defence: The Concept of Military Lien

War, by definition, must be a national effort up to the extremities of its resources and capabilities; it is the nation that goes to war, not just its military institution. Commitment of the entire range of national assets into war effort has therefore been a standard practice ever. In modern times, with development of robust civil wherewithal and infrastructure on the one hand, and a marked diffusion in war waging capability among state, quasi-state, non-state and in-state rebel insurgencies on the other, marshalling of dual-use resources to the furtherance of military operations under different situations becomes even more of an imperative. That is a condition in which the nation's all-round efforts are synergised not only to multiply military force-capability, but also to rationalise the overall burden of national security on the public exchequer. As a corollary, modern military institutions have scaled up their civil-sector dependency from a limited practice of 'civil-military coordination' to a higher level of 'assimilation' of dual-use infrastructure and assets to strengthen their operational plans.

In India, coordinated harness of civil-military wherewithal and infrastructure for the purposes of waging war has been an old practice, as it is duly sanctified by the provisions of the 'Union War Book' as well as various peace-time injunctions of the government. However, in the post-1971 War period of conventional peace, the practice has faded somewhat – as the trends of responding to military requisitions from various ownership ministries and departments suggest. Apparently, in its interpretation of benign liberty, the government itself seems to have allowed the very concept of military lien upon the civil sector to be smothered by a growing clamour for departmental autonomy which many times translates into exclusive self-centred priorities. In the civil sector, this development is evident from diffusion of control mechanisms from the hands of a single point administrative head – the Collectorate System for example – to that of the somewhat autonomous hierarchies of various civil departments. Such diffusion of control mechanism into the hands of departmental professionals may be understandable in a democratic civil sector, but when it comes to the assimilation of civil wherewithal into the nation's military preparedness, that is a dilution better avoided. Contrarily however, representation of military interests which was effected by embedding military professionals as well as the soldier-citizens of the TA and the 'Military Reservist Rolls' into various key civil departments – Home, Police, Railways, Industry, Transportation, Civil Supplies, State Administration etc. – has been diluted over the years, much to the detriment of the nation's war-waging effort. As a result, in the context of India's national defence, the scale-up to the level of 'assimilation' of civil dual-use infrastructure and assets to meet the imperatives of contemporary military operational plans, as referred to above, has not matured yet (4).

The need for better assimilation of the nation's civil wherewithal and infrastructure into military applications is a national cause towards economy of effort. However, its overlook is best depicted by the ambivalent manner in which the sentinels of internal security – the armed police forces – are expected to support any current or future military venture. Continuing from the discussion under the head of 'Goal Definition' in Chapter 4, it is reiterated that from the time policing was delinked from the military institution to be established as a distinct professional service, there has been in place an institutionalised arrangement for the former to relieve the latter from many of their rear area duties during war-like conditions – protection of vulnerable points, installations and assets, traffic control, impressments of transport and labour, marshalling of reservists etc. for example. Similarly, there is an institutionalised provision for the military forces to be called out in the aid of civil authorities or in suppressing armed rebellion which may have gone beyond the capabilities of the police forces to control. Indeed, this concept of mutuality has been in vogue in India, the synergy of 1971 War being a demonstrative example. However, as discussed in the preceding paragraphs, a double jeopardy has relegated this practice into obsolescence, firstly by the larger spill over of the nuances of modern war into the civil sectors of military significance, and secondly by the near complete dilution of military lien upon such sectors. This disability needs to be formally addressed by the DDE (5).

Proctor of Military Lien: A National Security Liaison Office

In the contemporary context of national security, the interdependency among the external and internal security forces has assumed more salience in view of the following developments:

a) Substantial expansion among the CAPF to fulfil the expanded scope of civil administration. During critical situations, these forces may also effectively bolster the strength of military forces by undertaking many of the second-line operational duties, provided the charter of responsibility is not allowed to be subsumed under partisan departmental exclusivity.
b) Emergence of a reckonable commonality between external and internal threats – such as rise of armed militancy, proliferation of arms-drug trade, sophistication of terror funding etc. – which require astute policing to support military forces when the latter are deployed to control threats to internal security which might have gone beyond the scope of policing.

It is needless to emphasise that apart from the police forces, similar interdependency and military lien is applicable to the Railways, Shipping, Airlines, the Ministries of Home, Industries, and Environment and Forests, the State governments and so on, the scale of interdependency having expanded in the prosecution of modern warfare. It is in this context of enlarged roles and their criticality in national defence, that the proposition envisages the creation of a 'National Security Liaison Office' with the purpose of duly empowered supervision, coordination and control the assets of military significance in the civil sector.

Apart from the national assets discussed above, the proposed structure of the DDE includes within its ambit control, many other Branches like the DRDO, Defence Estates Organisation (DEO), the Border Roads Organisation (BRO) etc. The roles and organisation of these Branches are already well defined and self-explanatory, which the DDE would undertake to uplift and synergise to the overall defence preparedness.

Finally, the idea behind the structure of the proposed DDE is that the commitment of protecting national security must lead to the institutionalised recourses for near-seamless and synergic assimilation of all of the nation's civil wherewithal and infrastructure towards that prime purpose. Heavy costs of national security and spill over of military concerns to the civil sector do not any more permit duplications, redundancies or last minute resort to ad hoc arrangements in the articulation of the nation's military power.

The State-Soldier Covenant

Before turning the discussion to other issues, the matter of Veteran's Welfare requires a brief mention. This is an issue of the hoary 'State-Soldier Covenant' which binds soldiers, sailors and airmen to uphold the nation's cause, at any cost, in return for state-protected security after his time is over. It is so that there are formally designated departments in the Union as well as the State government apparatus to attend to that Covenant – a unique commitment not applied to any other institution. In the recent years, however, this state-commitment stands vilified, much to the detriment of the majesty of the Indian State. This matter needs serious revisit at the highest policy-making levels if the nation is to harness the extra-ordinary loyalty of its ever-celebrated soldiery. The proposition therefore suggests a revamp of the functioning of the existing of Department of Ex-Servicemen Welfare, its re-designation, in substantive terms, to 'Veteran's Welfare Organisation' being a starting step.

Task Force for Defence Reforms

Before concluding the discussion on the proposed organisational structure for the DDE, it would be in order to touch upon the need to institute formal mechanisms to monitor the implementation of the entire gamut of restructuring and reforms as discussed in Chapter 4 and the current Chapter 5. This is a necessity to ensure that the goals are not lost sight of, the process is not diverted, and mid-course corrections, as necessary, are made without inadvertent goal displacement. Indeed, as discussed in Chapter 2 above, most nations, having started with their defence reforms have opted to institute such mechanisms, some even going to the extent of making the mechanism accountable to the nation's highest legislative body.

The task of implementing defence reforms is admittedly an extremely complex one. In advanced nations, the contents, range and scope of reforms are set by empowered group of top experts consisting of military thinkers who set the tone, and long experienced defence bureaucrats, sociologists, economists and legal experts, who pitch in to shape the endeavour. Once finalised, implementation of the reforms are effectively monitored through institutionalised mechanisms, so as to avoid stagnation of reform schemes, while at the same time retaining operational balance against the course and pace of changes among the various elements of military institution. Notably, these monitoring mechanisms operate either under promulgated legislative acts or formally enunciated policy instruments (6).

As described in the preceding Chapters, during the past decade or so there have been some attempts made by the Indian Government to tone up its system of 'Higher Defence Management'. Even if many of the easier and uncontested – and therefore of limited significance – provisions of the improvements sought out of those attempts have been instituted, the fundamental purpose, that is of modernising the national defence management organisation and thus to reform the system of defence policy-making in tune with the contemporary challenges, has more or less remained elusive yet. The difficulties encountered have been found to be as much in the superficialities in the scope and depth of the proposed vitalisation of the system as it has been in the failure to implement even that bit. It would therefore be wise to appoint a long-term Task Force to identify the reform areas and scope, holistically analyse these, specify the stages and timings of implementation, monitor progress, apply periodic course corrections and finally, put the new systems to validation tests.

For the fruition of the defence reforms, the above mentioned Task Force must take into account the past experiences and the reasons for the past attempts finding little success, the key ones being as follows:

a) The convening authorities of defence reforms – politicians, reform committees and bureaucrats – had been afflicted with inadequacy of strategic experience and expertise, which was further exacerbated by their reluctance to engage in wider consultations with the strategic community at large. These laymen therefore just could not fathom the range and scope of the task at hand. Then, opting for narrow and selective consultation, these authorities found themselves weighed down by trepidation due to divergence of professional opinion which appeared to them to be unknown, uncertain and contradictory. As a result, reform proposals came to be more of selective rather than substantial nature, and failed to logically conjoin with the rest of the defence management system. For example, in absence of compatible charters and personnel policies, integration of Service Headquarters into the MoD turned into a cosmetic exercise, just as the defence acquisition processes did not dovetail into the process of budgetary provisioning.

b) Options and analyses of defence reforms could not be freed from archaic notions of military administration which had been handed down by the previous generations of prejudiced governing establishments. Contrary to the pristine principles of exercising the right balance between political authority, bureaucratic responsibility and professional control over war and dual-use assets, finances and personnel management, the defence bureaucracy was found to be reluctant to let go of its disproportionate control over military administration. This charade was complemented by the military hierarchy either being unwilling or unsure of assuming more of it, while the political leaders remained ensconced in their isolation from defence matters. For example, the attempted reforms could not effect simplification of even in-house restructuring of military units, routine upgrade of weapons and equipment, and resolution of many sundry issues at the Service Headquarters level; these had still to be referred to the bureaucracy shackled Ministry. Resultantly, the past proposals for defence reforms failed to enthuse the executive level military professionals who could neither detect any advantages from the half-baked changes nor did they exert enough to optimise the implementation of such reforms.

c) Most importantly, looking through just the technical and organisational expediencies, the authors of defence reforms – civilian and military professionals – failed to appreciate the role of human element in implementation of the changes. Thus nothing was done to 'sell' the reforms to those who would actually implement these and so find ways to address organisational opposition, assuage innate fears, or bypass these to render these irrelevant, and so foster a win-win atmosphere wherein each participating group could be benefitted by the reforms (7).

Indeed, no appreciable headway to tone up the system of higher defence management could be made owing to a realistic organisational law which rules that, "a prejudiced organisational structure translates itself into similarly prejudiced organisational behaviour...and that renders even the most rational initiatives rather difficult to implement". This law explains the bureaucratic resistance against full scale reformation of the national defence management organisation and the system of defence policy-making. To avoid log-jam therefore, any new systemic initiative towards defence reforms must take that cultural hurdle into account and adopt a proven method of constituting an empowered Task Force – that would monitor and control implement the reforms – to consist of veteran and unencumbered military professionals and bureaucrats, besides of course the heads of each of the implementing organisations or departments.

Apart from attending to the causes of the attempted systemic improvements of the past turning out to be but half-measures, the Task

Force would therefore have to be competent in orchestration of planning and implementation of reforms against the usual resistances to be encountered. The purpose would be to nurture the reform schemes against odds in a seamless and balanced manner, and so, avoid incompatibility between one scheme to another at any point of time.

Competence of Reform Implementation and Audit

Advanced nations invariably have statutory in-built mechanisms for monitoring, stock-taking and course reviews in their system of defence management. The British, realising their inability to absolve possible deviations and redundancies in implementation of the razor-edge provisions of their 'Strategic Defence and Security Reviews', went a step further by composing a dedicated committee for implementation of reforms which took care of removing impediments, undertook the review of long embedded organisational cultures, addressed vested interests and reported to the Parliament through the Defence Secretary (the Minister) on annual basis.

In India too, we have the 'Parliamentary Standing Committee on Defence'. However, neither its membership subscribes to any strategic or military experience nor are its reports taken seriously by the Government. For the much overdue defence reforms to bear fruition in line with its fundamental objectives, this situation must change. Formal professional testimony, parliamentary debate and assignment of responsibility and accountability must form part of the statutory initiatives in this regard. The vast amounts spent, and societal costs borne in providing for the nation's military security, justifies such an arrangement.

The Proposition So Far

In sum, the propositions discussed above offer the advantages of professional thrust, astute policy making, expert handling from trained and experienced professionals, discard of redundancy and duplication, achievement of synergy, and focused management of the nation's defence. Even from the point of view of preservation of departmental sanctity, the proposition, with due elaborations and debate, may offer an acceptable win-win situation. In that, it is to be appreciated that contrary to superfluous perceptions, there would be no compromise of the existing bureaucratic and technocratic structure; in fact there would be the incentive of upgrade as well as expansion of professional perimeters, particularly so among the higher defence and public sector bureaucracy.

The discussion on the propositions related to the reformed structures of MoD, DDF and DDE naturally leads us to highlight certain broad parameters of defence policy reforms, enunciation and implementation of which are long overdue.

Long Term Guidelines for Political Stratagems

Organisation for a contemporary national defence management structure and its system of defence policy-making has been the issue of discussion in this chapter. However, for reforms on these aspects to be discussed in focused and conclusive manner, the key is to consider first the diverse political stratagems in the preservation of national security that may be open for the managers of national defence to adopt in a long term dispensation. Indeed, the stratagems of defending the national cause are many, and at the very first instance, purposeful adoption of most suited methods in the best interests of the country must be the guiding beacon for Indian leadership. Once the basic political guidelines get fixed, firm grounds of defence immediate, mid-term and long-term policy-making gets prepared. That in turn paves the way for emanation of the right defence policies for the system to manage the pending as well as rising challenges of national defence.

Accordingly, certain universally practised choices of defence policy stratagems might be enunciated along the lines as discussed in the subsequent paragraphs, the purpose being to see if any of these could be considered in the Indian context...

Convergence of Roles, Strategies and Resources

As mentioned in Chapter 3, in official communications of the Defence Ministry as well as the Service Headquarters, the role of the Indian armed forces has been officially defined as: One, to defend against external military threat; two, to assist in preservation of internal security and national integrity; and three, to provision aid and relief during natural calamities. However, in the first instance it is seen that enunciation of these roles has not been followed up with formal articulation of corresponding national strategies, military doctrines and optimised operating procedures – neither by the government or the CCS, nor by the military hierarchy – that are free of ambiguities and disconnections. In the second instance, notwithstanding the provisions of the 'Union War Book' and various departmental 'emergency schemes', over the past couple of decades have emerged many ambiguities and inconsistencies in policies and practices for the defence establishment as well as the other national assets of strategic nature – CAPF, Railways, etc. – to follow in fulfilling their designated roles in support of the military institution. The prime function of a reformed system of defence policy-making would therefore be to break free of the post-1990's state of policy-archaism, and with due alacrity promulgate updated policies to strengthen the cause of the military institution – and then to see to the promulgation of these in the best and cost-effective manner. Basically, the measures to be adopted in this regard are: One, enunciation of a 'National Security Strategy' and its implementation through periodic 'Strategic Defence Reviews' and 'Military Policy Guidelines'; and two, vitalisation of response and back-up mechanisms that the entire state-apparatus is obliged to offer, with due alacrity, to the sentinels of national defence (8).

Fiscal and Procedural Sustenance of National Defence

In tune with the modern parameters of defence management, a major consideration in formulating India's defence policies must be the existing imbalance of the equation between her defence needs that dictate the size and competence of the nation's military force on the one hand, and the fiscal sustainability of that force on the other. That equation tends to be unbalanced when over a third of the budget goes into personnel emoluments and another third in essential capital acquisitions, albeit with rather disconcerting slippages year after year, thus leaving the revenue budget at starvation level, archaic procedures of fiscal management adding to the mismatch. Thus when the annual raise in budget is pegged at around 10 per cent, the basic and routine requirements of the forces as large as what India has to maintain out of the defence budget tend to get neglected. Primary wherewithal as per the scales of hardware being vital to warfare, that indeed is a dangerous situation for any military organisation. Military history is replete with examples of such disastrous mismatch and the severe consequences of such situations. Managers of national defence have to find measures to break out of that debilitating log-jam (9).

Management of Military 'Hollowness'

When basic scales of weaponry, equipment, expendable hardware and munitions, operating systems, training etc. – the foundations of fighting power, in sum – are allowed to fall in short supply, the military institution, behind its stoic facade, turns 'hollow'. One example of policy disorientation that allows such situations to arise comes from short-indenting, induced by fund-starvation, of even the lower cost basic weapons and equipment, ammunition, mines, fuzes, spares and accessories. The trick of 'fund appropriation' is a convenient ploy adopted by fiscal managers, which in the first place leads to the much discussed military 'hollowness', and that affects the battle worthiness of capital weapons and equipment – at humungous dead cost to the exchequer. Such 'hollow' military institutions are liable to instigate impractical political expectations and then fail to deliver at crucial junctures of war-posturing, thus creating militarily irretrievable situations – as it happened in 1962 and again during Operation Parakram in 2001. In fact, as past experiences point out, it is more sensible to have smaller, a better kitted and fitter military institution than having a huge one that is 'hollowed out' by equipment and accessory deficiencies, organisational voids and operational inadequacies. India's political leadership have to take a call on that issue.

Restoration of 'Strategic Levers'

Besides the dangerous fallouts of 'military hollowness', an equally damaging effect upon the efficacy of national defence arises from a seldom discussed condition which may be described as 'strategic imbalance'. Self-inflicted by misinformed policy-making, this imbalance causes depletion of the reinforcing elements of military actions – such as the capabilities of military-focused collection and interpretation of intelligence, intelligence based quasi-military actions, overt and covert sub-conventional or 'special' actions, sharp mobilisation procedure, etc. – adverse fallouts of which remains unseen till a disaster appears. An apt illustration of this kind of flippant policy-making is offered by the Government's decision to convert the post-1962 created 'Special Service Bureau' (SSB) from a sub-conventional partisan force mandated to undertake clandestine operations in and across the border belts. Over the years, this potent force was first weaned away from its military character and then designated into a 'Shashatra Seema Bal' with a comparatively mundane role of policing the Indo-Nepal Border. Thus, in one stroke, a key operational capability and a feared military deterrence had been dismantled – a classical example of disorientation over national defence. Strategic imbalance caused by thinning out of military professionals from intelligence agencies and weapon research and development are some other example of misinformed policy-making against the interests of the state. There are many such examples as already discussed under the concept of 'military lien'.

Dynamism in Force-Mobilisation, Defence Industry and Military Diplomacy

Another ruling parameter of defence policy formulation is dictated by a nation's efficiency in mobilising and sequestering their military capability, in quick time, in response to unforeseen churnings of the real-politick – the US, UK and Germany being the examples. This policy permits a nation to keep its military structure alive and vibrant while lying dormant against major operational engagements, and yet retain the ability to mobilise and build up forces at short-whistle, the advantage being in keeping the overall defence expenditure down. There are, however, certain conditions to fulfil in this regard. Firstly, the state-apparatus and its mobilisation procedures have to be highly responsive to fast turns of external politico-diplomatic necessities. For India to adopt that policy, her present day elephantine and red tape bound system of emergency management would need to be vitalised – indeed, this has been done before in 1971. Secondly, being one of the most remunerative investments both in terms of political influence and profitable trade, defence industries are continued to be run in full gear even when military undertakings are dormant; this practice also permits the mobilised forces to be equipped with modern war wherewithal. Given the so far side-tracked course of defence industry, even that advantage would elude India for some years to come, after the present thrust on defence industry bears fruition. Lastly, in contemporary practice, military diplomacy is not necessarily linked to military mobilisation; its articulation is but a part of regular diplomacy by the means of training events, non-lethal military cooperation and sale of military hardware. Of late, India has so engaged with many nations; expansion of such engagements is a foregone multi-lateral commitment. Participation in military diplomacy also entails due modernisation of forces and to that extent, India's military modernisation cannot be stymied any more – in national interest. In sum therefore, these are three highly advantageous options that India's managers of national defence would be wise to adopt.

Review of Defence Logistics at National Level

In the contemporary world of defence management, military logistics is a national endeavour. No doubt, in India too, there is much cooperation between the three services as well as between the military and civil sectors which are connected with national defence. However, there still remains a vast scope for improvements in institutional back-up of military logistics –

in terms of civil supplies, labour, transportation, warehousing, workshop, engineering and medical services etc. – which, besides strengthening the operational teeth, would also result in better overall fund utilisation. Formal structuring of a national level logistic system, to be operative in peace and war, to dovetail with due certainty the civil dual-use facilities and infrastructure into the military logistic system, would meet that purpose. Such a system may be fostered by specific assignment of responsibilities, with due accountability, to various civil logistic providers under the supervision of the CDL and the 'National Security Liaison Office' of the DDE. Committed response from such diverse public and private service providers may need to be ensured through legislation of rules and policy promulgations; this practice has been adopted by some countries to regulate the provision for out-sourcing of services.

Congruence of Goals and Policies

Nations that play significant role in global affairs are usually destined to protect their interests by proactive diplomacy, duly backed up with robust military power – the US, China, Russia and Iran for example. It is therefore natural that the defence policies adopted by them are shaped by their political and economic aspirations and which are sought to be achieved with the due investments on their military establishment. Then there is also a second category of nations which find it impossible to sustain military power commensurate to their politico-military goals. These nations therefore opt to either scale down their political goals or enter into alliances as equal or junior partners, or even as facilitator-beneficiaries to cover their limitations. UK, Japan, and Pakistan are some countries which adopt such policies. It would be wise for India's political leadership to deliberate upon these two options and adopt a suitable one that meets national aspirations as well the resources.

Long Term Defence Stratagems

The preceding discussion offers certain options which have the potentials to bring major advantages to the nation's defence preparedness. However, adoption of these stratagems would have associated implications on the nation's overall governance and therefore these have to be considered in totality at the highest political level. Indeed, in multi-sector application of the stratagems discussed above, there would emerge many contradictory concerns. These concerns have to be accommodated by suitable customisation of the nuances of the stratagems, without diluting the core purpose, and finally reflected through the national security policies. In so doing, the desired parameters of national security policies may be defined, in broad terms, by the following measures:

a) Formal enunciation of a 'National Security Strategy' to vitalise national level responses and back-up mechanisms to conjointly and effectively uphold the cause of national defence. A continuous process of transformation of the military institution into a modernised, strongly structured, fiscally provided for and cost-efficient force would be an endorsement of that strategy.
b) The incongruities between the force levels, their state of preparedness and fiscal sustainability need to be redressed. This would entail rationalisation of the nation's defence imperatives, our political-military aspirations, serious rather than shifting committal of funds and the update of the policies and procedures that govern military administration.
c) Adoption of stringent policies to maximise military-diplomatic power according to the modern standards of synergic application, rather than just 'coordination', of intelligence, diplomacy and industry. Besides, in modern warfare of various shades, quasi-military, sub-conventional, conventional, 'intelligence' and 'special' actions play crucial roles in maximisation of power, and therefore, these supportive 'levers' of strategy need to be build up.
d) Adaptation of multi-sector policies in a manner as to resituate the lien of national defence over the nation's assets of strategic value – defence enterprises, logistic infrastructure, CAPF, Railways etc. – in substance rather than in form.

Finally, the point to appreciate is that it may be sensible to have a leaner and fitter military institution than a fatter and hollow one. To that end, besides the above listed measures aimed at maximising the power of a military institution which is affordable, build-up of effective reserve forces and institution of efficient mobilisation procedures, backed up with due legislation, may be considered to compliment the overall military force-structure. Going further, capability gap with respect to the possible emergence of powerful adversarial coalition, the nation's political leadership may consider building up alliances or strategic partnerships – there can be nothing 'not done' in the preservation of the nationhood.

Having thus defined the long term guiding parameters for the reformation of defence policies, we may proceed to touch upon certain key policy issues which have been calling out for attention since the past quarter of a century of inaction, and therefore, qualify for revisit at the very first instance.

Policy Issues of Foremost Instance

During the discussion over 'Goal Definition' in Chapter 4, four objectives of the reform of the national defence management structure and its system of defence policy-making had been identified. To recapitulate, these are: One, formulation of a 'national security strategy'; two, fusion of defence-specific inter-ministerial objectives; three, synergic coalescence of external and internal security mechanisms; and four, modernisation of the military force-structure and transformation of the military institution in tune with contemporary requirements of political, societal, economic and military security. Taking off from that definition, it may be in order to identify certain priority concerns for the restructured system of defence policy-making endeavours.

Policy on Balanced Political Directive

The first priority here would obviously be to frame a more elaborate 'political directive', duly corroborated by fiscal and industrial back up, for the military institution to develop appropriate strategies as well as the right force-structure in its fulfilment of the national mandate. In similar vein, that political directive would have to be translated into charters and tangible outputs for the nation's defence establishment, and to subject these provisions to periodical reviews. To elaborate further in tune with the contemporary practices, besides the military institution, a balanced political directive would also cover the strengthening of the national as well as military intelligence capabilities of forewarning impending hostilities, intelligence preparation of battlefields and situational development by means of intelligence operations. Similarly, it would reiterate the ability to cover the insurgency areas with adequate numbers of 'boots on ground' in conjunction with intelligence and socio-political development frame work. The directive would also aim at strengthening defence research, production and the linkages of all these with defence diplomacy.

In other words, enunciation of balanced and practical political goals should pave the way to the formulation of defence policies in two distinct aspects: those directed at the military institution and those meant to orient the defence establishment. It is only after the 'balance' has somewhat been matured – which, given the right impetus, might take some years to achieve – that the mangers of national defence may contemplate over, and finally promulgate, India's 'National Security Strategy'. Significantly, it needs be appreciated that formal coalescence of inter-ministerial policies and institutionalisation of their commitments to the overall strategic effort would be truly effective only when the said 'National Security Strategy' is promulgated (10).

Policy on Application of Political Directive

As a corollary to the issuance of a better articulated political directive, priority attention for the system of defence policy-making should be directed along the following lines:

a) Issuance of an elaborate 'political directive' from the CCS for the MoD to implement. This directive must be optimally balanced in terms of the nation's political aspirations, economic capacity and industrial strength.

b) Translation of the political directive into distinct policies for the military institution as well as the defence establishment to implement. For the military institution, the policies would favour redress of the 'hollowness' in its force-structure, not just by robotically filling in the hardware deficiencies and systemic voids, but by: First of all, reassessing the very purpose and performance criteria of the hollowed force-elements in modern warfare; next, 'right-shaping' the force-structure in tune with the political directive; and finally, devising ingenious military strategies to fulfil the mandate within a rational fiscal provision. In effect, the policies should promote the cause of military modernisation and transformational initiatives.

c) In respect of the defence establishment, the political directive would offer the right guidance in supporting and sustaining the war-strategies as subscribed to by the military institution – and in repudiation of deviations.

d) Finally, once reckonable headway has been achieved in institutionalising the principles of national defence, it would be in order to promulgate an appropriate 'National Security Strategy' for its conjoined application at inter-ministerial level in particular and the national level overall.

As we have found from the preceding discussion, government's 'policy directive' as well as the system of defence policy-making, in whatever form these exist, do not at present fulfil the above listed obligations (11).

Policy on Management of Military Reserves

Diffusion of war-fighting abilities among state sponsored proxies, powerful non-state organisations, radical groups and criminal conglomerates has necessitated substantial revisions in the military strategies in tackling these. Thus while classical prosecution of military operations have shrunk in its spread – but emphatically, not in their intensity or destructiveness – a vast space has emerged, alongside active or dormant conventional warfare, for the conduct of sub-conventional or neo-classical combat. The latter kinds of warfare require less of professional hard-kill acumen and more of comparatively softer, lower precision, but yet effective methods to execute. Resultantly, to reinforce conventional operations, conjoined line of communication military duties have to be undertaken by formally organised 'citizen-soldiery'. Another salient aspect of this development has been in the citizen-soldiery's assignment to larger war-time roles in military-civic actions, information, cyber, psychological and legal warfare, transportation, tele-communications, enforcement, intelligence and so on. Needless to emphasise therefore, 'military reserves' have emerged as high-skill, high advantage and low-cost national security providers.

In most advanced nations, as in India, this concept of citizen soldiery is applied in the form of the 'military reserve liability' and the Territorial Army (TA). Variations notwithstanding, there are duly instituted mechanisms for mobilisation, when needed, of the rolls of the 'Reservists' who are soldiers released from 'colour service' into 'Reserve Liability' for a specified period. On mobilisation, these troops marry up with their units and join active duty with the equipment earmarked for them to undertake combat roles of more or less equal less intensity, their civil employments remaining assured on demobilisation. The TA is a similar form of soldier-citizen force. The advantage of TA in modern warfare is in its flexibility of human resource management which permits the force to recruit high experts from diverse fields of professionalism – like communications, automation, cyber, psychological and legal fields – and embody them quickly to boost the so far lesser operationalised activities of modern military ventures.

It is therefore imperative that on the lines as discussed in Chapter 4 above, the policies governing the Reserve Forces and the TA be updated to the contemporary context. The reservists and the TA personnel have to be suitably incentivised and maintained in good trim to be ready to answer the 'call' at the times of need. More importantly, the process of 'call up' to arms needs to be bolstered with appropriate legislative sanctions. This would offer, at an appropriate time, an option to the Indian military institution to trim its standing regular formations. Indeed, this is one step that would pay out of proportion benefits to the cause of national defence, as indeed it has to the best military institutions the world over.

Policy and Procedures for Defence Procurements

An updated DPP, well-honed over the past decade or so, has been enforced by the MoD in 2016. A serious handicap in the process of defence procurements, much to the detriment of the military institution, has been addresses thus. However, issuance of the Policy needs to be bolstered by an efficient procurement and induction process through activation of the various components of the DDE described above. Since defence procurements would more often than not be mired in business competition, manipulations and even legal hurdles, the concept of military necessity may be accorded overarching priority as a matter of policy; the military institution may not be held hostage to the trade proprieties, as it has been happening since the Bofors case.

Policy on Defence Logistics

Here again, much has been achieved in synergising defence logistics at the inter-service level. Better coordination with national logistic infrastructure has also been achieved over the years of coordinating efforts. However, there has emerged a trend to among the public as well as private service providers to dilute, delay or even neglect their roles in provision of logistic support to the military ventures, as noticed by tardy response to defence funded railway projects, land allocations, road and pipeline extensions etc. New initiatives to integrate purely military, defence and national logistics systems would therefore remain incomprehensive and even strategically amorphous unless the concerned agencies are regulated by formal bindings of their specified assignments. The DDE, under the aegis of the MoD, and in exercise of the role of the CDL and the National Security Liaison Office as envisaged in the propositions, would be in the right position to institute such a mechanism for seamless and dependable integration of defence logistic commitments at the national level.

With the coming convergence between war and peace time, time has come to convert the 'Union War Book' to a 'Union Defence Guidelines'.

Policy on Role of the 'Other Armed Forces of the Union'

Formally referred to in the Constitution as the 'other armed forces', the past practice of invocation of the nation's military lien upon the CAPF – in terms of operational control in field, joint training and tactical communications – has been allowed to weaken over the years. This situation is a draw-back from misconceived interpretation of the democratic environment which has encouraged rise of autonomous culture and myopic distractions of partisan motivations – the CAPF officials are not comfortable in having to follow military 'diktats' even if they expect the military to take the brunt of emergencies. This weakness needs to be redressed in order to strengthen national defence and render the defence expenditure more remunerative. Indeed, other democracies do not permit such misconceptions to take shape when it comes to national defence,

As a corollary to the theme discussed earlier, the dated notion of internal security being exclusive to external threats needs to be revisited, and accordingly, closer association among the two kinds of forces fostered. Appropriate policies to govern effective assimilation of the vast organisations and strong capabilities of the CAPF into the nation's defence efforts should follow. Needless to emphasise, such operational re-assimilation of the CAPF should entail reinstitution of the past practice in which the overall command, without distractive stipulations, devolved upon the military commander.

Fiscal Policies

Fiscal allocations against defence budgeting and the provisions governing expenditure are subjects by themselves which need the attention of financial visionaries. Suffice to state here that taking off from the discussion over this aspect in Chapter 3 above, fiscal policies related to the defence sector have to be tailored according to the Indian conditions as dictated by its import dependency, nascent stage of research and technology development and limited industrial capacity.

In spite of all measures of formal management, there would still occur unwanted deficiencies in the scales of military hardware – particularly the expendables, as well as the cropping up of emergent requirements for defence works. To prevent such requirements from affecting logistic preparedness and eventually blow up into military 'hollowness', appropriate financial powers would need to be devolved, firstly, to the Defence Secretary to attend to the unforeseen and emergent requirements of the defence establishment, secondly, to the CDL to attend to the priority capital and revenue requirements of military institution, and thirdly, to the Chief of Joint Logistics and the Directorates General of the services' logistic branches (or the Chiefs of Materials), parts of the DDF, to meet sundry requirements against unforeseen delays, procedural hold ups and emergencies in joint and single-service logistic support system respectively – similar to the existing provisions in respect of the operational commanders.

As for the policies of fund allocations and expenses against pre-planned capital and revenue expenditures on structural upgrades, personnel management and hardware procurements are concerned, these too should be dealt under the concept of military necessity. The policies should be conducive in terms of practicality of time stipulations, exercise of financial powers, informed audit, balanced payment schedules and prevention of vendor mischief – all aimed at maintenance and upgrade of forces in step with advancements in military technology and rising standards of personnel management in time bound routine.

MoD Rules of Business and Procedures

Framing the right policies and promulgation, implementation, performance evaluation, course correction and audit of these policies are but bureaucratic exercises which require long experience, depth of understanding and deep vision. Therefore, the entire gamut of effective policy-making can succeed in making mark in the contemporary dictates of national defence only if this task is attended to by a dedicated defence bureaucracy that is made up of a right mix of civil servants, technocrats, diplomats, and of course, military staff. Even among the civil servants and technocrats, the mix must possess expertise on various domains such as public goods, personnel and training, finance, transportation, infrastructure, scientific research, procurements, manufacturing etc.

Defence dedicated bureaucracy would require modern defence dedicated tools – rules, regulations and procedures – to operate the reformed system of national defence management and defence policy-making as discussed above. Most of the defining rules and procedures in the MoD are of British era, modified as considered expedient in the 1950s' and superimposed with elaborations, amendments and additions from time to time thereafter. Indeed, this hotchpotch of archaic processes need to be contemporised, corrected and rationalised to be pitted against the modern imperatives. If therefore we are to modernise the ambit of national defence, one key to success in that venture is the modernisation of the defence bureaucratic system. Accordingly, in order to synergise the vast range of bureaucratic activities in preservation of national defence, there is a need to elaborate and improve upon the current 'Allocation' as well as 'Transaction of Business Rules', as followed by the Government of India. In similar vein, the wide range of office procedures that are currently adopted by various departments and branches of the defence bureaucracy, too need to be made result rather than procedure oriented.

END NOTES AND SELECT REFERENCES

(1) Prosecution of warfare being an excursion of unlimited permutations and combinations, it requires a wide range of weapons and equipment, each in turn having scores of variations, accessories and attachments. Most of these items harness different technologies and have different life cycles, which in some cases may be extended through mid-life overhaul and upgrade. Build-up of huge inventories and massive procurements to replenish these is therefore an imperative. In case of munitions, procurement plans are further complicated by the contending factors of high lead time, economic rate of production, operational dictates for stocking and judicious rate of expense on training. All these considerations add to the complexity of inventory management.

(2) Import dependency for high-end military hardware has led to vendor manipulations and corrupt practices at the highest political and bureaucratic levels. Many of these having been exposed as 'scams', capital defence acquisitions had been held up, much to the detriment of the military force-capabilities. The government was thus pushed into formalising a near-fool proof DPP. Over the past decade or so, this Procedure has been honed up and is presently ready to deliver, with the usual periods of gestational delays.

(3) To ensure long-term development and sustenance, the policy on defence procurements is classified by the provisions of 'Indigenous Designed, Developed and Manufactured' (IDDM) or 'Make (Indian)', 'Buy and Make (Indian)' and selective 'Buy' through import. Thus encouraged by opening up of defence production to the private sector, many small, medium and large entrepreneurs have joined the indigenous defence industry and tied up joint ventures with foreign manufacturers, the Tata Advanced Systems Limited, Mahindra Defence Systems and Larsen & Toubro being the big names in business.

(4) Unaccountability of these civil sector service providers is evident by their tardy response to the defence projects – duly paid for in advance – like provision of rail rakes, construction of bridges and sidings, extension of oil pipelines, grant of forest and environment clearances, maintenance of roads and canals etc. More seriously, the practice of consulting the MoD on various road, rail and waterway projects of strategic significance seems to have become optional.

(5) Dilution of military lien on armed police forces – a national cause towards economy of effort – is evidenced by the failure of the concept of unified command in vulnerable border and insurgency affected areas, and proliferation of CAPF organisations with duplication of roles. One of the most self-inflicting step taken by the Government has been the diversion of the post-1962 created 'Special Service Bureau', that was meant to organise resistance against military aggression, into the' Shashatra Seema Bal' (SSB) with a rather mundane role of guarding the Indo-Nepal Border. Considering India's volatile and vulnerable border areas, this step must qualify for a glaring example of strategic innocence that afflict India's defence policy-makers.

(6) Most European nations have implementation monitoring processes embedded into their defence ministries, while some like Australia and USA prefer to exercise parliamentary supervision. In China, such accountability is integrated into the governing system.

(7) Unable to break free of ingrained bureaucratic apprehensions, the custodians of national defence just could not bring themselves to let the military professionals lead, alongside themselves, the process of defence reforms. The range and scope of defence reforms were thus displaced by impractical expectations, disenchantment of military professionals and tardy implementation by civil and military executives. The fate of the Defence Planning Staff and many of the military automation and digitisation schemes are just two examples of such displacement from the path of reforms.

(8) As it was evidenced during the mobilisation for post-Parliament attack 'Operation Parakram' in 2001-02, response of the railways, the police, district administration, DPSUs, etc. to the emergent situation had left much to be desired. This led to the forces taking a long time to mobilise, and so lose certain operational opportunities. In this instance, even if the Union War Book was not invoked, many of its provisions had been formally promulgated.

(9) The mismatch is best exemplified by the analogy of guns and ammunition. The idea of possessing more guns with insufficient ammunition, or vice versa, has always been a matter of contention – what after all is the use of possessing guns that are starved of ammunition or ammunition that have no guns to fire. Striking the right balance in this context is contingent upon political, fiscal, industrial policies and procedures, as much as it is on the relative military equation vis-à-vis our potential adversaries.

(10) Jumping into enunciation of a vague or ambiguous 'National Security Strategy' cannot be in India's interest before the right 'balance' between military institution, defence establishment and fiscal provisions has been achieved. Before that happens,

what could after all the policy articulations in respect of the neighbourhood – the main audience – be? Will India promulgate her intent to regain the Pakistan Occupied Kashmir and the Aksai Chin, or would she accept status quo, or indeed might give-in due to any reason conceivable or not. Will she challenge the usurpation of the Indian Ocean, or declare her stake by joining in military alliances, or just reconcile to playing second fiddle on that arena. How could her strategic articulations with respect to the topsy-turvy situations in Sri Lanka, Afghanistan, Nepal and Bangladesh remain relevant for at least some years? What response would India offer in the matter of 'hot pursuit' or precision targeting of terror outfits and then go on to honour the credibility of that policy? The answers to these queries seem to suggest that till India marshals her mind and muscle, articulation of a rhetorical national security strategy might not be a noble idea.

(11) In 1990, the then Defence Secretary stated during an evidence, "If you ask is this the Defence policy, I would not be able to say the answer is in the affirmative because India's Defence Policy ..., from 1947 onwards, more precisely from 1950 onwards, has been basically a policy to defend our territory, our sovereignty and our freedom and no more than that."

On 16 May 1995, the Prime Minister and Minister of Defence, Shri P.V. Narasimha Rao, stated, "I would only confine myself ... to a very few matters impinging on the defence policy of the Government and I would like to take the House into confidence .... to the extent I can ... The first criticism has been ... we have no National Defence Policy .... this is not true. We do not have a document called India's National Defence Policy but we have got several guidelines, which are followed, strictly followed and observed, and those can be summed up as follows:

a) To defend our National Territory over land, sea and air, encompassing among others the inviolability of our land borders, island territories, offshore assets and our maritime trade routes.
b) To secure an internal environment whereby our Nation State is insured against any threats to its unity or progress on the basis of religion, language, ethnicity or socioeconomic dissonance.
c) To be able to exercise a degree of influence over the nations in our immediate neighbourhood to promote harmonious relationships in tune with our national interests.
d) To be able to effectively contribute towards regional and international stability and to possess an effective out-of-the-country contingency capability to prevent destabilisation of the small nations in our immediate neighbourhood that could have adverse security implications for us".

In a more vibrant regime for management of national defence, it would have been in order for the military brass to translate these political guidelines into concrete military objectives to identify and prepare for, and for the defence bureaucracy to create conditions conducive for the implementation of defence plans. Sadly, that did not happen in India.

(12) The following references are of salience:

a) Baylis, Wirtz and Colin Gray, Strategy in the Contemporary World, Oxford University Press, London, 2013.

b) James Blaker, Transforming Military Force, Pentagon Press. New Delhi, 2008.
c) Restructuring India's Military: Out of Box Options by Rear Admiral (Retd.) A.P. Revi, Delhi: Gyan Publishing House, 2012.
d) Ed Vinod Mishra, Core Concerns in Indian Defence and Imperatives for Reforms, Pentagon Press, New Delhi, 2015.

CONCLUDING OBSERVATIONS

"It takes all the running you can do to keep in the same place. If you want to get somewhere else, you must run at least twice as fast."

– **Lewis Carroll**

The world is changing at a rate faster than even before in the history of mankind. There is spread of democracy, individual freedom, worldwide communications and global exchange, technological tools for better living and so on. But these gratifying changes bring their own side-effects to disturb global peace and stability. In many ways, individual, group and nationalist empowerment translates into banal popular aspirations not only of exclusive economic aggrandisement, but further beyond to the cultural dominance, even usurpation of sovereignty over foreign societies. It is so that nation-states are being pushed into adoption of potentially exploitative, predatory and ultimately intrusive foreign policies, and when that does not satisfy impractical aspirations, non-state marauders take over in their bloody attempt to impose their brand of societal order – a brand that finds no attraction from the target nations. This indeed is the narrative that influences the secular world powers as well as those demonically empowered non-state factions to declare their monopoly over interpretation as well as imposition of political, ethnic and religious propensities beyond their borders. Developments in West Asia, Indian Ocean Region and South China Sea are some manifestations of that kind of international friction. War, in its different hues, will therefore remain an endemic nationalistic and sub-nationalistic affliction, exactly as the spread of the world wide conflict map, the brisk trend of global military spending, and the rising profitability of military trade indicate. Only fools would contest that counsel – a counsel that is eternally true but yet need to be dispensed every now and then to rationalise the romantic call of universal peace, prosperity – and *Vasudaiva Kutumbakam* (the noble Indian idea of the world being one family).

India has done well so far in preserving her sovereignty and internal order – albeit tenuously and by dint of its resilient military institution – at a 'competitive' cost, so to state. Presently, the sign of times seem to have attracted the concern of India's otherwise stoic defence planners. Recent initiatives of the Indian government in restoring the 'War Wastage Reserves' of weapons, equipment, and even more importantly, the ammunition stocks, and pushing through the ever-stagnant force-modernisation schemes are pointers to its commitment to redress the military 'hollowness' that was allowed to afflict the military institution over the past quarter of a century. But the modes, manners and methods of warfare are undergoing quantum changes, and so are changing the strategies and structures of the military institution. These changes must be accommodated into the ambit of foresighted planning for national security, its corollary, national defence, its instrument, the military institution, its foundry, the defence establishment, and finally, its term of reference, economic affordability. It would do us no good to try to fight newer and more complex challenges with wherewithal gone obsolete and costly to sustain (*).

As discussed in Chapters 1,4 and 5, time is ripe for India's organisation for national defence to be upgraded and modernised, right-structured and right-sized, right-oriented in strategic articulations, and finally sustained by affordable investments from the national exchequer. In other words, the entire gamut of national defence calls out for 'transformation', nothing short. To that end, defence reforms are imperative, nay obligatory, to bring about such a transformation.

As discussed, defence reforms have to be directed at the following aspects of national defence:

a) Modernisation of the military institution, involving force-restructures, command and control hierarchies, joint inter-service force-application, logistics and training.
b) Rationalisation of manpower to fund modernisation. This would involve trimming of regular manpower in favour of TA, Reserves and a competent system of force-mobilisation.
c) Institution of a defence acquisition and procurement processes that deliver rather than just promise.

As the American, British and Chinese experiences indicate, an endeavour so fundamental and profound cannot be met by a system so restrained by bureaucratic resistance and military inertia. Defence reforms therefore have to be initiated, implemented and monitored at the strength of political authority that is triggered by a concern for fiscally sustainable national defence.

Finally, at this stage we may momentarily divert from the main topic to point to certain imperatives at the CCS level which, even though left out the scope of discussion here, have to be undertaken for the defence reforms to be comprehensive and profoundly successful. In brief, these imperatives are:

a) A good option to strengthen the course of defence reforms would be to constitutionally sanctify the process. This could be done by the appointment of a Parliamentary Commission to approve and monitor the process of reformation of the structure of defence management and the system of defence policy-making. Due military representation, in appropriate form, should be mandatory in this process.
b) By its scope and implications, both political and fiscal, defence reforms are no less important than what the Indian state seeks to achieve through the Finance Commission, the 'Niti Ayog', and such other institutions. It would therefore make sense to institute the defence reforms through the sanction of an Act of Parliament. Re-structuring of the MoD and the functions of the consultative as well as executive mechanisms in the DDF and the DDE under the direction of the respective MoS, with the RM in overall control, may thus be sanctified and sealed.
c) It would be wise to form a close-knit group – in the nature of a 'Defence Council', to wit – headed by the RM and with the Prime Minister as its patron, for the military professionals to articulate their concerns in free, friendly and forthright environment. Most nations have such groups; in India, such groups had been in session during the 1960s and 1970s.
d) Issue has been raised occasionally regarding the constitutional status of the nation's grand strategy bodies like the NSC, NSA, NSAB, SPG, Joint Intelligence Committee (JIC), NCA etc. Since at that level it is advisable to redress ambiguities, the Government could formalise the status of these bodies, or better still, keep the advantages of having such bodies unencumbered by the bindings of the political system.

e) There are detailed provisions to be made before the institution of the CDS is installed. These provisions relate to the role of CDS in functions of the CCS, the abovementioned RM's Defence Council, the DDE, the Parliamentary Committee on Defence, the NSC, NCA and the JIC. Similarly, provisions related to the administrative and financial powers of the CDS, as well as the duties and powers of the two VCDS and the proposed National Security Liaison Office of the DDE have to be formalised before the system is created – the list of preparatory work is not exhaustive.

Reverting to the scope of the discussion, it is needless to state that the foremost act towards the goals sought here would be to reform the national defence management structure and its system of defence policy-making.

NOTE

(*) Reportedly, the severely depleted and obsolescent 'War Wastage Reserves' of military hardware to fight 20 days of 'intense' and 20 days of 'normal' engagements are to be recouped by 2020 while ammunition stocks are to be restored to 50 per cent level by 2019. In similar vein, two lakh crore of 'Buy and Make' schemes have been sanctioned by the government (regular press reports, Economic Times of 09 September 2015 and Times of India of 19 March 2016, for example). That must be good news, but the range of such recoupment indicates the mindboggling debilities of the military institution.

*

PART 2

MILITARY REFORMS AND MODERNISATION OF MILITARY INSTITUTION

"When the pace of change accelerates, the militaries that change and adapt are likely to gain massive advantage over potential enemies who are less agile."

– **Lt Col Scott Stephenson**

Overview

Core Purpose of Military Reforms

The ultimate objective of defence reforms at the national level, as discussed in Part 1 of this book, is to be able to shape a modern and competent military institution that can answer to the national mandate within an affordable investment. Further, within the overall ambit of defence reforms, reformation and modernisation of the military institution must be the topmost priority. Indeed, the fact, that India's external adversaries, internal insurgents and neighbourhood terrorists, all three are continuously mastering the exploitation of modern military technology to upgrade their methods to cut India down, renders the modernisation of India's military capability ever more obligatory. Accordingly, the call during the past two decades has been for the Indian Armed Forces to modernise in step with the times. In this Part of the book therefore the focus homes on to the matters related specifically to military reforms and modernisation of the military institution.

As a corollary, true fruition of modernisation would require comprehensive restructure of the nation's military institution in which ingenious tactical procedures are assimilated into modern war-waging hardware – to the extent affordable by the national exchequer – to shape an integrated force-structure that is configured to deliver across the entire spectrum of contemporary warfare. The Indian military institution of the day is definitely not in that shape – there is much scope for enhancement of its force-capabilities and so extract higher returns from the investments made on national defence.

To stand up to this challenge, defence policy-makers in India have to appreciate that just the aspects of induction of modern weapons and equipment, and raising new combat formations – long pended matters which have come to their focus at last – would not be enough to achieve cost-effective military security for the nation. For that to happen, it would be necessary to think beyond hardware modernisation and delve into the realm of profound military reforms, which must encompass the adoption of more potent strategies of force-application, restructure of forces to execute those strategies, and revision of tactical procedures to get better of the enemy, and so fulfil the political mandate within the ambit of fiscal affordability and industrial competence.

In other words, indigenous military reforms would entail definition of the politically mandated military objectives, evolution of a military doctrine that is adoptable to fulfil that mandate, formulation of military strategies in conformity with that doctrine, and finally, identification of the means, methods and tactics of implementing those strategies. Crafted with due strategic acumen, such a reformation – or transformation, so to state – must be a mandatory commitment for the nation's defence planners.

Roots of Military Reforms

The geo-political environment across the world has undergone profound changes during the course of past quarter of a century or so. As a corollary, nations have had to reconfigure their politics of international engagements to accommodate the changed environment. And since warfare is but a political recourse, it is only natural that the objectives of engaging in war and the manner of prosecuting it are recast in tune with the contemporary political, strategic, societal and economic dispensations.

Stimulus to the military institution's alacrity to conform to contemporary operational realities comes from two factors: one, infusion of high technology into the wherewithal's of war; and two, a universal transformation in socio-political culture, particularly in relation to the causes, means and methods of warfare. In the furtherance of political ends, these realities have necessitated the emergence of new methods of applying military forces which facilitate in complementing extreme reach and lethality of armed actions with the least of collateral destruction. Accordingly, the very concept of force-application at strategic, operational and tactical levels has had to be remodelled to assimilate the various new nuances of prosecuting warfare.

Prosecution of warfare in the contemporary era involves deployment in varying combinations of conventional and unconventional operations, each with varying composition of force-elements that may range from diversely committed light Special Forces squads to concentrated deployment of heavy battle formations. These are but revolutionary changes that have inspired the leading countries around the globe to revise the configuration, organisational structure, equipment profile, training and manning of their military forces. Advanced nations have accordingly devised their own versions and parameters of Revolution in Military Affairs (RMA), the core purpose being to assimilate high-technology into military art in a manner so intimate and profound as to open up new vistas for application of innovative strategies in the exercise of military power. As however, measures were instituted to integrate political objectives, tactical ingenuities, military hardware and force-structure, it became clear that for such integration to bear fruition, it would be imperative to undertake a holistic 'reform' of the entire military structure – just elemental and incremental 'military modernisation' would not do. That imperative is being defined as 'military transformation'.

Idea of 'Minimalist' Military Capability

During the past six and a half decades of its existence, the Indian State has mandated its military institution to the preservation of the nation's external as well as internal security besides in dealing with natural calamities. On its part, the military institution has restructured itself from time to time while doing its best to find an optimal equation between the war-wherewithal placed at its disposal and the mandate ordained upon it. To its good luck, the equation of foreign policies and international order over the past seven decades has so far permitted India to subscribe to rather tentative defence policies and 'minimalist' thrust on military preparedness in preservation of its integrity against a state of perpetual aggression from external and internal enemies, more or less, the exceptions being the foreign occupation of parts of Kashmir and Ladakh. Presently however, a spurt in aggressive political activism and military muscle building in India's ever-inimical neighbourhood has changed that equation. Resultantly, India's past datum line of 'minimalist' military preparedness has gone higher.

It is no secret that since the early 1990s', finding a balanced equation between the two prime determinants of the nation's defence preparedness – resources allocated versus the roles assigned – has been eluding the nation's military institution. Thus there has occurred a degree of incompatibility between the performance expected of the military institution and resources allocated to that purpose, which in turn has led to the body-military going 'hollow' and rendering a part of the military forces as hors de combat. The nation thus lands up maintaining a partly 'unusable' military force while incurring substantial dead expenditure without commensurate returns in terms of defence preparedness. As a result of this incongruity, India remains denied of the full security dividend that could accrue from maintaining the third largest defence force in the world, and that at excruciating costs to the hard pressed state exchequer. Further, there being no option of lowering the benchmarks of national defence in a region so dangerous, keeping the military institution as a partially starved, partially usable force makes little sense. Wisdom therefore dictates that it is imperative for the Indian political and military leadership to devise ways to empower the military institution through right funding, strategic innovations, modernisation and manpower rationalisation – military reforms in short. Notably, the suggestion here is not to 'maximise' military power as many nation's do, but to maintain the 'minimalist' military preparedness on even keel.

The proposition for Defence Reforms to revamp the national defence management structure and its system of defence policy-making, as deliberated upon in Part 1 of this book, are actually meant to facilitate the achievement of just that purpose. But structures and systems are just the tools; it is for the craftsmen to wield these to create a masterpiece. Within a governing system that is so less appreciative of military culture, so gripped by fear of losing control, and so listless in management of its military institution, the burden of initiating, securing political endorsement and steering India's military reforms could be borne by the military hierarchy itself. Regretfully however, beyond pining for some modern weaponry, and that just for the predominant service-arms, that hierarchy has so far shown little non-partisan concern in wholesome restructure of the military institution, and so modernise its overall war waging capability. Indeed, long restrained by budgetary starvation and apathy over systemic and procedural modernisation, that hierarchy prefers to make do with its old, so called 'time tested' ways and continues to prepare for the last war with some selective induction of operational increments thrown in from time to time. The purpose seems to be to project an impressive façade of tanks, guns, ships and aircraft, even if the secondary support and logistic systems, which are fundamental to the optimal deployment of those, remain bereft of compatible capabilities. Besides causing debilitating imbalances in orchestration of combined and integrated battle-worthy force-composition, such inadequate body-mass of the military structure prevents development of flexible, audacious and ingenious strategies to fully exploit the true potentials of the 'fist-arms'. Herein lies the dilemma (*).

As it has happened in all modern militaries, modernisation and reforms have always been imposed by political will, which in turn is backed up with the national leadership's deep understanding of the native military institution. That is not the situation in India. The remedy therefore is a tough one, as it requires an extraordinary group of visionary military leadership to devise and administer the reforms, the cause being duly backed up by an equally visionary political leadership and a proactive bureaucracy. That expectation remaining somewhat implausible in the foreseen future, it may be wise to adopt a realistic and practical approach to the theme of military reforms that might find the favour of consensus in the Indian dispensation – that is, reforms that least petrifies the political leadership and their bureaucratic mentors at the one end, and the 'stone wall' of rigid, inward oriented military brass at the other. It is hoped that, as substantiated by past lessons, once such an endeavour gets going, the bandwagons would be increasingly crowded.

Theme for Modernisation of the Military Institution

It is in the backdrop of the causes enumerated above that modernisation of the Indian military institution, which is true to the native context, assumes salience. Consequently, the intended range and depth of modernisation may have to be identified and conditioned according to the issues raised in the subsequent paragraphs.

Firstly, within the ambit of the country's distinct political culture, manner of governance and fiscal commitments, what might be the appropriate political mandate for the Indian military institution for it to stand up to the rigours of the regional strategic matrix.

Secondly, how might the Indian military institution be optimally structured to meet that political mandate within the capabilities of India's indigenous science, technology, military industry and regulated import, as well as the fiscal parameters which may be affordable in relation to other national commitments?

Thirdly, how should the inevitable disconnect between the political mandate and the resource-wherewithal allocated to that purpose may be covered by devising ingenuous war-strategies and tactical procedures. In that process, how might the military institution take advantage of India's indigenous strengths while covering up for her limitations? In other words, how might the Indian version of warfare be waged with synergic application of conventional and sub-conventional strategies with IW, special operations, irregular warfare and nuclear posturing, to deny to the enemy his objectives of opting to go to war in overt, covert or proxy mode?

Fourthly, over the years, the military institution has experienced many increments of technological infusions, induction of new weaponry and war-like equipment, and modifications in its organisational structure. Conversely, it has also been afflicted with debilitating deficiencies in arms, ammunition and war-like equipment, besides of course, shortage of combat leadership and tactically and technically skilled manpower of the kind that are needed to engage in modern warfare. With so many additions and subtractions, the existing organisations of battle formations and units remain no more as 'balanced in composition' as these had been when these were conceived at the time of World War II. As a corollary, it needs to be decided as to what re-structuring might be needed in the organisational framework, weapon and equipment profile, training and personnel management to make the current military institution more worthy of modern warfare.

Lastly, under the Indian dispensation, what might be the exercisable options – conceptual as well as practical – that might be adopted to foster jointmanship, net-centricity and achievement of asymmetrical advantages in prosecution of military operations? How these concepts and practices might be factored to multiply force-capabilities, impose deterrence and prevent potential adversaries from benefitting by military aggression, should the deterrence fail.

Primary Issues for Military Reforms

Military modernisation is a long drawn process that requires steady progress towards fixed goals and flexible options, elaborate exercises and experimentations, and professional monitoring and course corrections – all these over a period of time. Obviously, these involve issues of debate and deliberations at such a widespread level and extent that it is impossible to cover the subject within the confines of one book. However, it would yet be feasible to touch upon certain primary issues of military reforms which have come to the contention among the managers of national defence; forward movement over these primary issues might set the stage for the launch of comprehensive modernisation of the Indian military institution.

Accordingly, in the chapters following in this part of the book it is intended to provoke wider professional debates by highlighting, but little beyond, certain key determinants of military modernisation, and in its wider sense, comprehensive military reforms.

Chapter 6: The Mandate of India's Military Security

The matter of formal promulgation of a National Security Doctrine and its elaboration through a National Security Strategy is the topic of discussion in this chapter. As a corollary, promulgation of an unequivocal Political Mandate upon the Indian military institution would follow.

Chapter 7: Strategy Update and Force Modernisation

Discussion in this chapter would commence from the propagation of a comprehensive 'Joint Services Military Doctrine' in the fulfilment of the political mandate. Update and adaptations of strategies for the prosecution of integrated military operations would be touched upon next. Identification of the objectives of Military Deterrence against compulsively aggressive adversaries would follow as a natural corollary.

Chapter 8: Joint Warfare and Integration of the Indian Military Institution

Build up and modification, as necessary, of an integrated military force-structure in conformity to the abovementioned doctrinal principles would be discussed here. Complementarities of this force-structure to the joint strategies of force-application would also be highlighted.

Chapter 9: Network Centric Warfare

Major nuances of application of the above listed determinants through adaptation to the concept and practice of network centric warfare, both in terms of cultural, structural and procedural customisation of the military institution would be touched upon in this chapter.

Chapter 10: Training for Modernisation

In this chapter, cultural as well as professional training of military personnel has been highlighted, as indeed it must be, as the prime mover of military modernisation. The current anomalies with respect to the modern societal culture and youthful inclinations, and its disconnect with military ethos are discussed with certain suggestions to close the gap. Similarly, the basic dichotomies between younger intake, higher education and wider canvas of military professionalism have been touched upon.

END NOTE

(*) Resource crunch and misplaced attitude of partisanism among the military's predominant arms have caused serious imbalance in the three service's force-composition. Thus tanks, guns, ships and aircraft are short of accessories and attachment packages which are needed to turn main weaponries into lethal fighting systems. The state of secondary combat support systems – surveillance, protection, mobility, stealth and camouflage, battle field survivability and logistic systems – are below par when it comes to operational orchestration of the full 'orbat' of combat formations. The imbalance in force-structure thus gets pushed under the carpet by pompous demonstrations that are organised from time to time for the benefit of public morale.

*

CHAPTER 6

THE MANDATE OF INDIA'S MILITARY SECURITY

"Assessment of defence preparedness is a dynamic process, keeping in view the threat perception. Government takes appropriate measures, including modernisation, to maintain operational preparedness of the forces..."

– Defence Minister Shri Manohar Parrikar in Lok Sabha, 13 Dec 2014

Enunciation of a Formal Political Mandate

It is understandable that a nation of India's size, population, economic rise and geographic spread would cause her to be targeted by regional rivalry, even animosity, from immediate neighbours, and so oblige her to possess a vast military institution. It may therefore also be understandable that many foreign strategic analysts find it hard to believe that India has no formally promulgated national security doctrine or even a national security strategy that could guide the nation's defence endeavours to be prepared and progressed in a focused manner. That India is destined to exist between two powerful neighbours, one of whom would cut its own limbs just to see the Indian nationhood decimated and another who has chosen to perceive India as an upstart challenger to its 'rightful' supremacy who need to be kept in 'her place', and that double jeopardy obliges India to maintain the world's third largest military establishment even at the cost of her primary resolve to banish poverty, makes the matter even more astonishing to them. Similarly, when it comes to the native strategic community, this policy-reticence is viewed as a systemic debility and thus causes consternation among them. Indeed, it is difficult to disagree with such observations because formal articulation of national security doctrine and its corollary, a national security strategy, are imperatives for the right alignment of policies, processes and resources in the management of the complexities of national defence, and accordingly, in providing the right guidance to the military institution to structure itself in convergence with the national objectives.

Many opine that India lacks the wisdom to factor military power in her policies and that she lacks a 'strategic culture'. However, the very severity of that opinion calls for deeper scrutiny before it could be considered with due seriousness. After all, just the public dissemination of a national security doctrine or strategy can by no means imply a mature strategic culture, particularly when much of such pronouncements well could well turn out to be either vague or vain, and un-implementable due to imponderables beyond the state's control. Indeed, constrained in building up her defence capabilities by contending fiscal priorities and import dependency for key military hardware, it could be impractical, even inflexible, for India to formally commit to unequivocal and diligently deferrable national security doctrine or strategy. Conversely, any inability to enforce such sacrosanct promulgations being a more serious debility in geo-political messaging, the case for the Government of India's formal promulgation of its national security doctrine (or national security strategy) may be better rested, for the time being. Notwithstanding that, continuous and long drawn processes of military reforms and modernisation must proceed based on the indicative ordinations of the Indian political leadership. Accordingly, the discussion may be focused on purely military aspects of formulation of appropriate 'military doctrine', 'military strategy', and organisation and force-structure for war based on such indicative political ordinations.

Viewed from purely military angle, the point to note is that adherence to a deliberately considered doctrine and its tangible expression through strategies devised are imperatives for the military institution to structure and prepare itself by the best utilisation of resources made available to it. But for that to happen, it is necessary for the national leadership to specify a political mandate for the military institution to devise its war doctrines and amplify these objectives by outlining appropriate guidelines for the entire defence sector to follow. Obviously, rather than straight application of foreign templates, these objectives would be have to a reflection of the Indian political culture. Similarly, the means to achieve such objectives have to be customised according to the native conditions.

At this stage therefore, it makes sense to: One, define a broad 'political mandate' for the military institution to fulfil; two, devise a compatible 'draft military doctrine'; three, translate the doctrine into a set of corresponding 'draft military strategies'; and four, perform according to the principles and concepts enunciated in these draft policy documents while letting these to mature over time. Formal promulgation of a fine tuned defence policy may then follow at an appropriate time (1).

India's Political Culture

In one perspective – a stronger one that prevails among the nation's ruling establishment – successive governments have been wise to remain committed to an agenda that subscribes to the primacy of societal progress. This commitment remains inviolable even in face of all the existential, and mounting, threats to India's national security; what after all could there be to defend if the state cannot keep its citizens provided for – materially and spiritually. No doubt, it is that wise policy which has banished – nearly so – the recurring famines, epidemics and societal malpractices in the post-independence India. But then, statecraft is not a one-track journey; there is the other angle to it which posits that for societal progress to be sustained, the nation's sovereignty must be insured against military aggression.

Propensity of the Indian political leadership in maintaining just what they considered as a 'minimalist' military force in conformity to a policy of 'minimalism' in application of military power, has been discussed in Part 1, Chapter 3. Indeed, having been forced ever since to bank upon military force to keep the nation from disintegrating against an unending chain of external and internal assaults, the dominant political culture in India veers around to the purpose of safeguarding the nation's territorial integrity by denying success to her incorrigible adversaries' military aggression. In fact, that political culture leaves no opportunity to remind the world that India covets no one's territory and that she does not believe in taking recourse to military aggression to solve her disputes. The idea that any more than that 'minimalist' approach to military preparedness would set India back from her agenda of poverty alleviation and societal egalitarianism thus continues to persist, ostensibly with due electoral endorsement (2). That indeed is a noble policy which may have worked through the usual swings of accommodation and disconcert in the neighbourhood political relationships. But that policy does not cater to India's geographical situation between two culturally inveterate adversaries and their relentless assault upon the very foundations of her nationhood. So far, that 'minimalist' approach to military preparedness has led to the imposition of as many as five wars in six decades of independence (stalemates in 1948, 1965 and 1999 when Pakistan was prevented from achieving her goals, one defeat in 1962, and one conclusive victory in 1971), confrontation in five local skirmish or near-war operations (Kutch in 1965, Nathu La in 1967, Sumdorong Chu-Khinzemane in 1986, and Western Borders in 1990 and 2001) and engagement in a succession of proxy wars since 1956 (in various North-Eastern States, Punjab and Kashmir). To top these all, there is China's creeping encroachment across the otherwise geographically well-defined McMahon Line in the East and the Line of Actual Control (LAC) across the Aksai Chin, besides of course, her fait accompli take-over of Shaksgam Valley and recent intrusion into the Pakistan Occupied Kashmir (POK). Obviously, India's policy of maintaining 'minimalist' military preparedness has succeeded but only partially. Further, as geo-political indicators reveal, that 'minimum' needs to be redefined in order to protect national interests in a world that is increasingly tuning violent, militant and power hungry.

To that extent, the ill-advised quarantine of the nation's military institution, neglecting it to the extent of allowing it to be afflicted with 'hollowness' and stone-walling its modernisation, shows the nation's policy-makers' wisdom to be in half. More disconcertingly, the non-existent half of that policy-wisdom has led to the installation of a system of defence management which prevents the military institution from the best utilisation of even the 'minimalist' resources that are allocated for it to achieve optimal operational efficiency. No doubt, had not the policy-makers persisted with their ill-informed wariness of the military institution for most of the post-independence era, had they not opted to free the defence bureaucracy and research and production establishments of accountability, restrain the defence industry, stymie military participation in defence decision-making, allowed the forces to run into severe shortages of every warlike item, and finally, had they not been disparaging of the military personnel, then India would have been in possession of stronger military power at a lesser cost to the exchequer – and that without having to compromise on her goals of societal progress.

In nutshell therefore, the following inferences may be drawn from India's political culture as it relates to the articulation of military power:

a) Having followed defence policies that have, over the decades, debilitated India's military capability, the defence policy makers have to be sensible enough to be – actually they have little choice but to be – reluctant to rely on military power to seek India's political agenda.

b) As a corollary, defence policy-makers, during their short electoral cycle, are chary of investing in build-up of military power any more that what they considers absolutely 'inescapable'. Insensibly however, their assessment of that minimum inescapable level of military power falls short of what it actually should be, as indeed the frequent show of aggressive military designs from the neighbourhood goes to prove.

c) Further, India's political culture demonstrates that even if the her national leadership does not cringe from using her military power to deny to the adversaries the objectives of their military aggressions, it is reluctant yet to favourably conclude wars when such opportunities are at hand (e.g. 1948, 1965 and 2001). Further, she lacks the confidence of extracting political advantages from her military successes (e.g. Kashmir-1948, Haji Pir-1965, victory in 1971). Even in operations in support of Bangladesh, Sri Lanka and Maldives, that placid political culture has prevailed.

d) In fact, India earnestly believes her policies to be just, reasonable, benign and inoffensive – as indeed every other of her adversaries too believe to be their cause. The problem, however, arises when in a naive interpretation of real-politick, India expects her detractors to give weight to her belief rather than their own understanding, and rely on intelligence and diplomacy, to the exclusion of credible military deterrence, to send that message.

There could be reasons to suspect that possession of a large military force, controlling it through bureaucratic proxy, and keeping it a state of partial operational effectiveness – inadequately equipped, structured and provided for – could well be the consequence of the political culture as discussed above. There may well be merit in that kind of political culture since it is a reflection of the people's will and therefore it needs to be appreciated. This sentiment, however, does not absolve India's political leadership from its responsibility to spell out clear cut political mandate that it requires the military institution to fulfil, particularly when it remains obliged to allocate a very substantial part of national resources in maintaining it. Needless to state, intrinsic to the enunciation of the political mandate must be the commitment to empower the military institution to that level of operational efficiency which enables it to fulfil that mandate ordained.

The political culture as discussed above must form the basis of a practically implementable native military doctrine and its corollary, the appropriate military strategies.

Political Mandate upon the Indian Military Institution

As it is gathered from End Note 10, Chapter 5 of Part 1, India has no formally articulated defence policy, though ostensibly there is an 'understanding', to quote the Defence Secretary in 1990, to "defend our territory, our sovereignty and our freedom and no more than that". Further, to quote the Prime Minister's statement in 1995, "there are several guidelines which are strictly followed and those can be summed up as follows:

a) To defend our National Territory over land, sea and air, encompassing among others the inviolability of our land borders, island territories, offshore assets and our maritime trade routes.
b) To secure an internal environment whereby our Nation State is insured against any threats to its unity or progress on the basis of religion, language, ethnicity or socio-economic dissonance.
c) To be able to exercise a degree of influence over the nations in our immediate neighbourhood to promote harmonious relationships in tune with our national interests.
d) To be able to effectively contribute towards regional and international stability and to possess an effective out-of-the-country contingency capability to prevent destabilisation of the small nations in our immediate neighbourhood that could have adverse security implications for us" (3).

In a more vibrant regime for management of national defence, it would have been in order for the military brass to translate these political guidelines, even if rather ambiguous, into concrete military objectives, to devise strategies to achieve those objectives and to prepare accordingly. Similarly, it would have activated the defence bureaucracy as well as the nation's entire defence establishment to create conditions conducive for the implementation of such strategies. Sadly, with the military leadership excluded from national level defence policy-making, political class languid in its disinterest, defence bureaucracy in the hands of armatures and an unaccountable defence establishment engaged self-service, that did not happen in India.

What however did happen was that the military brass drafted what is known as a 'Political Directive' and had it 'approved' by the Ministry. An in-house and classified document, it is purported to specify the stock levels of war waging wherewithal to be maintained in terms of days of 'intense' and 'normal' fighting, besides certain general stipulations. Reportedly updated recently, implementation of this political directive, however, turned out to be an illusionary exercise because none, barring the military brass themselves, having little authority to do so, considered it necessary to adhere to those stipulations. That was the origin of 'hollowness' afflicting the military institution. To that extent, the military leadership may have to be excused if they failed to cull out a formal doctrine out of the political guidelines or the said Political Directive.

In defence of this policy ambivalence, it must be acknowledged that political mandate for a military institution is difficult to formalise when the nation's defence oriented technological, industrial and fiscal capitals are way below par. That is the cost to be paid by the current generation for the Indian State's past naivety when it found comfort in tying its politics of peace with anti-military demeanour, isolating military hierarchy from apex level decision making, strangulating defence industry under notions of disarmament and divesting defence research and production from military supervision. Indeed, all nations at some time or the other negotiate through similar ambivalence in promulgating their political mandate. Really therefore, Indian defence planners too could make an effort in that direction – particularly since the threats are well identified – for the military leadership to pick up the cue and proceed to devise a native military doctrine in full confidence that their professional articulation would find the favour of politicians, bureaucrats and financial mandarins, much to the efficient optimisation of the defence resource-allocation.

Indeed, during the past one decade or so, taking cue from the aforementioned political guidelines and astutely assessed strategic challenges, and shaped by professionally informed assumptions, the military hierarchy was wise to take the initiative from time to time to proceed with evolving beaconing military doctrines. However, in so doing, each service and their different arms, all of them turned somewhat partisan in over-defining their part and then pine for resources around their self-centrality. Needless to state, even the current doctrines remain but little more than single-service aspirations, thus leaving many overarching capability voids, operational contradictions and unresolved logistic requirements which render these to be less than comprehensive or practical. Even the three joint forces doctrines – a 'Joint Forces Doctrine', a 'Joint Special Forces Doctrine' and a 'Joint Amphibious Operations Doctrine' – that had been stitched together by the designated fountainhead of inter-service jointness, the Integrated Defence

Headquarters (IDS) of the MoD, has stayed clear of contentious issues to confine itself into a limited band of consensual articulations. Further, politicians, bureaucrats and financial controllers have not found it compelling to join that exercise, and so with the rest of the Ministry watching uncommitted, these doctrines and most of the associated implementation schemes could neither pass muster nor could see materialisation apart from bits of progress here and there.

With the government's recent focus on national defence – arguably compelled by rising aggressiveness of the adversarial neighbours and demands of regional power play – the situation is expected to change in the coming years. The change comes not just to tackle the peripheral, cross-border and internal challenges, but also to answer the call for international obligations that are being increasingly expected from an emerging power, as indeed, India is stated to be. Conversely, in managing national security concerns, the scope and depth of government's efforts cannot but remain bound by domestic consensus over economic priorities, besides being beholden to civilian institutions that, barring exceptions, are uninitiated to the complexities of nurturing balanced military power. Obviously therefore, till the government's intended vitalisation of national defence starts showing concrete results and inadequacy of military preparedness is reasonably covered more or less, strategic articulation of military power cannot be on its high agenda. Considering all angles therefore, the time when the political leadership is able to spell out a clear-cut military mandate and back it up with the right allocation of resources is yet far away.

Wisdom therefore dictates that even in the absence of a more explicit, focused and provided-for political mandate, but taking cue from the new awareness towards national defence, drafting of a comprehensive, native joint-service military doctrine may yet be undertaken in consultation with the policy makers and with their endorsement and commitment to the marshalling of the state institutions to purpose. Thus might emerge the best options, in tune with the political guidelines and within the resources available, to devise a practical and implementable doctrine. In so doing, the political leadership, military professionals and bureaucracy would bring about a regime of national defence in which the military institution focuses on doctrine-sanctified strategies, the defence establishment prepares the forces to fight the kind of wars that the doctrine envisages, and the Government allocates appropriate resources to the purpose.

In other words, it would be wise to extract an effective military doctrine from the prevailing strategic situation, the available and observable political inputs, and professional military appreciation (4).

Contours of a Joint-Services Military Doctrine

A military doctrine is an expression of political culture. It translates into a statement of intent to achieve specified goals. It therefore must proceed beyond text-book definitions, and rooted in actionable possibilities, indicate the strategy to harness the resources at hand in moving towards such goals. Most politically mature nations therefore beacon their military leadership through formal promulgation of their defence policies in the form of 'defence white papers', 'strategic defence reviews', 'military strategy guidelines' etc. – the nomenclature varying from one nation to another. These policy promulgations are preceded by a host of studies, experimentations, confabulations and debate which invoke the qualities of strategic foresight, prudence, practicability and pioneering. But even after such deliberations, wisdom of statesmanship makes it incumbent for the visionary political establishments to revisit such promulgations at regular intervals and make due course-corrections. A native military doctrine is thus rooted in ordination of formal political mandate, and revised according to the strategic dynamics that confronts a nation from time to time.

In the Indian dispensation, decision parameters being hazy and the terms of references being dictated by intangible factors, doctrinal inquisition and related prosecution of warfare must be an exercise intellectually challenging and procedurally excruciating. Unpredictability of future equations of global as well as regional power adds to that complexity. In spite of such hurdles, as India finds her space in the contemporary world order and gears up to deal with its challenges and adversities, the idea of a truly meaningful military doctrine may not be stifled any more. The cause is ripened by the post-2010 measures by the government to energise the defence research, technology and industrial sectors, because convergence of these aspects with an appropriate military doctrine would integrate the nation's entire defence system into one whole and leave out redundancies. Such an optimally focused, credibly deterrent and cost-efficient military security is a national call, no less.

The proposed joint-services military doctrine, besides being aligned to the political culture, would aim at orienting the military institution towards a set of military goals. In so doing, the doctrine would have to specifically address military engagements in conventional, sub-conventional and strategic partnership modes and thus initiate the process of 'strategising' according to the geo-political theosophies of modern warfare. Obviously, the doctrine would cover the aspects of inter-service interoperability and multi-dimensional operational capabilities, just as it would profess joint-service analyses of redundancies in induction of weapons and equipment and the economics of inventory scales. In this, the purpose would be to complement the war-wherewithal's on land, sea and air – fire power and mobility, for example – rather than allowing duplication among these. Besides, while dealing with the aggressive impositions of China and an ever antagonistic Pakistan, the doctrine would need to promote favourable asymmetries to bear upon future military engagements.

A doctrinal inquisition is an undertaking of great intellect, knowledge, experience and debate. It requires extensive deliberations that cannot be performed within the confines of a book; however, it would be in order to discuss some of its defining features as these apply to India.

Conventional Warfare: China

To dissuade China from attempting to secure her territorial claims by means of her overwhelming military power, the politico-diplomatic cost of such a venture on China has to be rendered unprofitable – just the military cost may not deter her. One way to do so may be to bank upon defensive strategy, executed with extreme aggressiveness in conformity to the advantageous features of the extreme terrain, and duly bolstered with special and behind-the-lines land-air operations, opportunity actions in the seas and covert exploitation of the Tibetan discontent. The purpose could be furthered by the continuation of a long-drawn war of tempo varying from intense to dormancy, and so denying to the aggressor the satisfaction of proclaiming victory. Achievement of a strategic stalemate while imposing high cost in men and material, and so preventing China from emerging 'victorious' could thus be the focus of the proposed joint-services military doctrine. By all reckoning, that goal should be achievable within the parameters of national defence as discussed so far – apart from the voids and deficiencies, much of the structural capability is already in place. A demonstrated prospect of achieving such a stalemate may run afoul of China's global ambitions, and so could arguably discourage her from military adventurism to settle her territorial issues with India in preference to peaceful, political means to manage that quest.

Conventional Warfare: Pakistan

In dealing with Pakistan, the current concept of launching strong manoeuvre forces to conduct sharp, intense and destructive operations would remain relevant. However, the doctrine could revisit the idea of marshalling a humungous force-structure, including as many as three strike corps, to conduct territorial offensives across what is a recognised International Border, and with the purpose of destroying the opponent's forces. The political bargain achievable from such offensives could also be built into that doctrine. Further, while that option must remain as an effective counter to Pakistan's congenital intransigence, but its ultimate gains could be weighed against the more remunerative options that are offered across the unsanctified Line of Control and into the POK as well as the Arabian Sea Coast. Thus there may be a case for a more balanced force-deployment across the mountainous, plain, desert and maritime sectors of India's Western Frontiers. Lastly, to call Pakistan's nuclear bombast, the doctrine may profess the composition and deployment of effectively tailored and equipped combat forces to neutralise Pakistan's nuclear assets in passive and active modes, which may then be formalised, promulgated and demonstrated to impose higher levels of deterrence as befits a habitual offender.

The Nuclear Angle

India's 'minimum nuclear deterrence' may not overly concern China, neither in counter-force nor in counter-value mode, as she has shown in her nonchalance over massive casualties of the Korean War, and acceptance of mass deaths and destruction during the Great Leap Forward, the Cultural Revolution and the construction of the Great Dam. In any case, with her overwhelming conventional superiority over India and the latter's posture of pure defensive, and of course, going by the either side's nuclear doctrines, China would more likely than not refrain from initiating nuclear exchange. The issue therefore boils down to the Pakistan's nuclear brouhaha. Strangely, Pakistan's presumed nuclear 'rational-irrational' paradox seems to impose caution against India's exercise of her superior conventional military power. It is a case of the weak deterring the strong, wherein Pakistan's paranoid anti-India afflictions on the one end and the cacophony of jihadi 'self-extinction for faith' on the other contrive against the very fundamentals of India's nuclear deterrence. Conversely, suggestions are contrived to place the onus of restraint and repudiation of destruction and war on India alone – supposedly because she is a mature nation! Thus having acquired nuclear weapon capability, India is expected to recess that and then lose its deterrence value against brisk stockpiling by the adversaries. Meanwhile, there has emerged a crop of Indian policy-makers, who finding her conventional superiority of little use, posit that military modernisation may not be a priority. A doctrine free of such self-condescending impositions may release India from her strategic trepidations. Indeed, there is a case for the nuclear investment to be paying more reasonable dividends.

Sub-conventional Warfare

The fourth doctrinal consideration could be aimed at dealing with the current trends of politico-military subversion, like China's building up of Pakistan's conventional, nuclear and logistic capabilities. More directly, the doctrine should focus upon Pakistan's unrelenting export of insurgency and terrorism, and various forms of internally instigated and externally promoted sub-conventional wars, prospects of which loom ominously over India's security. To that end, India's sub-conventional doctrine could be elaborative in its linkage with the conventional one, and so find appropriate roles for her conventional strike forces in the overall scheme of counter-insurgency and politico-military subversion.

Strategic Partnerships

Finally, to be counted in the global politics, the Indian military institution will have to gear up to participate in UN assignments and various military manoeuvres. These are the engagements undertake in strategic partnerships and alliances, for the preservation of global peace against the rising violence that finds support from state as well as non-state intransigence. To meet this end, organisation of highly capable Special Forces, backed up with modern conventional battle formations would be necessary. Much of this purpose could also be met through dual-use capabilities that are built-up to manage the global humanitarian responsibilities against natural and man-made disasters. That would be another consideration in evolution of a competent joint-services military doctrine.

Harness of Native Assets

History teaches that a military doctrine has to be customised to exploit national strengths while covering for its limitations – and that must be another consideration in making of the joint-services military doctrine. Even if dependent on import of major weaponry and equipment, India is competent in construction, transportation, communication, IT and space engineering. Therefore, while imports and indigenous development of sophisticated military hardware may continue, effect-multiplication of such hardware, which would always be limited in numbers and sophistication, would be a welcome advantage. Harnessing this advantage through technological and logistic enhancements that are within the indigenous capabilities, may be a key doctrinal consideration. For example, effect-multiplication of combat forces by the harness of indigenous strengths in terrain doctoring, camouflage and deception, construction engineering, transportation network and transporter fleet, communication grid-work, IW, cyber operations, space-based surveillance, electronic warfare etc. maybe some of the themes enunciated in the doctrine. Indeed, factoring these measures into the doctrine would enable the military forces to deceive the adversary and disorient his command and control set up, while providing themselves with more tactical flexibility to deploy their dear resources in tandem or in succession, and so make up, to some extent, for the forces' limitations in numbers and sophistication of weaponry at hand. Similarly, taking cognisance of India's capacity to produce modest designs in large numbers, the doctrine could hedge technological sophistication of imported weapons and equipment – tanks, guns, ships, aircraft, radars etc. – with swarming numbers and ingenious tactical solutions, and so cover up, till the indigenous military industry comes of age, qualitative superiority with quantity, and indirect, asymmetrical tactical options of the use of these (5).

Military Technology

Secondary fallouts of a competent military doctrine would help the cause of development of native brand of military technology. For example, whereas global military technology does not find it profitable to develop hardware customised to the kinds of terrain that the Indian military forces have to operate upon, hardly any indigenous effort has been made in the past six decades to fill that void. Doubtlessly, development of medium technology mobility and survivability hardware, for example, could offer distinct advantages to own forces in war. A native military doctrine would see to amelioration of that oversight.

Military Tradition

Finally, ingenious, fearless and hardy soldier being India's best asset, the doctrine could propose to tap his faculties to create favourable tactical asymmetries against powerful adversaries to compensate, to some extent, for tactical and technological limitations. Besides conventional tactical acumen and physical and spiritual endurance, the Indian soldier is ideally suited to be trained as special operations troops and has acquired unparalleled competence in high altitude and extreme cold survivability, attributes which could be factored carry warfare of varying tempo across unexpected terrain and non-campaign seasons. The doctrine could thus profess higher investment on his training and morale to compensate for indigenous technological and fiscal limitations and yet place the adversary in situations of tactical adversity.

Guiding Factors in Doctrinal Inquisition

It is futile to devise a military doctrine that is disjointed from the nation's cultural demeanour. Rational or debatable, India's native cultural demeanour would inexorably find reflection in her political culture, and that in turn would influence the political mandate for the military institution. That is a fact that may not be overlooked in the interest of making the joint-service military doctrine practically implementable under the Indian dispensation.

Even if it is envisioned purely from military intellect, proposition of a joint-service military doctrine must be an endeavour of the entire state, and as a corollary, upheld with matching alacrity by the civilian sectors. One foremost factor in this regard would be the quality and depth of the nation's intelligence set up. Though much progress has been made during the past decade in vitalising the Indian intelligence system, there yet remain divergences in terms of data-mining of military-specific intelligence problems and co-option of military expertise in that set up. In similar vein, conjoined organisational set up in the fields of IW, defensive and offensive cyber operations and space applications must be the guiding factors for a competent military doctrine to evolve. Lastly, the considerations of imposition of military deterrence and achievement of favourable tactical asymmetry must be factored into the professed joint-service military doctrine.

Factoring Deterrence and Asymmetry

Strategists define 'deterrence' as a form of 'negative incentive' to defer an adversary from actuating his hostile intent, either proactive or reactive. Consequently, it addresses the adversary's reason, beckoning him to understand that actuation of his hostile intent would fail to bring the intended advantages commensurate to the costs suffered. Military deterrence therefore needs to be backed up by credible capacity for the infliction of unacceptable losses in terms of military assets, civilian infrastructure or territory. This is the tangible part of deterrence that is easier, if costly, to achieve in measurable terms. The real complexity, however, lies in putting on line the adversary's political prestige that decides his standing in the domestic as well as global economic and political equation. Obviously therefore, deep knowledge of the target society's values and the construct of its rationalities as well as delusions are necessary for deterrence to be pursued.

It is important to note that the act of being deterred has cultural connotations, and therefore, determinants of deterrence are somewhat different in the context of the South Asian neighbourhood. The Western ideals of sanctity of life and liberty, preservation of societal assets, and most of all, the expected norms of rationality in decision making, may mean differently to the power-wielders in this part of the world. Many of these, having been seeped in nihilist perceptions, have given themselves over to senseless delusions. To them, recovery of self-certified 'lost territories' or revenge against 'humiliation' and defence of 'religion and ideology against non-believers' may take precedence over socio-economic prosperity, even their existence as individuals, groups or nation. Obviously, India has to devise her exclusive formulae to deter military adventurism against her interests in the Asian context. Factoring India's own political culture into those factors, it may be appropriate to term that formula as 'dissuasive deterrence' – a possible mix of hard, soft, covert and recessed means.

Key agents of instability in the Indian neighbourhood are: One, a common phenomenon of internal instability; two, a fanatically obsessed Pakistan; and three, a power hungry China. In the course of assuaging the first listed, the last two are bent upon usurping parts of India even if that may lead to the fracture of their own national integrity. Besides, there are past lessons to appreciate that this predatory duo's relentless anti-India mission must go beyond China's occupation of the Aksai Chin and Shaksgam Valley or Pakistan's possession of Kashmir until the very idea of Indian nationhood is run down. Obviously therefore, in a neighbourhood wherein xenophobia and predatory urge are so emphatic, there must exist the seeds of war. To protect her existential integrity, therefore, India must remain obliged to commit substantial resources from her meagre kitty to deter the duo from keep launching schemes to dismember her by military means.

Experience shows that military deterrence has to be but case specific, to be construed in terms of the particular mode of warfare that it aims to prevent

– conventional, sub-conventional and nuclear modes for example. Further, it has to be customised exclusively to address each particular adversary. For example, Pakistan's hostility against India needs to be deterred at the conventional, proxy war and nuclear modes while neutralising her sponsorship of terrorist groups. This one is an example of 'complex deterrence' that involves, firstly, deterring each of the hostile players, state as well as non-state, who set the aggressive agenda both in China and Pakistan, and secondly, institution of credible measures to defeat hostile acts in all of the above mentioned modes. Obviously, India's deterrence has to be comprehensive, credible, cost-effective and demonstrative.

Deterrence in Sino-Indian Context

The aura built up by China is a perfect example of 'existential deterrence' over India. This is so that contesting her, diplomatically or militarily, has so far been practically unthinkable amongst the Indian policy makers. China's deterrence is so effective that the Indian government feels it necessary to rationalise with the former's diplomatic provocations and regular incursions across the Line of Actual Control, while all that China does to keep her border inviolable is just to make occasional appearances. Notwithstanding that uneven equation, so far in the post Nathu La-Sumdorong Chu period, and helped by China's inward focus on economic progress, India's subtly dissuasive posture has kept the Sino-Indian border-line quiet. It has even attracted China's endorsement – albeit tardy in observance – of various 'confidence building measures'. But since China is emerging out of her contrived quietude that she had adopted as a state policy to nurture her 'four modernisation' schemes, and when trailers of her instinctive hegemonic designs are finding evidence, there arises the question as to how strong must India's military deterrence be for China to keep the issue of borders settlement reserved solely for a politico-diplomatic solution. Indeed, considering the high and ever increasing capability gap, India's deterrence over a much stronger neighbour – arrogant super-power in the making – would have to be rather extraordinary.

It would be banal to expect China to be dissuaded from her goal of 'reclaiming' her self-sanctified territories by the disincentive posed by India's a dozen or so army divisions and modest fleets of naval men-of-war and air squadrons. Similarly, a dozen or two missiles are unlikely to make China suppress her 'will' to fight, particularly when the Chinese autarchy has stoked a sense of nationalistic fervour to makes it her citizen's patriotic duty to arrogate territorial aspirations. Further, by coupling her economy to the global structure, the Chinese leadership may not find any threat of economic sanctions too fearsome to deal with; in fact her economic clout deters other nations from coming out openly against her brazen highhandedness. Therefore, as she gears up to flex muscles in her traditionally methodical manner, something more than substantial has to be devised to deter China from 'teaching' India another 'lesson' (6).

For India to pose a workable deterrence against a severely unfavourable power differential, asymmetric methods may have to be adopted to exploit China's sensitivities. China's priority goal is to retain power in the Communist Party's domain, which is considered imperative to her second priority, that is, the achievement of her super-power aspirations. Both these priority objectives are contingent upon the prevalence of her internal stability. Therefore, an Indian military capability that does not permit PRC to proclaim clear-cut victory in a short campaign, ties down the PLA in a long drawn-out engagement, and provokes instability in Tibet, would more likely than not dissuade China from seeking a military solution to her problems with India. The PRC's entrapment in such a strategic quagmire might encourage other external and internal victims of its high-handedness to coalesce to contain China's great power ambitions. That kind of gathering alliance of the tormented weak, as history tells, is a sure formula for the powerful bully's fall. China should know that.

India's cause may take encouragement by the fact that in military conflicts, smaller powers have in the past, and may in future, genuinely hope to defeat larger powers. However, a determinant to note here is that a weaker contestant is certain to lose if it adopts a strategy that is symmetrical to that of the stronger opponent; Belgium-Germany 1914, Falkland 1982, Iraq-Coalition Forces in both the Gulf Wars etc., are some examples. Conversely, they do better by adopting asymmetrical strategies to resist their more powerful opponent – French Indo-China, Algeria, Vietnam and Afghanistan, for example. To contest any aggression from the North therefore, India could adopt a strategy that would hinge upon aggressive defence, offensive riposte and special operations deep into the Tibetan hinterland to present a prospect of, as discussed earlier, the aggressor falling into a deep and sticky cesspool – 'deterrence by denial', to wit.

Two other aspects merit consideration in the context of India's deterrence against China, in which diplomacy and signalling would play key roles. Firstly, the recent posture adopted by PRC indicates that in finding its objectives it would prefer to depend upon superior conventional military power, while articulating her nuclear power in the form of an 'existential deterrence' to keep other great powers from spoiling her sport. Given her comparatively modest substance, it would therefore suit India's deterrence to be construed by the possession of adequate conventional capability to prevent China from gaining from military aggression, should China decides to adopt that course, and leave the situation well short of driving the PRC towards any justification for nuclear strike.

Secondly, in a worst case possibility, danger lurks in the form of China's further pumping up of her designated trouble-making lackey, Pakistan, and a remote possibility of offering covert support to Indian insurgents. To cater to such eventualities, India's conventional 'deterrence by denial' may have to be complimented with 'reverse deterrence' in two aspects. One, it has to be demonstrated that the imposter stand no chance of succeeding against India's resolve, and therefore, any support rendered to him would be but a sheer waste if not downright embarrassing; and two, covert support to internal pretenders would leave India free to pay back in Tibet, Xinjiang, Bay of Bengal et al. In either case, astute diplomacy would need to be bolstered by display of military resolve – backed up by conventional military power.

Deterrence in Indo-Pakistan Context

As with Pakistan, India's deterrence has been a success to the extent that the former has reconciled to the fact that her dream of capturing Kashmir through conventional military aggression would never come to fruition. It was thus that the case of 'proxy war' found favour in her strategy to satisfy her anti-India obsession. Here, there are two facts to take note of. One, India's conventional military power is adequate to prevent Pakistan from capturing Kashmir but yet insufficient to impose the requisite level of 'deterrence by punishment', thus allowing Pakistan the freedom to persist; and two, through her nuclear posturing Pakistan communicates her belief that her nuclearisation has defanged India's conventional deterrence as she continues to prosecute proxy war with immunity. Actually, one school of Indian analysts feel the necessity to endorse that notion. Thus while Pakistan's nuclear deterrence over India works beautifully, the same may not be true of the reverse – India's huge military spending notwithstanding. The matter is not helped when the possibilities of Pakistan outsourcing the management of Occupied Kashmir and Northern Areas to China and turning into China's surrogate nuclear arsenal become more and more of a reality.

The inference is that except deterring conventional aggression, India's current military deterrence over Pakistan fails both at the sub-conventional as well as nuclear levels. The failure in the first instance is attributable to India's inability to make Pakistan pay for terrorism, while that in the latter case India's nuclear 'non-strategy' – but not the nuclear doctrine per se – hands over to Pakistan the ignition-key of nuclear exchange. This non-strategic equation becomes even more baffling when viewed in the classical perspective. India hints at adoption of a military strategy that, flouting all principles of war, envisages attrition attacks all across the heavily fortified Western front-line, and having broken through, obviously at humungous costs, terminate operations soon after capturing insignificant objectives at shallow depths – all this to avoid provoking Pakistan's nuclear sensitivities. Then there is the latest insinuation to suggest that Indian political leadership may not have the stomach to implement its policy of inflicting 'massive retaliation', should Pakistan opt to use nuclear weapons, particularly the 'tactical' ones. Indeed, it is a strange case wherein India, a superior power, remains deterred from using that power and is reduced to preaching such innuendos as 'war is not a solution', and that 'nuclear weapons are not meant for war' – that indeed is a case of a state undermining its own deterrence – whereas Pakistan, flouting brazen irrationality, brinkmanship and blackmail, unleashes a three decade long mayhem of 'war through terrorism' into India's hinterlands. In the international order, there are but few instances of such a state of helplessness.

India's said joint-service military doctrine needs to focus on turning this farcical equation around. In that, the Indian statesmen have to realise that Pakistan's nuclear tantrums notwithstanding, military response to aggression – and proxy war is an aggression – may be recessed only at the nation's peril. To give shape to that understanding, the focus may be on innovative military strategies and modernisation of force-restructure within affordable defence allocations. Indeed, the litany of humungous defence expenditures, at the cost of bread and butter, need to be scotched – these are but banal and exaggerated. Whether it be 'cold start', 'hot pursuit', conventional retribution at a 'time and place of own choosing' or launch of 'special operations', and whether it be in 'limited', 'conventional', 'hybrid' or 'covert' mode, the joint-service military doctrine must devise strategies to relieve India of the disconcerting log-jam, including recourse to neutralise Pakistan's nuclear assets in passive and active modes, as discussed above. Indian strategists, going beyond attrition minded direct actions with superior numbers, have in the past devised strategies to generate favourable asymmetries in terms of tactical audacity, logistic flexibility, irregular warfare and covert 'punishment' operations – duly provided for, they would do so again. Indeed, when dynamically demonstrated, such strategies, with a range of robust asymmetries duly built-in, would foster credible deterrence against Pakistan (7).

Deterrence through Asymmetry

The matter of asymmetry is intrinsic to military strategy and tactics. It is at the core of doctrinal as well as strategic consideration, as indeed it has been built into the arguments above. There is however, one exclusive consideration for the drafters of the proposed joint-service military doctrine. May be, a doctrine of deliberate build up over a longer period in simultaneity with diplomatic hedging and option of engagement in longer war could be more appropriate in deterring both China and Pakistan. Given India's geographical depth, a terrain that saps offensive intrusion, a vast industrial base and cultural resilience, it may be worthwhile to examine if long-drawn war with cunningly articulated tempo to selectively and successively decimate the enemy at the wrong end of terrain, before switching over to deliberate offensive, could offer advantageous in the contemporary dispensation. Indeed, such campaigns, in which successive tactical surprises are achieved in terms of time, place and strength of operations over a long spread of time – rather than the achievement of strategic surprise through quick mobilisation and fast-strike, as it had been attempted during Operation Parakram – have historically proved to be overwhelmingly successful. A quagmire of conflict, from which it is difficult to extricate swiftly and with honour, is a nightmare to any of the aggressive powers of today. India therefore may create a favourable asymmetry out of this strategy (8).

Investment on Peace Dividend

For the near future, it is certain that India will continue to be tormented by proxy war and terror acts emanating from Pakistan, while being needled by China's over territorial claims and land-sea encirclement. There is no doubt that when these inimical forces orchestrate to stalk conjointly, it cannot portend well for the Indian nationhood. As a corollary, it would be an abject failure of her state policies – diplomatic as well as military – if India is unable to deter these inimical powers to desist from their compulsive mission of undermining the Indian nationhood.

History proves that inter-state tolerance is best nurtured under an incentive of military deterrence. Thus motivated, there are hopeful signs of matured realisation among the polity of the rising threats to national defence and a strengthening of resolve to protect self-interests among the custodians of nation's defence. As stated earlier, given the right impetus, it will take a decade or so to turn around India's somewhat out-dated and placid defence structure. Meanwhile, to reap the right value for money, the national leadership may assiduously undertake to advance the cause of India's military modernisation. It would do further better by directly involving the military leadership in policy confabulations rather than through the medium of bureaucrats, scientists, auditors and arm-chair strategists who are unqualified for that role. Indeed, the same MoD had accomplished such a task in the aftermath of the Chinese aggression in 1962. The wise ones need not wait for another catastrophe to awaken.

Then let the defence investments deliver dividends, let military power keep peace.

Conclusion

Having discussed the ambient aspects of native political culture, its reflection in the government's informal political mandate and its formal issuance of political directive to the nation's military institution, and finally, the contours of a proposed joint-services military doctrine that would meet the contemporary demands of the strategic situations confronting India, stage is set to delve into broad parameters of a prospective military strategy that, in conformity to the doctrinal orientations, would answer to the calls and complexions of modern warfare. Discussion in the next chapter is devoted to that issue.

END NOTES AND SELECT REFERENCES

(1) Under the convention adopted in this text, a 'national security doctrine' is a conceptual framework for the preservation of overall national security. It balances the goals of national security with the resources that can be committed for the purpose in terms of military power and binds the defence establishment as well as the entire national infrastructure in supporting the cause of the military institution. To be implemented in true spirit, the national security doctrine has to be translated into 'military doctrine' which guides the identification of the objectives of use of military power and the 'strategies' adoptable to secure these. In other words, a security doctrine balances the nation's security needs with the material resources at

hand – military as well as back-up defence assets – to meet such needs. 'Strategy', on the other hand, flows out from the doctrine and guides the means, manners and options of application of military power in preservation of national security. Some facets of arguments, though not directly related, are to be found in:

a) Changing Perspective on National security, Ed. P C Dogra, Lancer's books, New Delhi, 2004.
b) India's doctrine Puzzle: Limiting War in South Asia, Ali Ahmed, Routledge, New Delhi, 2014.

(2) Neighbourhood adversaries differ. According to them, India possesses disproportionate military power which she uses to keep territories which she has already captured in Jammu, Kashmir, Ladakh, the Central Himalayas and Arunachal Pradesh. They go further to state that her demeanour of peace, maturity etc. is a cover for her 'Brahminical subterfuge' to disintegrate her neighbours and ride over them to be a world power. May be, history would vindicate them!

(3) In his long career, the author did not come across any such formal political-military 'understanding' or 'guidelines'. May be, these had been there between individuals, say the RM and one or more Service Chief(s) – but individuals change.

(4) This is one initiative the nation's military leadership has to take, without waiting for a formal political enunciation because ultimately the responsibility to organise and execute modernisation, strategising and force-restructuring would fall upon them. Taking the lead therefore would make the exercise more deliberate and controlled.

(5) A transformational doctrine could be shaped to enhance the 'relative combat effectiveness' of Indian military forces by the strength of indigenous IT-induced surveillance, command, control and deception mechanisms. The doctrine could also profess the harness of indigenous engineering expertise to bolster strategic and tactical mobility in deploying and re-deploying in quick time, and so optimise operational dividends from what military hardware is available.

(6) As demonstrated during the war in Korea, the 'Great Leap Forward', 'Cultural Revolution' and building of the 'Great Dam' over the Huang He, in securing her controversial goals, China could not care less about triggering innumerable casualties and widespread devastations. Even if faint voices of dissent are heard these days, the situation has not changed substantially. The CPC's hold remains absolute, all-encompassing and unchallenged

(7) India's nuclearisation of did not stop Pakistan from intruding into Kargil, nor could Pakistan's nuclear voodoo dance stop India from evicting that intrusion.

(8) It was so that Babur created asymmetry in his favour by introducing front-line deployment of field guns to rout the numerically much superior Lodi army in the First Battle of Panipat. Similarly, the Marathas adapted to the tactics of mobile warfare with light cavalry against the vastly superior Mughal army in the Deccan; contrarily, they also invited disaster by adopting symmetrical tactics that suited the Afghan army in the Third Battle of Panipat.

*

CHAPTER 7

STRATEGY UPDATE AND FORCE MODERNISATION

"At a time when major powers are reducing their forces and rely more on technology, we are still constantly seeking to expand the size of our forces. Modernisation and expansion of forces at the same time is a difficult and unnecessary goal. We need forces that are agile, mobile and driven by technology, not just human valour."

– Prime Minister Narendra Modi, Combined Commanders Conference, December 15, 2015

The Cause of Strategy Update

Self-incited by ideological revisionism, there are fundamental disputes in the Indian neighbourhood, of which India is the convenient target at hand. That situation in turn is fed by aggressive militarism on either of her flanks wherein even if it takes two to fight, just one party is enough, and willing, to start it – in many ways the start has already been made long ago. Therefore the threat of warfare – or arguably, escalation of the on-going latent war – looms heavy over India, the prosecution of which would be dictated by contemporary means, methods and objectives. There would thus be the need to contemporise Indian military strategies and update these at regular intervals. 'Strategising', therefore, must continue to be a dynamic process in the coming days.

As a matter of fact, each of the three services of the Indian military institution have been diligent in working out their strategies in keeping with the dynamics of operational challenges confronting them, besides of course, honing these through elaborate field manoeuvres. Further, even if service-centric, these strategies converge at the delivery end to conjointly secure the end-states of national objectives. In this respect, record of the Indian military leadership has all along been a matter of exemplary professional ingenuity and astute orchestration of the available war-resources. That indeed is so that India has successfully negotiated through a near-continuous period of military hostility all through her independent existence, even when the military institution has seldom found priority political interest. But presently, the situation has exacerbated beyond what could just be a matter of passing concerns. With far-reaching changes in the objectives, means and methods of prosecuting military operations in the contemporary era, the nature of war has undergone a conceptual as well as practical 'transformation' in which technology and budget are key components – our adversaries have accordingly taken full cognisance, and concrete action, to raise their military capabilities.

To keep up to assimilate such concepts and practices, the Indian military institution must elevate to the tenets of joint-service strategising in which combat, combat support and logistic systems of each of the services bolster each other for the achievement of best operational effects. Doubtlessly, in so doing, even if tactical actions and manoeuvres could remain single service-predominant operations of war, the overall force-application would have to be integrated from tactical level fire and manoeuvre upwards in order to optimise capability-multiplication and to manage redundancies. It is time therefore for the Indian military institution to contemporise itself into the propagation of 'integrated military strategies'. But just that would not be enough.

Military studies tell as that conduct of war has much to do with intellect, creativity and initiative; it is much more than just a 'bull-fight' of brawn and muscle. In standing up to aggression from professional, better provided for and powerful adversaries therefore, it is imperative for the Indian military institution to elevate its conceptual inquisitions, with the purpose of not only instituting more effective methods of applying concurrent military strategies, but also to expand the repertory of strategic options of prosecuting warfare in more ways. In other words, in the rising heat of the coming future, while it would be imperative to widen and strengthen our strategies to deter and defeat cross-border attacks, border encroachments and overt and covert military aggression, it would also be necessary to innovate new strategies of surgical, special, irregular and hybrid warfare in dealing with escalated natures of hostility. The situation thus requires the Indian military leadership to take up the cudgels of devising a range of adaptable strategies of force-application and then to create commensurate force-structures – all within the resources affordable.

In so doing, it would be wise to remember that military strategies are but the functions of societal culture and national wherewithal's, and when the three mesh well, the results are much amplified. Therefore, the native strengths of warrior culture and military intellect could, to much extent, cover for the limitations of war-wherewithal which, as history tells us, would never be found to be sufficient.

A Framework for Integrated Military Strategies

Taking cue from the discussion so far, it would be realistic to postulate that the military strategies adaptable to translate the military doctrine into implementable courses of action could be outlined as: One, to defend against China's attempt to secure her territorial claims by military means; and two, to defeat Pakistan's never-ending military campaign – proxy, subversive or regular war. Further, a direct fallout of such strategies could be to raise the level of deterrence against either of the adversary indulging in military adventurism in the future – the present level of deterrence that was instilled during the period of post-1971 War with Pakistan and stand-off at Sumdrong Chu in 1986-7 with China have obviously lost effectiveness in the current dispensation. Further, the commitments to suppress insurgencies gone out-of-hand, participate in UN and allied operations and respond to disaster relief could be built into such strategies. Thus the discussion in the previous chapter on joint-services military doctrine could be inferred to the adoption of integrated military strategies for the foretasted range of applications of military power, the overall purpose being to secure India's national security goals.

As a corollary to the theosophical exercise of doctrinal inquisition, formulation of extra-ordinary and yet practically implementable military strategies is an exercise of astute professionalism. Bound by innumerable tangible and intangible factors of extreme complexity, military strategies are dynamic action plans that are dictated by the operational situation prevailing, the immediate, interim and final objectives of engaging in military action, and the relative combat ratios, resources at hand and the state of preparedness, amongst many other factors. In this respect of 'strategising', the record of Indian military leadership has all along been more than adequate –

notwithstanding occasional criticisms in hindsight, many times with superfluous situational understanding. Therefore saving ourselves from groping in the maze of imponderables, the purpose of the discussion here would be served by confining to some of the core considerations of integrated 'strategising', without prejudice to the actually adoptable military strategies to deal with the challenges confronting India from the North, West and the Seas at relevant the times. Towards that end the following key considerations could be the terms of references for the formulation of integrated strategies:

a) Customisation of strategies across the spectrums of conventional, sub-conventional and nuclear warfare.
b) Options of fighting within and across into enemy territories, preferences of short or long-drawn state of war, and conjoined leveraging of land, sea and air power across more than one theatre of operations.
c) Adoption of one or more alternatives of pre-emption, pro-active defence and riposte, denial of objectives and punishment.
d) Intelligence based special operations, hybrid warfare and conduct of irregular warfare.
e) Nuclear posturing, and the options of nuclear disarming.
f) Coverage of geo-strategic military obligations against peace enforcement, stabilisation and disaster management operations under the aegis of the United Nations' Organisation or strategic partnership commitments.

Strategy Options: Northern Borders

To take the discussion further according to the conventional doctrine discussed above, India's integrated military strategies could envision a native version of ingenious defence against China's military aggression within nationally affordable means. One way to do so could be to harness the advantageous features of the forbidding terrain, and display characteristic Indian resilience, perseverance and audacity to prosecute an endless series of short and intense battles, intermittent low-intensity engagements and special operations deep across, all these actions being interspersed with varying periods of dormancy and escalation to keep the powerful enemy on the tenterhooks. Advantageous tactical asymmetries may thus be achieved through committal of infantry-mechanised, 'special' and 'irregular' operations capabilities, duly backed up with multi-dimension all-terrain mobility, robust logistical support and audacious application of firepower and air interdiction. Having mastered high-altitude and extreme cold weather operations over the decades, the land-air strategy could bank upon continuation of military operations during non-campaigning seasons and across treacherous terrain, and so to put the aggressor to asymmetric test.

Lastly, defensive contests astride the border belt could be reinforced by conventional riposte-type offensives across relatively dormant or exploitable sectors, and by inducing conflagration of internal insurgencies in Xizang and Xinjiang. Similarly, well-conceived and audaciously executed naval actions – a forte of the Indian Navy – across the choke points in Indian Ocean could add to the aggressor's discomfiture. In short, the classical Strategy of Sustained Attrition and Denial, through the prosecution of traditional but recently reiterated concept of 'Hybrid Warfare', could be an adoptable strategy in this instance. Stretched over a longish existential period, this strategy could be one option to hedge and wrestle against a powerful enemy, trap him down into a strategic quick-sand and so make his venture as painful in success as in stalemate or defeat (1).

Strategy Options: Western Borders

In similar vein, strong manoeuvre forces of balanced composition, to be launched to conduct deliberate and intense operations to decimate opposing forces may continue to be the recourse to defang an intransigent Pakistan. Even then, rather than being bound to 'international pressure' and so confining just to 'short' engagements, there could also be the option of prosecuting an intermittently sharp war that is long enough for the advantages of the nation's intrinsic strengths to manifest. In fact, the strategy of swift, short and intense offensives may be revisited in light of the fact that it is workable only when the best part of the military institution is maintained at a state of ever-readiness and the stocks of consumables of war are full. These are difficult and costly conditions to fulfil. A short war would also dilute, more or less, India's favourable differential in war-waging capabilities. Whereas recourse to intermittent spurts of sharp and moderate engagements over a longer period may be adopted to keep escalation in control, offer scope for diplomatic moderation and most importantly, render irrelevant Pakistan's nuclear bombast.

Further, there may be also be a case to revisit the current matrix of terrain and force-application astride the Pakistan front. Given that Pakistan has opted to attack India at the sub-conventional level while flaunting irrational nuclear threat to save herself from the latter's conventional retaliation, it is time that the three decade long aggression be upturned either by any of the various options of conventional offensive action, or by triggering sub-conventional conflict in the POK. Towards this end, the notion that the onus of keeping Pakistan away from her nuclear trigger, indeed even to prevent war, must be on India, needs to be scotched, banal as it is. As discussed under the doctrinal aspects therefore, the strategy may shift its weight to the recovery of some or all of the occupied territories across the irrational Line of Control in the state of Jammu, Kashmir and Ladakh, and accordingly, open up an option of restructuring India's offensive forces. The corresponding integrated military strategy could then be articulated according to the classical Strategy of Deliberate Annihilation, and profess the application, at chosen time and sectors, of overwhelming 'main', 'strike' and 'special' forces, each having its integrated joint-service 'manoeuvre' and 'precision-attrition' elements (2).

Strategic Options in Sea and Air

The adversaries' aggressive intents being focused on land territory, it has been an expedient practice in the strategic fraternity to elaborate comparatively more upon ground operations – an indeed has been the case in this book too. To some extent that is understandable as long as the all-pervasive salience of service-specific, as well as integrated land, sea and air operations are kept in due contention. Factually, with the Indian Ocean Region occupying China's strategic perspective, much to the chagrin of other global and regional powers, the seas have already turned into another focus of inimical designs against India. Similarly, the factor of air power would be the main determinant in defending the Indo-Tibet border belt. Obviously, such a situation requires stronger sea and air capabilities to be assimilated into the proposed integrated military strategy.

In any case, according to the universally followed principles of RMA, imperatives of military modernisation call for integration of highly potent land, sea and air forces. To that end, a potent force-integration can be economically and technically achievable only through modernisation of the usually large and loose land forces to turn these trim and lethal, and the corresponding up-sizing of sea and air forces, not just to fill the gaps in operational capabilities, but actually to enhance and expand it. Needless to reiterate therefore, India's deliberately defined and duly contemporised integrated military strategies would assimilate a better proportioned combination of land, sea and air power to secure her military and finally political objectives of the coming era.

Strategic Partnership Missions

Strategic considerations that influence the make-up of India's conventional military structure would in most part also fit into the integrated operations which may have to be undertaken under the aegis of the UN or global alliances for peace-enforcement or disaster response tasks. In fact, the necessity of inter-operability among advanced militaries would facilitate the upgrade of equipment profile and battle procedures of the Indian military forces.

Control of Internal Insurgencies

Extreme challenges in terms of poverty alleviation, managing a bulging youth versus growing old population, and leaping popular aspirations, against fixed resources that the Indian lands and seas may offer, would keep India vulnerable to the continuation of internal rebellions in the coming decades – the instigations may come from employment, economic, ethnic religious, and such issues. Mostly, such rebellions may be arrested by armed police actions and various development initiatives aimed at denying to the rebels their rhetorical goals. However, armed insurgency, when supported by external forces, can be decimated only by military-incentivised offensive counter-insurgency operations, even when these have to be described as 'police actions'.

Subduing insurgencies from blowing up into national threat, and so to create conditions for political accommodation of angst within the framework of Indian Constitution would require application of unit level light infantry forces, supported by military logistic system and sustained from civil administrative infrastructure. Much of that capability is already in place in the form of the Rashtriya Rifles, Assam Rifles and Coast Guard. These would have to be appropriated into the military modernisation schemes. The strategy adopted in this instance could be the classical Strategy of Containment and Exhaustion.

Effects of Nuclear Doctrine on Conventional Military Strategy

India's current nuclear doctrine is arguably China-centric; its Pakistan-focus arises by default. As its nuclear force-deployment indicates, the PRC is apparently wary of possibilities, if remote, of adverse results of its conventional military aggression upon India, should that be necessitated in the future. A long-term visionary not given to romantic idealism, China may even suspect the emergence of an assertive India-Tibet combine to her detriment. In either case, China seeks to back up her conventional military designs with nuclear threat should she find herself in a militarily tight corner. Further, China's stance of desisting from 'first-use' of nuclear weapons is also characteristic of her characteristic ambivalence when considered in the context of territories that she claims to be hers – as indeed Arunachal Pradesh or much of Ladakh are – and therefore, arguably, outside that stipulation. To that extent, India's imposition of 'minimum nuclear deterrence' against China may be appropriate, firstly, as long as the inter se nuclear asymmetry is not allowed to go out of hand, and secondly, India wields a demonstrated conventional military strength that denies to China the fruits of military aggression. It is here that Pakistan fits in as China's nuclearised strategic surrogate to create a triangle of nuisance.

India's nuclear doctrine seems to suggest that Pakistan, taking note of India's assertion of 'massive retaliation' in response to any form of mass-destruction attack, will have a certain level of tolerance to conventional offensives, against 'shallow' objectives, before she opts to cross her threshold of nuclear first-strike – a threshold that keeps getting lower at Pakistan's convenience. That is a qualification, adverse as it is, built into what Indian strategic analysts refer to as 'limited war under nuclear overhang'. Besides, there is doubt among many analysts as to whether 'nibbling of some patches of land across the borders, at a heavy cost, only to have to return these at the end, would offer any real advantage to India'. The contradictions are further added to by some misinformed mandarins who propagate the illusion that nuclear missiles could cover the hollowness in conventional military prowess, and so find wisdom in depending on scientists and bureaucrats to deliver in a nuclear-conventional war, and leaving the military institution to undertake sundry chores. Such contradictions are dangerous portents of negating India's superior military potential – it is a case of absurd self-deterrence! Indeed, there is much wisdom in finding strategies to breakout of such disorientations – given due opportunity and support, Indian strategists have in them to deliver.

Pakistan fancies in her belief that her nuclear weapons are the bulwark against a militarily advantaged India that is committed to her destabilisation. This certainty may be but the conscious realisation of her uncontrollable urge to undermine India – irrespective of the costs that she has to pay. Thus, for a nation that even in her rational perspective is so congenitally afflicted with anti-India stimulus, the fanatic idea of 'jihad – at any cost' may render acceptable the fallouts of India's massive nuclear retaliation to her first-strike.

Presently, Pakistan, through investment in tactical nuclear weapons, has taken another step in nuclear brinkmanship. These weapons, she presumes, would further curtail India's option of inflicting conventional military retaliation, thus securing Pakistan's immunity against her incessant attacks on India, overt and covert – an instance of a weak but relentless power deterring a stronger but uncertain one. To make that hubris palatable, some analysts suggest that 'global powers may restrain India from going ahead with massive nuclear retaliation', or that the 'humane and responsible demeanour of the Indian leadership might cause them to retract from adopting a horrific recourse', or words to that effect; the insinuation being that India should be responsible enough to take nuclear attack and not retaliate.

Dangerous insinuations as narrated above, in effect, lead to degradation of India's conventional credibility while negating her nuclear deterrence. These are serious indictments against India's strategic responses in deterring nuclear war as well as her quest for military security against adversaries that are unable to shed their anti-Indian disposition. At the first instance therefore, the integrated military strategy might unequivocally reaffirm India's commitment to the policy of nuclear 'massive retaliation', while calling Pakistan's nuclear pretentions. Indeed, there are serious incongruities in India's conventional as well as nuclear strategies which need to be reconciled to the rightful purpose.

The Human Factor

Strategic formulations are matters of extensive deliberations. Conversely, professionalism and ingenuity of the majority of our military leadership, defence ministry bureaucrats, politicians responsible of national security and strategic think-tanks have for long remained shackled to a placid and obfuscating culture. The dearth of discussion and debate, both in the realm of possibilities and boundless military thinking, point to that void in India's strategic discourse. Time, however, has come to marshal native intellect and professional acumen and to breakout of that cocoon, and so to align the focus of national defence towards a better destiny. In that context, for the strategic innovations to be implementable, the managers of national defence have to invest in the excellence of those who would actually implement the change – that is, the executive functionaries, both within the military institution as well as in the defence bureaucracy. Modernisation and uplift cannot work unless the implementers are uplifted out of mediocrity.

This brings to the fore the necessity of the proposed National Defence University (NDU). This institution should offer a platform for innovative thoughts and original ideas on matters of military strategy. Besides, the NDU should aim at raising, examining, analysing and propagating hard and tangible issues of purely military nature as well as those in the wider context of national defence, rather than turn into another mundane secretariat for the serving officials of the MoD or MEA, as indeed most such institutions have done. Point to note further is that the NDU can bring relief from stagnation of military thought only if the study faculties of the top military training institutions uplift their curricula just from précis writing and reporting new developments to venture into theorising over the contemporary and future character of warfare.

Convergence of Strategies and Force Structure

It would be appreciated that the preceding discussions are but illustrative; much of the afore-stated strategy frameworks are already in place. Even then it may be worthwhile to factor the aspects discussed above in the innovation of the proposed military strategies without succumbing to past fixations. Indeed, there would be much to update and revise the current strategies, besides of course, devising ingenious ones. The purpose would be to achieve congruence of national objectives, military strategies and the force-structure within an affordable defence budget. In that, India's defence policy-makers have to visualise that beyond a point It is not necessary to be impressed by Pakistan's nuclear tantrums; after all, India's nuclearisation of did not stop Pakistan from intruding into Kargil, nor could Pakistan's nuclear voodoo dance stop India from evicting that intrusion. India's national leadership also needs to accept that military response to aggression – and proxy war is an aggression – may be recessed only at own peril, and whether 'cold start', 'hot pursuit' or retribution at the 'time and place of own choosing', or whether limited, conventional or hybrid, India must devise strategies to punish military aggression without being self-deterred. When credibly demonstrated, adoption of such strategies would foster credible deterrence – for the good of all. India's current strategic demeanour does the exact opposite, it rewards intransigence.

In other words, first, there would be the need to revisit and revise what had so far been declared as organisational voids and equipment deficiencies – the current extent of 'hollowness', so to say – in light of the contemporary challenges. In similar vein, the need would be to devise the most efficient operational concepts and practices to meet those challenges, and fit these into innovative strategies and corresponding force-structures to be applied when called upon to do so. Thus, in the overall context, the call of visionary national defence is to find the right congruence of professionalism, innovative strategic concepts, modern force-composition and affordable war-wherewithal.

Having discussed the key parameters of the integrated military strategies with the stamp of native characteristics, the next imperative would be to consider the principles which could guide a corresponding modernisation and restructuring of India's military forces.

Modernisation of the Force Structure

A continuous state of military challenges on the one end and budgetary limitations on the other have made it imperative for the military leaders to organise India's defence forces in a manner as to secure success within the resources obtainable. Resultantly, force-structure of the military institution is a well-conceived and effectively designed 'order of battle' that has been honed diligently and updated regularly to stand the test of times. However, accumulated deficiencies in equipment and personnel profile and a long period of stagnation against the call for organisational as well as systemic modernisation have caused reckonable imbalances in the composition of the combat forces. Notably, these imbalances manifest in three distinct but interlinked aspects, all leading to dilution of combat power. These aspects are as follows:

a) One, there is the imbalance due to capability deficit – inadequacy of modern scales of fire power, mobility, data communication, surveillance, reconnaissance and targeting, and IW capabilities to bolster the accuracy and lethality of battle units and formations, for example.

b) Two, there is also the imbalance caused by deficiencies of accessories, attachments and expendables which permit weapons and equipment to be exploited to the optimum design capabilities. Deficiencies of night fighting devices, precision weapon sights, full range of munitions, automated ammunition loading etc. are some examples in this context.

c) Three, continuation of redundant elements – obsolescent firepower sans modern target acquisition, archaic unit intelligence sections sans uplink with digitised data banks and idling supply chain installations, are some examples of this aspect. These dead weights affect combat power in an indirect manner by contributing nothing but wastefulness of scarce resources (3).

The process of military modernisation by itself would necessitate that these imbalances are covered, firstly as stated earlier through considered deletion of such deficiencies and voids which might have gone irrelevant over the past quarter of a century, secondly, through upgrade of obsolete entities to contemporary standards of capabilities, and thirdly, incorporation of modern combat, combat support and logistic capabilities into the organisation of various line units, field formations and command and control headquarters. Needless to state, these are the aspects of military modernisation that would necessitate substantial changes in the current organisation of the units, formation headquarters and the overall force-structure.

Further, as reiterated many times over, changes in geo-political challenges and the corresponding sequence of corollaries – in terms of, firstly, the political mandate, secondly, the military doctrine, and finally, the military strategy – would dictate the range and scope of force-restructuring. Notably, during the final stages of military modernisation, it would be necessary to address the incongruities that would invariable emerge, particularly when updated strategies are transmuted into a compatibly balanced force-structure.

Next, under the overall ambit of a native joint-service military doctrine and its transmutation into integrated military strategies, the right nuances force-structuring in the Indian military institution may be outlined in terms of the fundamental considerations as discussed in the succeeding paragraphs.

Spectrum of Warfare

The politico-military mandate calls for the Indian military institution to possess the ability to operate across an entire range of military responses. These responses are in the realm of low intensity counter-insurgency at one end, through various versions of joint-services conventional warfare, IW, nuclear posturing, and finally, the inexorable militarisation of outer space. Built into this scheme of matters must be the ability to operate in multi-national alliances and out-of-area assistances' that the neighbourhood might look for at times of their need. Thus besides the proposed integrated military strategies and its compatible force-structure, equipment profile and training, modernisation of the Indian military institution must encompass the ability to undertake such range of global partnership operations.

Force Restructure

Fundamental intransigence and hostile intents of the adversarial powers, and to some extent, the indigenous insurgencies, would be the determinants of the nation's overall military force-structure. When so tested with respect to the existing service-specific force-structures, there may not be a cause for great overhaul, so to say. However, advancements in military technology and tactical adaptations of these in conduct of contemporary modes of warfare having bypassed, more or less, India's stagnant military institution, undertaking of extensive modernisation of the existing single as well as joint-service construct of forces, for these to catch up with the contemporary tactical dispensation, must be a priority interest for the planners of national defence. In that endeavour, the existing organisation and composition of the forces – combat and combat support units and formations, and operational logistic establishments – would have to be reconfigured in terms of equipment, manpower and training profile for these to subscribe to the concept of integrated joint operations – presently, these exist in irreconcilable states of incompatibility. Thus while the current unit level scaling of fire power, mobility, electronic warfare, communications and logistic packages fall well short of what is needed to fight a modern war on land, sea and air, the battle formations turn handicapped in terms of 'balance in composition'; the expediency of resorting to ad hoc attachments to reconcile such mismatch might work in exercises, not so in war. Modernisation of would help overcome that anomaly.

Astute modernisation would also aim at correcting the expedient but irrational trend of falling for incremental introduction of arm-specific modernisation – a trend promoted by a system which favours materialisation of visible and easy-picking rather than operational-priority schemes. Mutually compatible all-arm and all-service upgrade of battle-formations would be a natural fallout of such corrections. That would afford to the battle formations the requisite operational bite as commensurate to the kinds of war propounded, the allocation of funds and priorities of new inductions being dictated accordingly (4).

Next, when the overlapping commons amongst the three services – namely, controlling headquarters, surveillance, communication, long range fire power and operational logistics – are integrated into the military strategies and managed by joint staff, it would lead to tri-service grouping of result oriented task forces in terms of various types of battle formations and the roles and compositions of these. Modern warfare being better conducted with highly capable special forces operating in conjunction with conventional battle formations, this factor would also have to be taken into consideration, just as must be case with recourse to the latest in deception, cyber and psychological warfare, and C4I2SR technologies; whereas these recourses are still treated in peripheral terms, there is the need to incorporate these capabilities into every level of the integrated force-structure. In the subsequent stage, such grouping of task forces would trigger a secondary reconfiguration of equipment profile, organisational structures, order of units and formations, and the system of operational logistics – modernisation after all is a dynamic process. It will also lead to formal assimilation of tri-service inter-operability, exercise of alternate means of securing an objective and discard of dead-weight redundancies.

Modernisation would thus optimise joint-service assignment of forces, introduce alternate means and methods of undertaking tactical engagements and manage the level of acceptable redundancies. More importantly, it would be cognisant of the trends of sub-conventional conflicts that could, in all probability, reign before, during and after a conventional war has met its objectives, and thus promote comprehensive integration of campaign-plans, with each service assigned its roles in all stages of a campaign (5).

In the overall context, a combination of force-modernisation, modular task oriented force-composition and complementarities in terms of tri-service as well as inter-arm interoperability may therefore be brought about to create an overall balanced and flexible military force-structure. Operational tasks could then be assigned to integrated tri-service battle formations – or task forces – balanced in composition according to the contemporary scales of firepower, mobility, command, control, communications, intelligence (C3I) and logistics, with specific roles assigned without duplication of effort, and yet retaining the flexibility of alternate recourses to achieve the desired military objectives. To illustrate, defence of an area could be organised with flexible combinations of troop deployment, fire power, air interdiction, Special Forces and sea blockade, each of the task and sub-task forces committed in varying quantum of availability and suitability to the achievement of the singular objective. A modernised force-structure would render such advantages feasible.

Force Density

It would be necessary to maintain adequate numerical capabilities of the three services, both in terms of battle formations as well as troop strength, to be able to meet the imperatives of the aforementioned range of operations. Critical troop-density, that would be necessary to keep the border secure and internal insurgencies in control, would have to be accorded due consideration, particularly because in such deployments usage of weaponry is limited in favour of boots on ground. This consideration might call for higher dependence on light infantry units – Assam Rifles and Rashtriya Rifles for example – because police forces may not succeed in reining in the highly fanatical externally propped up, trained and well equipped insurgent organisations, particularly when the spread of fighting affect large parts of India.

Force Multiplication

With runaway advances in technology coming at huge expense and the ever present constraints of resources to keep pace, dependence on 'force multipliers' or capability enhancement accessories for main weaponry and other military hardware would be an important thrust area of modernisation. Induction of balanced tri-service force multiplying capabilities would include early warning, reconnaissance, deception, targeting, strategic transportation, operational mobility, tactical manoeuvre, camouflage, protection and finally, precise destruction. Further, net-worked force multipliers – like satellite communication, aerial surveillance, command and control, precision fire power, precision guided missiles etc. – have to be accessible down to the lowest echelons of the combat forces for tactical empowerment. Accordingly, combat units and formations have to be restructured to accommodate, and exploit, these enhancements.

Usability Factor

The issue of force-restructuring of the Indian military institution would encompass a professional review of the concept of 'Usability Factor'. This is the factor that determines as to what force levels could be effectively deployed, committed and sustained in conduct of operations. Indeed, with threats looming from two fronts, in theory, there may be no limitations on India's force deployment, but for the matters of rationality and affordability. The test lies in the military institution's capacity to provide the optimum level of combat support and logistic back-up to all its standing forces, for the entire 'order of battle' to fight war either in simultaneity or in tandem. Indeed, one-time raising of forces is easier than maintaining these in a state of best preparedness in terms of full scaling of weapons, equipment and personnel, and supply of the scaled levels of ammunition and expendables.

Quantity and quality of military hardware are the functions of the nation's technological and industrial capacities, while personnel management and training are equally burdensome for the national exchequer. Therefore, to possess partially equipped and unprepared forces, for these just to sit out a war, or even to be employed below their designated capabilities, must be an systemic flaw and a failing of defence management – a costly one at that. In other words, the nation's capacity to sustain forces in war must be a guide to structure an entirely 'usable' force structure so that it enhances the overall Usability Factor of the forces (6).

Management of Operational Preparedness

High technology hardware and its fast obsolescence, and high-skill and high cost of personnel to battle with these, have made it extremely costly to maintain large military forces, not the least at the full state of preparedness. In fact, unless managed with professional wisdom, modern era high performance, high-precision military hardware impinge, rather than promote, organisational efficacy. This situation is addressed, firstly, by deliberately maintaining military forces at varying grades of preparedness as commensurate to varying periods of warning and mobilisation, and secondly, by adoption of flexible terms of engagement for the military personnel. Thus there are the standing 'regular' forces, one part of which is maintained at the latest state of modernisation as well as operational preparedness, while another part remains ready with comparatively modest state and grade of equipment. Then, to build up the regular forces, there is a third part arraigned by 'skeleton' units and formations that are scaled with hardware nearing the end of service life, and muscled up, when needed, by personnel having 'reserve' liability to recall at short notice.

India's military modernisation could consider such an option to maintain the forces at full, partial and sequestered states of manpower and hardware and so make the best out of a leaner and more lethal military machine. Thus while the second category would remain able to gear-up in quick time to assist the standing forces, the last category – 'mothballed forces' to wit – could be assembled within a specified period, when called up to arms in assistance of regular forces. Expansion of the Territorial Army to shoulder line of communication duties in war and exigencies of counter-insurgency operations could also be thought of, in order to fillin the periodical surge requirement of forces. Weapons of war having spilled out of the parameters of physical combat into money-trafficking, cyber-sabotage, media-manipulation, economic subversion and technology thefts, the charter of this force may be further expanded to induct expert 'soldier-citizens' whose expertise would complement the overall military security concerns related to banking, excise, engineering, cyber, financial, industrial, transportation and media sectors. Thus the rigid terms of engagement may be made flexible in favour of vocational reassignment and reserve liability. Changes of this nature may be incorporated under the overall scope of military modernisation.

Management of Intelligence

Over the past two decades or so, the national intelligence organisations have done fairly well in terms of improvement of in-house procedures as well as assimilation of high-technology in acquisition and dissemination of intelligence. The issues of inter-departmental disconnect in intelligence collation and dissemination, long term build-up of operating skills and fielding of a judicious combination of sources, including human intelligence, are also being well taken care of. Even then, the format of managing strategic intelligence as it obtains today remains afflicted with certain conceptual and organisational limitations. Some experts argue that even if the intelligence agencies have individually proven their competence, the state of higher synergy among various agencies and their function may still be achievable. In this respect, there are issues related to independent parliamentary oversight, reinforcement of the joint intelligence mechanism, and balancing of environmental bindings – for example, the matter of peer review, the notion of 'political correctness', individual privacy, cadre management etc. – which may need to be dealt with.

From the point of view of military intelligence, the art and science of 'intelligence appreciation', 'intelligence tasking', 'situational review' and 'military assessment' of information received from various agencies requires resuscitation. This key aspect of military preparedness has somewhat lost its prime status at the formation and unit levels, mainly because of obsolescence and inadequacy of the integral intelligence assets and its consequent lack of interest among the battle leadership – as exemplified by indifferent manning of intelligence appointments. As a result, there are reasons to suspect that full advantages of the capabilities of various intelligence agencies, as these relates to build up of timely and actionable military intelligence, remains below the optimal level of efficacy. This anomaly needs to be redressed if the fruits of military modernisation are to be secured for the benefits of defence decision-making in general and military decision-making in particular. Indeed, there is the need to strengthen the military intelligence apparatus at each level of the military structure.

Build-up of near as well as long term military intelligence has always been an imperative of warfare. In the current era of defence management, its scope and reach have expanded many folds, firstly, due to the means and methods of warfare as well as intelligence collection having turned into a technology intensive exercise, and secondly, by the spread of intelligence functions to cover the emergence of 'dual-purpose' security challenges like media-misinformation, money-trafficking, cyber-subversion, media-manipulation, economic arm-twisting and technology denial. Military intelligence functions are therefore no more to be confined to the traditional force and terrain information; societal, fiscal and political input are very much part of it, particularly in sub-conventional operations. Accordingly, modernisation of military intelligence must lead to revival of the traditional intelligence cycle with a modern construct. That would require strengthening of the system of collection and assessment by military professionals working at tactical and operational levels within the military structure, as well as those embedded in national intelligence agencies for the purpose of military-specific assimilation of strategic intelligence in a more institutionalised manner.

With particular reference to management of defence intelligence, it is imperative that its scope be expanded in keeping with the range and depth of operational level commitments as well as the tactical interests of modern field formations. Accordingly, synergy of intelligence functions in its entirety, starting from battlefield intelligence at unit levels and leading up to strategic intelligence at the national level would be an objective of military modernisation; the obsolete practices of field or tactical intelligence gathering would not suffice any more. Organisation of a corresponding system of intelligence collection, collation, inference and dissemination in near-real time would have to be incorporated into the modernisation scheme. As the voids in terrain and force intelligence, even at unit and field formation levels, showed up during the Kargil War – and that weakness persists, more or less – this revamp must be a priority concern of modernisation of the military institution.

Further, at various levels of command, the process of regulating the volume of intelligence inputs in tune with the necessity and desirability, as well as the ability to assimilate intelligence inputs into battle plans would need to be worked out in minute details before the necessary staff and equipment are added at unit and formation levels. Similarly, with the coming of an open society and access of military personnel to it, field security and counter-intelligence functions within the military institution needs to be freed from the traditional reluctance to watch over the own, and strengthened. The resultant high expertise-high technology driven system would have to be supported by elaborate automated data processing and communication networks. All these aspects towards achievement of true synergy of intelligence resources, including specialist training, must form intrinsic parts of military modernisation. In sum, revamp of strategic, operational and tactical intelligence setup would be an important part of modern force-structuring.

Logistic Framework

Classical 'defence' incorporates aggression and offensive conduct in good measure. But as it usually happens in any 'defensive' oriented military force that stands transfixed to static defences, inflexible options and confined areas of interest, operational logistic support often gets taken for granted while basic logistic infrastructure stands at low priority. Logistic capability and its flexibility thus becomes the first casualty in any military force-structure, and that keeps military commanders and staff hamstrung in their audacious and innovative thoughts and action, stifles their tactical initiative and leaves them to bank upon attrition to buy victory.

The case of the Indian military institution is not much different. Its military leadership, by its thought and action, seems to have grown so impractical as to consider modernisation without having to upscale to elaborate logistic support infrastructure. It seeks to cut down the 'tails' in favour of larger 'teeth' – the former term referring to logistics and the latter to the fighting arms – without seriously reflecting upon the fact that strong tail is mandatory in making a 'bite' strong. The result is stark: operations have to be confined to specific sectors that must remain aligned to logistic tails, and even then, battle plans peter out after a week or two of campaigning. Indeed, there is reason to believe that the fixated attrition and mass mindedness among most of the Indian unit and formation commanders and staff are imposed by an inflexible logistic back-up and its confined coverage in terms of force level, time and space, that leaves them little option but to follow pre-determined and rigid avenues of operations.

For a modernised force-structure to earn respect of the adversaries, it is incumbent upon the military institution to possess robust and flexible logistic support systems that can sustain the freedom of tactical operations. Similarly at the operational and strategic levels, it is also imperative to organise extensive spread of logistic nodes and bases to back-up long term military campaigns. When well located, stocked and suitably mobilised for forward supply and repairs, the purpose in the first two instances is met by services units and installations that are integral to field and static formations respectively, and who follow the courses of battle to back-up opportune exploitation of unforeseen battle situations. Similarly, the strategic purpose is met by developing research, manufacture, base repair, depot facility and robust chains of supply to the theatres of war. Presently, even if the logistic system within the Indian military institution and that coming from the defence establishment meets the basic requirements of war, the moot point is that its existing configuration requires expansion as well as elevation for it to be able to meet the demands of modern manoeuvre and offensive campaigns (7).

Finally, there has emerged a trend of 'out sourcing' the military logistic commitments. The idea has its advantages provided the local environmental conditions are taken care of. For example, the culture of placid response and casual contractual commitments against the slowness of legal courses has to be dealt with through legislative acts and special judicial processes. The formidable terrain where the Indian military forces are required to fight and where the outsourced agencies have to function, would also have to be factored in.

For military modernisation to bear fruition, a consciously professed enhancement of the present logistic system – to cater to the maintenance of high technology hardware, flexible positioning of munitions and supplies, and forward repair and refit – must come to the evidence. In specific terms, this means holdings of sufficiently cushioned quantities closer to the battle areas, keeping a part of the stocks mobile, battle field and forward repair and refit, and upgrade of the capacity and quality of the products of defence logistic installations. An optimally stout and fat 'tail' would then extend the range, depth and strength of the 'teeth' and make the 'bite' more petrifying (8).

Harness of Indigenous Competencies

As mentioned on the issue of military doctrine, building upon indigenous competencies would also be applicable to the articulation of modernisation schemes. There are remarkable indigenous competencies in the fields of transportation and mobility, communications, storage and material handling, field fortifications and earthwork, bridging, and electronic warfare. Equally salient would be the harness of IT expertise to deceive and disorient the adversary and corrupt his command and control set up, and so make up to some extent for our qualitative and quantitative limitations in sophisticated weaponry. Obviously, a modern force-structure would have to be strengthened with higher scaling of such capabilities to boost operational flexibility, and so provide to the commanders in field, more tactical freedom to deploy their cutting edge resources.

Advantages of Force Restructure

For the investment in military power to be worthwhile, the kind of comprehensive structural reconfiguration as discussed above must be a top priority for the managers of national defence, that would result in accrual of higher cost-effectiveness in protecting national interests, 'peace dividend' in short. In effect, the following advantages would emerge from the proposed structural modernisation:

a) The force-structure would be rid of the appendages that are necessary no more. In return, it would incorporate modern capabilities to execute focused and precision operations, free of redundancies as well as voids. New capabilities would permit conventional forces to execute flexible manoeuvre and precision targeting, and that in turn would lead to more efficient force-application. Inter alia, assurance levels of securing the political purposes of resorting to military action would be higher with leaner, muscular and manageable forces.
b) The force-structure would assimilate the advantages of native strengths – human resources, IT, engineering acumen and logistic potential. There would be found alternate courses to enhance the exploitation of imported hardware and so cover, to some extent, the limitations of indigenous high techno-industrial capacity. That would enable the military forces to overcome the current technological and fiscal deficiencies till the time these gaps are closed.
c) Build-up of integrated task forces for special or incisive information based operations at the desired times and locations, to tackle soft or hard objectives in conformity with the overall operational plans would be facilitated.

d) Ingenious management of latest, contemporary and near-obsolescent weapons and equipment in combination with regular, reserve and part-time personnel would be possible. This would enable exploitation of the forces' operational effectiveness from resources within.

e) Integrated joint-service logistic capability across successive echelons of force deployment – to include modernised production, procurement, inventory management, repair and recycle, stocking, replenishment and transportation systems within and beyond the battle zones – would be achievable within the scope of indigenous industrial and fiscal capability. Serving the purpose of force-multiplication of war resources, that would add to the overall military capability.

f) Indigenous defence technological and industrial development to support force-restructure and modernisation schemes would provider impetus to technology diffusion to all other sectors at the national level, as it happens in developed countries.

Managing Modernisation

As stated earlier, given the right impetus, it will take a decade or so start reaping the benefits of turning around the various organisations of the nation's defence establishment. The nation's defence managers – political, bureaucratic and military hierarchy – would do well to utilise this period to push the process of military modernisation in all its hues, and so make the overall defence investments deliver better dividends. Notably to do so, in contrast to the common perception, India may not need to spend high on defence, but rather work towards convergence between political goals, military strategies and modernisation of the military machine through better managed and regulated funding.

To reiterate, new initiatives should be aimed at update of military strategies, right-sized force-restructure to replace flab with muscle, modernisation of military hardware and optimisation of quality and strength of personnel. Above all, transformational upgrade of training and military acumen would marshal professional merit to shoulder the burden of military preparedness. In so doing, to reiterate, it would be wise to directly involve the military leadership in policy confabulations rather than through the medium of officials unqualified for that role, and so save bureaucrats and scientists from the burden of fiddling with what must be for them but an intelligent amateur enterprise. There is no need to be wary of that kind of charter; the same government had made that possible in the post-1962 period (9).

END NOTES

(1) 'Phyrric victory' is one in which there is little to distinguish victory from defeat, either outcome proving to be equally devastating, as the results of Phyrrhus' War on the Romans (279 BC) showed. Further, the most prominent instances of weaker contestants grounding their powerful opponents to the dust are: the Anglo–Spanish War (1570), Shivaji's Deccan War (1650-1700), Anglo-Indian Wars of 18th Century, Battle of Austerlitz (1805) and the Afghan Wars of 19th Century, to quote just a few. More recently, Gallipoli (1915), Indo-China (1945-53), Vietnam (1965-74), Afghanistan (1980-89) are some examples of superior force being trapped, straight-jacketed and defeated in detail. In a recent study, it is found that during the past century, as many as fifty per cent wars have been won by forces inferior.

(2) The strategy could be to choose the best suited time and terrain rather than racing to act 'pronto' as if there would be no tomorrow. Had such deliberate sense prevailed at the time of the Kargil Operations, the goal could have been met with lesser casualties and concluded at a better end-state.

(3) It is frustrating to attempt to reassign or relieve redundant manpower and replace obsolete equipment with modern ones; the government procedures are designed just to resist that. Thus these dead weights continue to occupy time and money. Redundant depots, obsolete workshops, mass of office staff of the days of the typewriter and the call bell, extra drivers and radio operators, obsolete field guns and old generation field engineering equipment and machinery (mine warfare, water supply, field fortification equipment), etc., the list of dead weights is long.

(4) Predominant arm specific modernisation has led to India's native electronic warfare and C3I potentials remaining untapped for military use while latest tanks are – with banal hope – expected to be supported by virtually discarded air defence and mobility support. Similarly, sea fleets and air armadas are expected to perform to the ideal levels even if bereft of key echelons of support elements. Then there are weapons without the complimentary stocks of munitions, surveillance capability of Unmanned Aerial Vehicle unmatched by corresponding action capability, and so on. Even if it does not make professional sense, partisanship of the 'predominant' in the face of inadequate funding causes this profane distraction.

(5) Higher mobility and sustainability in battle field would offer new tactical options in conventional operations while comprehensive campaign plans would help in controlling resistance from residual opponents forces which, as the trends indicate, would invariably persist.

(6) There is no sense in having fighting formations which are so denuded by deficiencies and voids that these cannot engage in battle to perform the designated role, and therefore are either left out of battle or used in sundry tasks. Similarly, there is no

use in raising armoured and artillery units when these cannot be fed with full quota of ammunition. In the case of naval and air assets, the implications of such mismatch are more severe.

(7) Like camouflage, concealment and deception dummies, forward repair of costly, complex and mostly imported weaponry and equipment too is more important than ever under the modern conditions. The heard often talk of discarding against forward repair of casualty equipment in a 'short war' is an obviously banal argument.

(8) Logistic flexibility to exploit tactical opportunities comes from wider grids of ammunition placements, pipelines for fluid supply, alternate echelons for sustained supplies, robust transportation capability and immediate forward repair and refit.

(9) In the past, society depended upon many such skills which were common to civil as well as military life. Today that is not so, and therefore modern day soldier has to be specifically trained to possess those skills – night work, jungle travel, camping practices, improvisation etc. for example.

*

CHAPTER 8

JOINT WARFARE AND INTEGRATION OF THE INDIAN MILITARY INSTITUTION

> "*There is time for everything, and time for change when you can no longer help it.*"
>
> – **Duke of Cambridge, in 1890**

Defining Joint Warfare

For any state, war is an extreme undertaking. Therefore, integration of all forms of state power – military, people, industrial etc. – and the joint application of these to defeat enemy forces has ever been a natural practice. In similar vein, within the military institution, leveraging joint effort among its constituent services has ever been a fundamental condition in prosecution of warfare. However, in the recent times, when military technologies and battle procedures for the application of forces have developed extreme complexities, and that demands high professional skills to exploit, it is essential that the three services, and even the arms within these, have to develop along separate, exclusively delineated courses. Conversely, the consequent compartmentalisation among the services and their self-autonomous inclinations have brought about a situation wherein it becomes necessary to call for special efforts to converge the focus of such divergent elements of forces on attainment of jointness to secure one singular and ultimate military objective. Propounding the concept of 'jointness' in modern warfare fits that diverse requirement.

Overtime, the term has come to suggest the following propositions:

a) Applicability of service-specific control over their exclusive domains of assets, capabilities and expertise;
b) Integration of operational planning and composition of balanced 'order of battle' in a manner that capability voids are addressed, tactical alternatives and options are offered and redundancies or duplications are avoided in the spirit of the hoary 'principles of war';
c) As a corollary, adoption of integrated approach to preparation for war-worthiness, to include tri-service rationalisation of military procurements and acquisitions, prioritised apportioning of budget, and compatible training and personnel management; and
d) Finally, at the point of reckoning, recourse to joint application of various force-elements to execute integrated war strategies.

Jointness signifies a flexible and judicious mix of full time tri-service integration when that is practical, and task and time specific integration of diverse elements of tri-service forces when that is not. It also signifies the nurture of service-specific combat and support assets, professional skills, battle procedures and organisational practices. Inter alia, jointness, and its corollary, integration, lead to the achievement of military security within reasonable and affordable fiscal investment from the state. In other words, significance of jointness comes from cognitive integration of tri-service planning and execution, and physical integration of war waging assets at their disposal, but not necessarily the merger of independent service-specific organisations or structures. Modern military institutions therefore pay much emphasis to joint conduct of operations in land, sea and air, with each of the three services – in some cases with Para-military forces to back-up – participating in appropriate and proportionate roles to put up one integrated effort to defeat the adversary.

The Indian military hierarchy, as also the nation's defence policy-makers, are well appreciative of this fundamental plank of modern warfare. Indeed, there goes on, in all seriousness since over a decade past, much confabulations and analyses to foster a regime of jointness in the Indian military institution. Many efforts had also been made to make tangible progress in that direction, but optimal applicability of the concept of jointness is yet to outscore against the compartmented functioning in single-service exclusivity. That indeed must be an indictment of defence planning in India wherein, firstly, there is an observable wariness among the services over a step that would ease their otherwise excruciating call of waging war, and secondly, the Government, reeling under exasperating fiscal commitments of a poor but aspiring nation, shows little enthusiasm in structuring its military institution to meet its political mandate while saving the state exchequer from duplication and redundancy.

Agreeably, tri-service cooperation had worked fine during the 1965 and 1971 Wars, as indeed it did in all past military ventures which called for that. But the point to appreciate is that when it worked more than four decades back, the three week long tri-service cooperation was cemented by the pressure exerted by war. In modern warfare, the dispensation needed is perpetual 'jointness', not just situational 'cooperation'. The former definition implies inter-service functioning, training, imbibing similar instincts and intents, and then proceeding to devote conjoined efforts to meet each other's operational goals not only under the excruciating circumstances of war, but on a regular basis; coming together occasionally for short periods to sweat it out at specified junctures before going separate ways and then falling back to ensconce in service-centric cocoon in the name of professional autonomy would not do any more. Indeed, future wars demand perfect fit of seamless joint-service fighting that might succeed only if congruence in thought and action become a part of routine inter-service military life even if the means and procedures of force-application must differ according to the service-specific exclusivities (1).

Jointness in Indian Military Institution

Before delving into the issue of jointness in Indian military institution, it would allay much of the negative reservations by pointing out that jointness, as described above, does not imply merger of professional concepts and the spirit driving these, nor the identities, organisational assets or battle procedures. It cannot be an invasive intrusion into the respective organisational turf and it does not call for turning the services into one monolithic structure of all pervasive uniformity; the depth of professional skills required to perform in each field of operational activity, the range and characteristics of complex hardware to be exploited and the elaborate logistic system to support all that do not allow that to happen. Each service would therefore continue to be what these are, having their unique force-structure, their exclusive parameters of professional skilling, training, hierarchy, and cultural peculiarities – to wit, even their idiosyncrasies. Jointness on the other hand, would make it more efficient to engage with operational challenges, and if astutely orchestrated, would bring results out of proportions as compared to each service fighting their own wars and opting to cover each other just at the margins of their activities only when there is no other option (2).

Wariness of jointness is actually an illogical line that stymies timely modernisation. This wariness comes from non-professional apprehensions which stem from systemic inertia that the defence planners inflict upon themselves – by binding themselves in a system that regresses and disables welcome changes; military as well as bureaucratic minds fertilized with fear of marginalisation in an untested dispensation exacerbates that effect. The result is that notwithstanding some flashes of momentary jointness which might be temporarily contrived under inescapable situations that appear now and then, manifestation of the kind of jointness that must answer to the call of modern era warfare remains but a chimera in the Indian military institution. Bluntly put, the show of jointness that are occasionally advertised during joint military exercises, natural calamities and operations of limited scope, are mostly confined to form rather than substance (3).

Experience reveals that individual entities join up only when subjected to external pressure which might be generated from social, economic or security considerations to threaten the roots of their survival. Military organisations are no exception to that rule. Indeed, apart from the original propagator of integrated military structure – Russia – wherever jointness has fructified, it has either been through stern political imposition or under painful surgery after a military disaster. Thus in the USA, it was the catastrophic experiences of the Vietnam War and an aborted embassy rescue mission in Iran that catalysed the promulgation of the 'Goldwater-Nichols Department of Defence Reorganisation Act, 1986'. That profound step was replicated by the UK through a sequence of 'Strategic Defence Reviews', just as France did so through her 'Defence Programme Laws', Germany by her 'Blue Ribbon Commission', and Australia by her own version of 'Strategic Restructuring'. Many others who saw the light followed, with the North Atlantic Treaty Organisation (NATO) and PRC joining the trend. Meanwhile, some nations – Canada, Belgium and South Africa, for example – not having militaristic adversaries breathing down their neck, went on to offer to their military institutions just two options: 'join up or perish'; the outcome was obvious.

Misplaced tendency of the government in seeking democratic consensus even on military matters may be playing a role in slowing down the process of jointmanship in the Indian military institution. The other reason is psychological; hoary military experience suggests that in battle, it is best to rely on capabilities under one's own control, while banking on committal of forces under other's control is avoidable – if it can be helped. Thus construed as having to share authority and control over assets with 'outsiders' who may not be initiated to the finer nuances of service-specific imperatives, jointness may not come through voluntary grace. Further, looking at militaries which have assimilated jointmanship as the cornerstone of their doctrine, it is predictable that when it comes to the Indian military institution, internal squabbling to focus solely upon narrower definition of service-specific interests may still continue, as indeed it has happened to the fate of DPS and its successor, the IDS; even the tri-service Andaman and Nicobar Command has suffered on this account. It would certainly open up another hue of ritualistic posturing, that of one contender trying to usurp more of resources, command more authority and be in limelight. Contentions over counter-air and ground-support operations and structuring of the Special Forces are some cases in point in this context, amongst a host of many. However, seen in true perspective, neither the matter of exercising full control over war resources nor the rituals of internal squabbling may contradict the necessity for jointness – these can coexist and yet bring benefits (4).

Even if the above mentioned reservations are exaggerated by inner fears, jointness in war-fighting – with integrated planning and execution – is a call of the contemporary period which must override all other concerns. Indeed, the cause of jointness must be espoused in the interest of building up an efficient national military machine – a machine that deters aggressive behaviour from the neighbourhood. Serious efforts to enforce the achievement of robust war worthy jointness, free of ambivalence, therefore must be made to hasten up the process under the overall scheme for military modernisation.

That endeavour leads to the question as to what kind of jointness might be looked at and who would it be to enforce it.

A Native Concept of Jointness

The political mandate upon the Indian military institution is much different as compared to our adversarial as well as the other world powers. Naturally, operational philosophies adopted by those militaries, which have much wider political mandate to fulfil, are not the kind that would apply in the Indian context. It would therefore be wise to be circumspect in taking cue from more advanced militaries.

Appropriate or not, the fact remains that the cultural construct of the Indian state does not envision posing pre-emptive or pro-active military threat or infliction of actual punishment to the forces inimical; it is satisfied if such forces are stalled from succeeding in their anti-Indian ventures. Therefore, to register as to what military objectives it may be looking for, the Indian military institution would have to devise its original, *swadeshi* brand of strategic thought process and format its own brand of jointness as it must sprout from native conditions. Besides, a devise for jointness would also have to address the contradictory imperatives which pose a major dichotomy in its development and application. This dichotomy relates to the imperative of building up specialisation in strictly defined but deeper spheres of tactical and technical expertise. With growing technological sophistication of military hardware and the complex tactical configurations in which these are to be deployed, there is the need to commit to narrower fields of life-long training, upgrade and practice among the military personnel assigned to various services and branches within these. This necessity fouls against the equally salient need to train and practice upon wider spans of joint-functional skills. The answer lies in a system of personnel management that permits a fine and flexible balance between domain specialisation and cross domain joint functions. The system of personnel management would have to be modernised thus (5).

To delve further into the kind of jointness which might answer the native call – and of course, within an affordable budget – the stage is now set to discuss the possible broad features of an indigenised version of inter-service jointness.

Tiers of Jointness

Even if it may have its exclusive characteristics, the Indian version jointness in conduct of military operations, as in its universal construct, would display distinct features at the political, strategic, operational and tactical levels. At the political level, all-pervasive jointness would pave the way to nurture a cost-efficient military institution that is fine-tuned to its national mandate and so brings the best dividends against the state's investments over its military institution. As stated, apprehensions of the unknown, that is borne out of inadequate strategic understanding, and which is further ensnared by procedural binds imposed by an archaic system of defence policy formulation, has so far precluded that advantage from fruition. Hopefully in the foreseeable future, the dawning of a new realism might rescue the politico-bureaucratic class of defence policy-makers from their incarceration in indecision, and enthuse the new generation of the military hierarchy to that cause, for the either to join hands in enforcing jointness – and integration when possible – much to the benefit of the national cause– both in overcoming military hollowness and securing the best value for the investment made from the national exchequer.

Jointness at the Strategic Level

Integration, as a measure of jointness at the strategic (tri-service, theatre and Army and equivalent) level, actually implies consolidation of managerial and administrative overheads at the one end, and optimal exploitation of executive and logistic infrastructure to control duplication and improve delivery on the other. Deliberately contrived integration may not necessarily lead to overall cut down of establishment or infrastructure, but it would definitely lead to consolidation and reassignment of these to permit upgrades in conformity with modern operational feasibilities without further bloating of the military institution in its practice of jointness.

As stated, at the strategic level, warfare of the modern era calls for seamless jointness among the three services. Conversely, viewed shorn of prejudicial afflictions, it may not appear to be ideal per se to have nearly one and a half dozen single-service theatre command headquarters in India, huge establishments each functioning in their own exclusivity, duplicating, sometimes even contradicting each other, and from time to time cooperating only when a necessity appears. Logically, the purpose of theatre command may be better served by 'integration' of these single-service theatres under joint-service headquarters. Introduction of intermediary tiers of 'field forces' could also be considered if and when necessary; any India-specific model that brings about true jointness while honouring the service-specific interests would serve the purpose. These matters have been discussed in details in Part 1 of this book.

There may be many options to achieve tri-service integration in the fields of training and logistics. Presently there are many single-service training institutions which cover either fully or partly overlapping syllabi – basic military training and various command level and engineering courses, for example. Integration of such training institutions for similar disciplines of education may be thought of. However, in examining the details of such tri-service integration, not just the training curricula, but the capacities of train facilities as well as administrative infrastructure like firing ranges, exercise areas, accommodation, essential services etc. available at such training institutions also would have to be factored to avoid falling for simplistic and short-sighted solutions. Similarly, there are single-service logistic installations which serve similar purposes – like base maintenance workshops, communication hubs, munitions depots etc. – many of which duplicate the effort not only at the management but even at execution levels. Though much progress has been made in cutting down duplications among such parallel chains of supply and maintenance, there is scope left yet to integrate the installations as well as the processes which meet the purposes of common tri-service end-use. Integration of that kind would lead to substantial cut down on overheads through across the board consolidation of the bloated managerial and administrative establishments. All told, it would do good to promote tri-service integration in training and logistics whenever feasible, and so find pragmatic and efficient upgrade of what are but obsolete practices. Of course, these are matters of deeper analyses and trials which have to be incorporated into the ambit of overall military modernisation and restructure.

While pitching for organisational and systemic integration in promoting jointness in war-fighting, there are cognitive issues to be taken into considerations. To begin with, there are certain genuine management concerns that defy efforts to find summary solutions towards inter-service integration. The geographical spread and holding capacities of immovable assets, institutions, installations and headquarters, dependence on service-centric battle procedures, exclusively dedicated communication networks, unique nuances of inter se cadre management and career advancements are some of the tricky issues which require extensive deliberations, trials and elaborate planning.

Next, any over-affliction of the Indian military hierarchy with the simplistic notions of having 'small headquarters' and 'short logistic tail' need to be reviewed. In the former instance, there is also the contradictory demand for larger headquarters, as much to accommodate new branches that are needed to control the increments of modern capabilities as to facilitate career advancements. As for the overplayed enthusiasm over 'cutting the tail', many of the frequently propagated measures might lead to compromise in the quality and timeliness of services support to the technology dependent modern forces – maintenance, overhaul, forward supply etc. Effects of these compromises might not be evident in the course of cross-border skirmishes and counter-insurgency operations, but the debilitating effects would surely be exposed in the conduct of deliberate warfare. Indeed, the necessity of modernising headquarters and logistic chains, for these elements to be fully competent in exercise of their substantially expanded range of charters – rather than falling for misconstrued and debilitating 'cuts' – must to be accepted to be a part of the intended military modernisation (6).

Finally, there would be genuine apprehension among the military hierarchy regarding the unpredictability of fallouts of the measures which could be adopted in good faith but with little experience or insight. Managers of national defence, too, would be chary of stepping into matters of which they may not have the knowledge or experience. These are genuine apprehensions which arise from unfamiliarity with modern military concepts and capabilities, and exacerbated by a system of defence management that stifles innovation. Therefore, the political leadership, bureaucracy and military leadership, each in their own field of responsibilities, need to overcome their reservations through professional debate, study of foreign military systems and experimentation. It also needs to be appreciated that modernisation through integration, jointness, and right force-structuring require high initial investment and allocation of additional resources before the advantages are felt and dividends are earned.

In sum, at the strategic level, jointness may be cemented by means of integration of command, control, training and logistic elements of the three services while the sanctity of service-specific domain expertise continues to be observed. Integration of the service-specific theatre commands into tri-service commands, each manned by joint staff, may thus be one of the priority goals of military modernisation. Such integration may further be extended to cover joint training and education wherever practicable, and as a corollary, to the management of jointmanship qualified and service-specific specialist personnel. Further, the construct of integrated organisations may be guided by modern tools and skills of prosecuting war rather than pre-conceived notions of 'teeth', 'tail' and 'ownership' of infrastructure, location etc. Finally, apprehensions over the unknown or unpredictable fallouts of integration may be discarded – experience shows that it not only works better and offers better dividends, it also raises the larger as well as narrower interests of the entire strategic community – military and civilian.

Jointness at Operational Level

At the operational (Army and Corps, and equivalent) level, jointness comes closer to its definition, this being the level where it is most practical to foster inter-service jointness in its true form. At this level, commanders, staff and battle formations from the three services can be formally grouped to act in unison to engage in joint war-fighting. In the conduct of modern operations at this level, jointness leads to convergence of application of service-specific assets and expertise, and thus, opens up vast ranges of enabling possibilities for the battle formations to take advantage of. To much extent, this purpose is presently met by the incorporation of sister-service branches at army command and corps headquarters levels, though the corresponding arrangement at higher naval and air headquarters may need to be strengthened. Further, jointmanship opens up new vistas for development of personnel skills, competencies and career opportunities in the field of jointness, the grace being that service-specific practices and conventions, rather than having to be transgressed, are actually found helpful. That indeed is a win-win situation: for the services in terms of professionalism, asset upgrade and opportunities for the personnel, for the entire military institution in terms of its competence to bolster national security, and for the people's exchequer in getting better value for money.

However, for the right conditions of jointmanship to flourish, the fundamental approach to inter-service inter-dependence needs to be reoriented. Thus from the current practice of one lead service seeking 'support' or 'co-operation' from other two, the approach must change to that of forming one joint entity to devise plans, structure forces, allocate resources, control and monitor execution, and manage the result. Obviously, to cultivate credibility in jointness, such entities have to be empowered in terms of operational and administrative authority to prevent these from turning into mere proxies of their mother service.

As one of the key aspects of jointness, cross-posting and exchange of appointments in joint command, staff and logistic establishments may be adopted at the level of corps, naval and air force stations. In that, the combined supply or ordnance depots may have inter-service composition – more to foster joint perspective and accountability, if not anything else. Inter-service exposure and experience may begin with selective adoption of common staff duty practices and procedures, intercommunication, information operations, logistic management, training curricula – training courses, simulations and exercises, for example – and of course, standardisation of common-use stores and equipment (7).

Jointness at the operational level would retain the present structure of service-specific organisations and hierarchies of command. Yet, with infusion of joint staff at key appointments, some degree of common stakes over inter-services assets would get formalised, much to the advantages in the overall war-fighting capabilities. Doubtlessly, jointmanship at the operational level, as it matures, would reinforce strategic jointness, and over time, address the concerns, remove apprehensions and benefit the Indian system of defence management.

Jointness at Tactical Level

At the tactical (Corps and lower, and equivalent) levels, jointness would be more of an indirectly articulated linkage between single-service forces, in which capability of one service reinforces another predominantly tasked service to deal with specific tactical situations. Integration of air power in ground operational plans, deployment of army engineer troops for naval beaching operations, and tasking ground troops to designate air targets are some examples of such integration that have been in practice, the modernity being in higher complexity, expanded scope, and of course, more profound results.

Modern war at its cutting edge requires tactical integration of tri-service inventories of weapons and equipment into any single-service battle or technical procedure, for a given operation and its duration. Across the board cognition to master tactical ingenuity, intelligence management, understanding of weapon and equipment systems, and robust bonding with the peers would be necessary to that purpose. Indeed, such a charter requires years of training, education, hands-on experience, regular exercises and discourses across successive echelons of command, staff and instructional personnel under the guidance of mature hierarchies. The challenge is exacerbated by the expanding spectrum of warfare, whence tactical commanders and staff have to gain concurrent skills in joint planning and execution of third and fourth generation's warfare, low-intensity operations and nuclear posturing. To that end, the cutting edge junior leadership would have to really 'master' – in war, being familiar is not enough – the tri-service inventory of battle assets accessible to them and the characteristics of these, gain expertise in exploiting these, and so marshal joint-service capabilities to beat an enemy who would certainly be equally competent and committed. Accordingly, at the tactical level – say up to divisional and equivalent level – the culture of jointness may be promoted through junior command and staff training, and interactive familiarisation during field manoeuvres.

Notably, experiences gained from joint war-fighting during the invasion of Guatemala, the two Gulf Wars, the Kosovo Campaign and the wars in Afghanistan and Iraq indicate that inter-service jointness at the tactical level does not necessarily imply exchange of personnel, or revision of tactical training curricula, or re-designation of intra-service hierarchies. Inter-service cross-postings at tactical levels are therefore to be confined just to such functions which require one service to seek access to another service-specific skill to better achieve its own tactical objectives – skills in gunnery, sapping, air targeting, amphibious tasks, communication interface, logistics, etc. for example. But more importantly, for jointness to be ingrained into the system, the authority to organise ready response to tactical level tasking sought by one service must be judiciously delegated to the tactical level commanders of the other services, rather than them having to go through the rigmarole of seeking approval from distant hierarchies at every stage. It would then be possible to let each service function freely within their fields of expertise and yet reap the benefits of integrated force-application. Application of distinct service-specific battle procedures in integrated employment of unmanned aerial vehicles, attack helicopters and tactical ground support fighters to secure totality of effects during the Gulf War II is an example of the gains of jointness at the tactical level without compromising the sanctity of service-specific roles and methods (8).

Within the parameters as discussed above, it makes sense to deploy tri-service capabilities to activate joint actions, and so to 'shape' tactical battle areas in more profoundly advantageous manner, the end purpose being to secure success more efficiently. As a corollary, combat elements of each service would, as a matter of fact, be enabled by more elaborate assistance from the other two in terms of surveillance, intelligence, mobility, fire support and logistics. Thus while the Army would reap the advantages of enhanced fire assault, interdiction, air cover, multi-dimensional mobility and intelligence support from the other two services, the Air Force would find more effective target designation and ground security for its installations, and the Navy would enhance its capabilities in coastal and island operations. All three would, of course, be sustained through nodes of joint logistic infrastructure.

Obviously, to foster jointness of the nature as discussed above, some bit of structural upgrade of tactical units and formation headquarters would be necessary. New branches or 'cells' with the necessary inter-service hardware and control mechanisms – networks for fire control, data exchange, communication, geo-spatial intelligence, battle field surveillance, etc. – would need to be built into formation headquarters of each service at the tactical level as well as in joint headquarters at operational and strategic levels. At user-unit levels, such skill-specific cells would have to be made organic or attached, as appropriate. Limited cross-postings of competently trained liaison officers or specialist advisors – even 'controlling officers' when the degree of inter-dependence is substantial – between the three services would then be obligatory; the past practice of deputing liaison officers, Forward Air Controllers, etc. would have to be revived and the appointments manned with due competency.

Fostering an Era of Joint Warfare

In the past decade or so, in the matter of jointmanship, besides the operational and logistic commitments, advocacy of joint training and cross-posting of key functionaries between the three services have been gaining ground. Creation of a tri-service apex appointment in the form of the CDS also continues to be discussed without making headway. Besides, integration of single-service theatre commands is also inviting attention – though not conclusively positive. Thus so far, the debate on integration and more institutionalised jointness has remained confined at the strategic level, and since no headway has been made so far, its percolation down to the operational and tactical levels stand stymied. That leaves the force commanders to take the initiative to 'co-operate' at their own level as and when necessary.

The preceding discussion opens up possibilities of early institution of jointness at the operational and tactical levels, these being implementable within the organisational order of the three services. Such implementations do not demand drastic changes in the existing structure, staff and battle procedures, and thus leave out the exclusive service-domains undisturbed. In fact, jointness at these two levels offers to each service many advantages in terms of operational efficiency, economy of effort and cadre progression. As for operational jointness and structural integration at the strategic and political levels, the nation may have to await the right commitment among its managers of national defence.

There remains a case therefore to out-reach and go ahead with what jointness may be introduced at the operational and tactical levels and hope that capillary action takes this development to the higher levels. In so doing, it may be wise to choose such methods which could circumvent the bureaucratic nay-sayers – military and civilian – disabling them from exercising their ever-honed competence in derailing a process that is perceived, undeservedly, as threat to their authority.

A Fulcrum for Jointness: The Institution of Chief of Defence Staff (CDS)

Integration of the processes of planning, command and control provides for the fulcrum upon which articulation of jointness takes place. For such integration to be subsumed into the system of national defence, there must be a singular military professional authority to preside over the military institution at the apex level – jointness in preparation, planning and prosecution of modern warfare does not come by consensus among equals having their own perceptions, convictions, compulsion and agenda, particularly under the excruciating conditions of war. Simply put, in India, there is a need to synergise the three services to propagate one strategy, and back it up by tri-service force-structuring, joint-training and fund-allocation. Obviously, this role cannot be shouldered by the three chiefs, committed as they must be to primacy of their own service, not the least by the defence secretary who cannot have the requisite military insight. Only a professional body, possessing the requisite authority, foresight and the ability to rise above all considerations but the national cause, can articulate that role. The institution of the CDS must be that fulcrum, to moderate, arbitrate and help devise balanced tri-service joint strategies, and offer focused single point military advise to the government's managers of national defence. That is a necessity which is accepted as such in all modern military institutions.

As described in Part 1 of this book, much has been discussed regarding the institution of CDS among the Indian defence fraternity during the past one and a half decades but no tangible result has emerged. Indeed, even if there is no contention over the need for the institution of the CDS, its fruition is blocked by lack of consensus among the military supremos, while a nonplussed political establishment, severely handicapped in its strategic awareness, wallows in indecision – of course with some subtle mentoring from the bureaucracy. It is so that true modernisation of thought, structure and application of the nation's military power stagnates on the face of mounting challenges of national security.

Given the range and pace of geo-political churnings of the contemporary era, it is a bounden obligation for both, India's political as well as the military leadership, to address the disconnect that has developed between the political mandate for national defence, its obligatory translation into the requisite military capability and a pragmatic fiscal affordability; that the requisite military capability is dictated, not just by the nation, but mostly by the adversary's designs, exacerbates that disconnect. On bridging that disconnect, the military leadership's part is to devise unique strategies for the best application of military power to secure the objectives of national defence within what best resources the nation may afford, and prepare the military institution accordingly. Salience of such strategies is further heightened when viewed in the context of technological and industrial limitations within which India's military security has to be achieved. Thus is necessitated a balancing act to reconcile India's politico-military objectives against the maintainability of a level of military power that fits within the resources that may be prudently committed to India's military preparedness. Indeed, innovation of such unique military strategies has to be a cognitive exercise to factor joint military intellect in achieving results that are higher than the distinct capabilities of the tri-service forces. In a converse option – as it has been adopted by many advanced nations – the limits of the nation's sustainable military capability may even call for revision of the political mandate for national defence. Whatever be the case, wisdom lies in reconciliation of the aforementioned disconnect. Only an empowered institution of CDS could play the decisive role in that reconciliation (9).

The institution of CDS would execute the military part of that balancing act and so offer to the political leadership various options to propagate a robust and cost-efficient national 'defence strategy'. It would foster in the Indian military institution, the right balance of tri-service operational capabilities and so assist the nation in reaping full benefits of its investments on military security. Notably, to fulfil the roles discussed above, the body of military professionals who would constitute the institution of CDS must be competent in control as well as advisory roles – half-measures would not do.

Charter of the CDS

Having established that a purposefully mandated institution of CDS is obligatory to tune-in the Indian military structure according to the national objectives within an affordable fiscal regime, a brief mention of its major aspects of charter would be in order.

The foremost charter would be the advisory role in the Government's formulation of the 'National Security Strategy', the current 'Raksha Mantri's Directive' may be needed to be elaborated to the contemporary context.

Next, it would be to act as a military interface to guide the convergence of various government departments and defence oriented public and private establishments to the focused implementation of the nation's defence policy. Finally, as already discussed, the CDS would be the prime-mover of strategising for joint-warfare, formulation of joint war-fighting doctrine, tri-service force-structuring, joint-training and overall force-modernisation. The practice of inter-service cooperation not being enough in contemporary warfare, the CDS would need to foster true 'jointmanship' in the nation's armed forces, cutting down on redundancies and fostering a regime of inter-dependency and interoperability among the three services.

As the shaping up the nation's the war effort must transcend the orthodox civil-military barrier, the CDS would also have an advisory role in the context of harnessing 'dual-use' resources. Indeed, civilian sectors such as law-and-order, transportation, supply chain, industry, communications, cyber activity etc. have more contributory roles to play in military strategy today than ever before. Many aspects of policy-making at the apex level therefore need to be tempered with military insight to reap the benefits of, firstly, harnessing the advantages of civil institutions, and secondly, dove-tailing dual-use resources into military endeavours. Obviously, a body of dedicated military professionals is needed to nurture that kind of inter-dependency which would promote the phenomenon of 'grand strategising' at the national level.

Thus besides its oft quoted necessity in managing India's nuclear weaponisation, there are wider responsibilities that the institution of the CDS would need to undertake. Today, in absence of that institution, these crucial responsibilities lie unattended, much to the detriment of the nation's military security and its fiscal management.

A Matter of National Interest

India's national defence is managed by a rusted and obsolete mechanism which depends on inter-service 'co-operation' – voluntary somewhat – at all of the aforementioned four levels – political, strategic, operational and tactical. Demand of the day however calls for 'jointness' of the nation's military institution in order to remove redundancies and duplications while multiplying force-capabilities. Jointness would therefore be the key element in bringing about military modernisation, which in turn would cover the matter of integration of service headquarters and the MoD, integrated defence policy making and exercise of integrated acumen in higher direction of war.

In the ultimate analysis, jointness should make sense at the policy making level, because the state would reap the reward of full dividends accruing from its huge fiscal investment at the cost of the society and the nation, the military institution will find it more efficient to secure its goals and the defence establishment would expand its industrial realm within as well as outside the nation.

END NOTES

(1) In the summer of 1999, Pakistan surreptitiously occupied, by combined military and irregular forces, a large swathe of Indian territory astride the Line of Control in the Kargil Sector of the state of Jammu and Kashmir. As a 'hollowed' Indian Army geared up its resources to evict the occupation under a political stipulation not to cross the Line of Control, there was reservation from the Indian Air Force in joining the operation, obviously due to genuine concerns as viewed from their angle. At that time, after some procrastination, the government had to clear the conduct of air operations to support the Army. As for the Navy, there was little thought given about its role; it was left to the Navy to undertake certain operations on their own. This is a classic example of military failure: the intelligence set up failed to predict and forewarn, the Army had gone complacent on surveillance over the Line of Control, the Air Force found itself unprepared for high altitude operations, as if it was expected to fight only over flatlands, and the Navy, probably because the sea was far away from Ladakh and therefore it was not expected to bolster the effort, was left out to gallantly conjure up its contribution to the effort entirely on its own. This is exactly why formal 'jointness', and not just 'cooperation' is needed in the prosecution of modern warfare.

(2) As exemplified by the experiences of modern militaries, jointness leads to optimised resource management, higher skilling of personnel and better career opportunities.

(3) A sense of autonomy has so seized the group notions that the services find it impractical to adopt common communication assets and practices, joint staff duties and procedures, single recruitment and training organisation when feasible, even common military laws. Each service views the other as another, competing organisation rather than another part of their body.

(4) Inter-service squabbling is moored at the misplaced interpretation of democratic practices, wherein the government of India is beholden in seeking all round consensus even in matters of military urgency. It thus subjects such matters to legal, environmental, fiscal and populist stipulations, just as these are applied to its civil departments like agriculture, transport etc. When applied with mindless stringency, these standard stipulations lead to virtual stoppage of progress – for example, acquisitions of weaponry, development of roads, notification of firing and manoeuvre ranges, acquisition of training areas, etc. One result is that the soldiery is left holding the banner of procedural propriety while having to bear with unreliable and obsolete weaponry, and strategic projects languish for decades,

all this to cover for systemic indifference and scams. Unlike other governments, here there is no special provision to meet military necessities through special provisions which may not always – actually more often than not – be according to routine – barring certain recent exceptions. As for internal squabbling among the services, the regressive attitude against the Integrated Defence Staff and the still floundering Andaman & Nicobar Command, usurpation of Unmanned Aerial Vehicles by the Artillery, attack helicopters by the Air Force, and IW by the Signal Corps, even the indifference over close air support to ground forces are some examples. Jointness and integration would keep such attitudes in control, and take these in stride.

(5) Mastering the sciences of near-perfect handling of highly sophisticated weaponry and equipment and then artfully applying the capabilities of these in equally challenging terrain and tactical configurations are imperatives of engaging in military operations. Such acumen requires lifelong training, experimentations and practice to develop. Development of equally demanding joint operational expertise that would survive the vagaries and exertions of war therefore becomes an additional venture. Meeting these contradictory criteria calls for certain deliberately devised compromises from all round perfection among the personnel. Experience shows that it is not a tall order to achieve, but it needs to be taken cognisance of and planned for.

(6) Modern expertise needed in formation headquarters and even in units relate to harness of Geo-Spatial Information Systems (GIS), comprehensive administration of cantonments, finer aspects of financial planning etc. Requirement of additional expert staff may partially be met through automation, but that still leaves the need for creation of new branches or cells for high-skill harness of modern wherewithal of war. As for the distorted notion of 'tail cutting', some of the past examples of short-sightedness was the downsizing of the personnel strength of Ordnance Corps which led to combat units having to divert fighting troops to run forward ammunition supply chain, reductions in Electronic and Mechanical Engineers which led to long queues for overhaul of tanks, guns and vehicles thus causing loss of service life of costly and imported stocks, and disband of Pioneer and Animal Transport units which had to be re-raised after the Kargil War.

(7) For example, a corps headquarters may have in its 'G', 'A' and 'Q' staff, appropriate representation of air force or navy officers and men. Creation of distinct naval and air branches of appropriate construct would be a natural corollary that would bring far-reaching operational and logistic empowerment at the corps level. Similar modifications, as appropriate, may be considered in formation headquarters of all the three services.

(8) To illustrate, whereas in the yesteryears, one was a top company commander if he could site his platoon and lead patrols well; today he has to be equally good in leading his men through different hues of sub-conventional warfare, besides having reckonable understanding of administrative, legal and civic affairs. This is a tall demand on young military leaders. Conversely, the imperative of sustained skill-acquisition and grooming in leadership attributes stand increasingly undermined

over the past three decades, what with shortage of officers, absence of mentors, tight training schedules, short tenures of appointment and the ever-increasing burden of administrative commitments that bring along a mountain of paper-work. Indeed, it is quite usual to find sub-unit commanders just about superfluously familiar with the weapons and other war-like assets placed under their command. Unit commanders – the steel frame of military structure – are only a shade more accomplished, while staff in headquarters is nonplussed when confronted by finer nuances of operational, logistic and internal administrative management, thus creating 'fire-fight' out of even routine functions. Inadequate exposure to the hoary charters for each duty thus chokes opportunities to commit mistakes and learn, and consolidate the acumen of command and staff responsibilities with the warrior's attitude. Jointness therefore also calls for a restitution of carefully crafted regimen of general, specialist and joint operational training.

(9) Major Powers, who have opted to scale down their politico-military goals, are: Britain (acceptance of supporting role to US, UN and NATO so as to reduce military expenditure), France and Germany (scaling down the level of military preparedness in favour of long mobilisation time) and China (freezing attempts to 'liberate' Taiwan by force). Notably, these nations had the option to do so – India, incessantly targeted, may have that luxury only in exception to her current national and international posture.

*

CHAPTER 9

NETWORK CENTRIC WARFARE

"No army of fifty years ago before the date selected would stand a dog's chance against the army existing at that date."

– **Major General JFC Fuller**

Defining Network-Centric Warfare (NCW)

The technology revolution of the current era has brought about many defining developments in the sphere of military science. 'Network-centricity' is one such development in the sphere of military technology. 'Network-centricity' is actually an overarching system made up of many specifically customised systems, significance of the whole lying in its superior properties of marshalling and synergising the application as well as the effects of all those diverse but equally salient elements of combat, combat support and logistic forces that go to constitute an operationally integrated military force. Synergic effects of NCW finally translates into optimal integration of the performance of weapons, equipment and personnel with the military units, combat formations, and support, reserve and logistic echelons to the near-perfect exploitation of each of their design capabilities and so achieve a near-perfect matrix of force-effectiveness. This effect is achieved by way of marshalling diverse and dispersed elements of warfare to converge their focus at the point of interest, maximising their capabilities and accuracy, and minimising response time, idling of assets and redundancy. NCW is therefore a tool of warfare which permits near-seamless and quick-time convergence of the capabilities of all the relevant elements of warfare, multiplies the conjoined force-effectiveness and thus empowers the military forces to achieve optimal synergy in prosecution of precise and predominant operations.

In this chapter, first the generic nuances of NCW would be touched upon before proceeding to examine its various aspects in relation to the Indian military institution.

Remarkable Prospects of NCW

A simple illustration of the properties of NCW is offered by an Unmanned Aerial Vehicle picking up a potential enemy target, say a groups of regulars and terrorists moving towards the Line of Control to infiltrate into own territory. Well-designed network-centricity could then transmit the description, location, movement and all such necessary data to the control room in near-real time, identify the nearest troops and weaponry available within range to engage the groups thus facilitating the command and control headquarters to exercise its options, transmit executive instructions, navigate the troops, guide with precision the long range stand-off weapons, and finally display the visual results of the engagement. In another illustrative situation, aerial sensors pick up enemy formation's movement, thus enabling the command and control headquarters to adjust its defensive and offensive deployment of forces, engage the enemy at successive stages of its movement with precision fire from integral as well all those additional weaponry which might be found within range, alert the flanking formations and feed the progress to superior headquarters for it to react as necessary – all these in near-real time. Meanwhile, the enemy's follow-up and logistic echelons are 'fixed' by the higher headquarters and the 'sensor-shooter loop' is activated to wring destruction with just few precision guided bombs. In another section of the headquarters, a group of technical experts would have by now deceived the enemy regarding approach of a 'virtual' counter-force or existence of a non-existent mine field. A third illustration could exemplify a rifle section fighting to clear a section of urban area. The commander presses a few buttons on a key-board strapped to his forearm to focus on his helmet head-up display to observe the street ahead that is obscured to him by buildings but visible to an aircraft or a satellite, and surveys the location of opponents. He then warns his scouts and adopts the best formation to outwit the opponents. If necessary, he may call for all or any available fire support from ground or air in quick time and with lethal precision, while directing each soldier as what he needs to do on minute to minute basis.

Network-centricity turns such imaginations into realty. The pictures may be replicated in any terrain, day or night. Of course, the enemy too will do the same and that will have to be countered and counter-countered. Nevertheless, NCW is a concept which quickly and accurately integrates all relevant operational assets – through an efficient network of sensors, navigation systems, vertically and horizontally spread high-capacity data-communication links and artificial intelligence processors – to assist in logical decision making under the fog of war in a manner that leads to the achievement of tactical objectives with least of difficulties and destruction. To elucidate further, net-centricity of the war machine is brought about by the conjoined function of transmission networks, processing hardware and skilled personnel to process and exchange intelligence, command and control, and logistic data through dedicated hubs, nodes, networks and links, and integrating all these into one 'system of systems' that may be accessed at even the lowest fighting, supporting and logistic echelons. Obviously, the side that mixes its tactical wit with technical skills better will win the day. Therefore, right grounding of the military leadership in science education becomes mandatory to garner real benefits from this new tool of warfare.

Basic Features of Network-Centricity

While it is not the intent to delve into the details of network-centricity in just one chapter of this book, it would still be appropriate to touch upon its basic activities to progress the discussion on its organisational aspects. Accordingly, the basic functions of networked 'system of systems' may be summarised as follows:

a) Access to the object of information may be accomplished both in static mode – such as surveillance radars, geo-synchronous satellites, laser designators, aerostats, human observers and 'moles' – or in manoeuvrable format – such as orbital satellites, air craft based radars, unmanned aerial vehicles, balloons, reconnaissance radars, intelligence teams and agents. Basic or primary information pertaining to static attributes like terrain, weapon and equipment characteristics, organisation etc. is made use of in gaining that access.
b) Having gained access to the objects of information, the next step is to register the signatures emitted by these objects. The system of collection of information related to the areas and objects of interest is operated by means of arrays of suitably focused sensors. These sensors are deployed in multi-dimensional mode – under or over

ground and in sea, aerial and space modes – and work on various scientific laws like radiation – optical, infra-red, thermal, etc. – acoustic and seismic waves, for example. To retain focus, sensors are articulated remotely and redeployed as necessary. Registration of the input signatures is carried out in digital rather than analogue mode for ease of processing these into 'information'.

c) At this stage, the information accessed and registered is in raw form, besides being burdened with unnecessary details. These have to be transmitted to be filtered, collated and analysed to cull out the relevant intelligence. Thus transmitted to NCW nodes, auto-process units carryout programmed filtration of unnecessary 'noise' from the inputs, before subjecting the data to formatting, collation, assessment and evaluation of logical response measures. Here again, the pre-loaded bank of primary information comes into play in combining with the information collected and so shaping the collated information into actionable intelligence. Finally, the processing units are programmed with tactically construed algorithms to apply the gained intelligence in supporting informed decision-making.

d) The next step is the dissemination of the intelligence as well as command and control instructions to the intended recipients by means of transmission links. In execution of the task, this step may be followed up with navigational assistance, precision weapon guidance, selection and engagement of targets, and finally, assessment of effect.

A common impression that net-centricity is all about transfer of data signals of various operational content through a mix of state-of–the-art electronic and electro-magnetic media is only partially true. Apart from high capacity, high speed and wider connectivity through vertical as well as horizontal media communication grid, the cause of net-centricity must be served by its equally salient platforms, viz., digitised data bank, collector sensors, data converters, processors for intelligent computation and input filters, all these managed by cadres of tactical and technical specialists, and regulated by logical protocols and procedures. Each of these assets have their own attributes and therefore have to be specifically designed, designated, authenticated and finally construed for a net-centric force to have good prospects of getting better of an adversary in the field of battle.

Digitisation, Sensing and Communicating

Digitisation of data, and programmes to manipulate these for use, are imperative for the system of net-centricity to proceed beyond the drawing board. This is a process of recording inputs from the external and internal sources in electronically digitised from and format into digitised data or information banks, such data lending itself to mathematical manipulations and reformatting according to the operational requirements. Digitisation therefore is fundamental to the conduct of NCW by the means C4I2SR systems.

To elaborate further, one category of inputs involves digital conversion of basic attributes pertaining to the terrain, weapon, equipment, personnel and other war-like assets – 'primary' digitisation, so to say. This primary data is to be complemented by 'secondary' digitisation which pertain specifically to each of the user services and the arms within these services and involve creation of their dedicated libraries of tactical, technical, management and decision support information. Digitised data bank is thus created by feeding primary as well as various services and arm specific secondary information into the system. Obviously, the process of primary as well as secondary digitisation is an extremely laborious undertaking that requires sustained engagement in field work – over many years – to acquire, update and authenticate the items of information.

The second category of inputs pertains to characteristics of tactically significant objects at a point of time. These have to be digitally recorded in real time from dynamic signatures emitted by enemy's or own activities in the war zone. The recording is executed through suitably positioned collectors or sensors of various working principles to gain the advantages of wide coverage, near-perfect accuracy, high resolution and near real-time transmission. Of course, raw signatures have to be converted to a standard format before analysis. Marshalling of elaborate digitised data banks, high-technology sensing hardware and robust communication media are the issues to be settled before a true regime of NCW may come to fruition.

Network-Centric System Architecture

To meet the purposes of NCW by the harness the C4I2SR capabilities, network-centric systems adopt suitably customised architecture which may be designed and modified as necessary according to theatre, campaign, or even force specific requirements. Modern technology enables the networks so architected to be operated through grids of 'control stations', 'hubs', 'nodes' and 'entities', all of which may be integrated into one wholesome system across the entire war zone, and so enables access to heretofore inaccessible objects therein, register relevant information, synthesise and disseminate these in near-real time. The main components of such architecture may be, for management purposes, grouped under the following categories:

a) Extensive digitised data bank or information library to store properties, attributes and specifications of the objects of relevance, such as terrain, communications, weapon systems, tactical and logistics management, personnel and so on, both in respect of own as well as adversarial forces. These elaborate digitised data banks of pre-set information are to be matched and meshed with the currently collected information and manipulated in the desired manner by pre-designed software programmes to paint the latest intelligence picture, the programmes being customised according to user-interests.
b) Variety of hardware to search, access, sense and register information of tactical relevance in digitised form – arrays of vehicles, sensors, switches, routers, transmission media, processors etc. These high-technology hardware are tactically deployed all across the front and depth areas of the war zone in static or moving mode, in one or more dimensions, and inter-connected with secure, high-speed, high-capacity data-communication linkages. The hardware requires expertise in design and manufacturing technology, specific skills to operate and maintain, and high investments in periodic upgrades.
c) Specifically designed and secured software, developed in-house to suit indigenous characteristics, and conjointly validated by composite teams of tactical and technical experts to cater for all conditionality's of war. These software programmes are to be run through the processing hardware to convert the inputs into actionable intelligence, in formats desired. The point to note is that the software are but the translation of tactical requirements into mathematical algorithm, aimed at drawing tactical inferences from real-time collected intelligence and so provide for the decision support system.
d) Grids of communication networks to connect the sensors, processors, command and control set up, and the forces consisting of troops and weapon systems, for the purposes of dissemination of intelligence, command and control instructions, monitoring of

planned operations and periodic report and feedback.

e) System management through groups of technicians, operators, system auditors and maintenance and repair crew, with each individual trained in specific fields of expertise.

The point to note is that the tactical decisions regarding areas of search, timings, objects of interest and informational queries continue to remain in the realm of military art – technology is therefore best harnessed by the elevation of military acumen. Further, for the configuration to function as a complete tactical tool, the entities and nodes are to be spread vertically and horizontally across all echelons of military hierarchy so as to architect a theatre grid of systems and sub-systems. Obviously, there are certain contingencies to be addressed in order to render the configuration fit for war. Some of these concerns are:

a) Ensuring security of the network against physical destruction, intrusion, technical sabotage or subversion through embedded programmes – the last named is most serious when the system components are not all indigenous.
b) Notwithstanding smug claims, automated networks of hardware and software are prone to frequent corruption which are tedious to locate and repair, thereby causing situations of utter helplessness. Many times, algorithmic faults remain unnoticed while continuing to generate corrupted outputs till something goes horribly wrong. These situations could lead to tactical disasters like fratricide, accidents, collateral damage and political mess up. In short, automated networks can create such adverse situations which even the enemy may not, and therefore the initial design has to be robust and emergency response mechanisms have to be in place. That entails placement of a fairly large complement of dedicated staff and specialist technicians to work on various aspects of the system on regular basis.
c) Another contingency in network-centricity is the possibility of infusing distraction among subordinate commanders over orders passed and objectives assigned which might be caused due to their access to vast array of hazy inputs coming from multiple sources. Senior commanders and higher staff, on the other hand, tend to usurp the intermediate commanders and pass direct orders to lower commanders even when their perceptions may be divorced from the realities on ground. Thus, the system creates its own version of

tactical dilemma. Further, war-fighting being an exacting and many times a dirty business, access to net-communication results in spread of potentially harmful perceptions thorough the media, thereby causing potentially distracting pressure from higher commanders, politicians and relatives. Therefore, a well-considered policy of access control and authorisation, so as to avoid, firstly, overload of unintended inputs, and secondly, dissemination of contradictory instructions to the intended and unintended recipients, is a necessity for effective network-centricity.

d) IT enabled network systems are cost-intensive and subject to frequent upgrades. Besides, the entire military network has to be maintained at full scale and latest generation of technology; phased installation or upgrades will lead to serious functional breakdowns. Consequently, the fiscal burden of maintaining the networks operational would be recurring. Financial managers will have to be sensitised of this matter.

e) Lastly, the inherent dynamics of a network-centric military organisation would translate into emergence of interest groups of technical personnel, vendors and developers. There would be perpetual migrations and rivalries among them which might lead to trade-war, security leaks and even monopolist dependency of the forces. Further, with the commanders and staff becoming utterly dependent upon technological tools, technical personnel will seek equality, even precedence, over the generalists, as it has happened in the civil sector.

These are the challenges of network-centricity which have to be addressed in the cognitive domain, for it to play its true transformational role in prosecution of warfare.

Operational Hierarchy for NCW

As in case of traditional methods of command, control, exchange of intelligence and execution of battle plans, NCW too requires to be conducted according to a set of hierarchies, branches and subscribers amongst the headquarters, forces, formations and units who are duly networked according to their roles and responsibilities. However, since net-centricity offers wider coverage, higher volume and quicker exchange while having to remain within the parameters of pre-determined algorithms, its effective and reliable exploitation is contingent upon building up the right hierarchy for the conduct NCW that would have to be a combination of regular or permanent features at the strategic and operational levels, while at the tactical levels it will have to be flexible enough to respond to the dynamism of situations.

A typical hierarchy for simple order of battle may be illustrated, looking from top down, as follows:

a) At a theatre or campaign level, there could be the integrated Network-Centric Warfare Command Centre (NCWCC) to perform the overall strategic and operational functions of C4I2SR.
b) The second tier of hierarchy at the operational level may be made up of 'command and control hubs' where of converge the networks which perform the operational functions of command, control, intelligence and logistics. To assist in decision making, this tier of hierarchy may also have ready access to those 'task-specific hubs' which control the networks dedicated to surveillance, fire support, electronic warfare, movement control, mine warfare, nuclear warfare, inventory management etc.
c) To obviate over-crowding and yet leave open the choice of access across the standard hierarchies, networks at the third tier could be role-specific. It could consist of varying numbers of networks that are specified to serve various role-specific units within a field formation, fire power units for example. In this, network-centric synergy may be furthered by extending such networks to similar role-specific units in flanks and rear as well. For example, networks dedicated to fire power within a formation could connect various inter-formation fire support assets like air, field and medium artillery, multi-barrel launchers and missiles, as well as those ancillary elements that serve the purpose of acquisition, analysis, designation and damage assessment of targets. Similar provisions may be extended to intelligence, obstacle, missile, electronic warfare, and logistic functions.

There is really nothing new to NCW; when amalgamated into one whole, these hubs, networks and nets coalesce to conform to the eternal modes of controlling battles. What really makes difference in the contemporary era is that data input collection, processing and transfer functions across the top to bottom as well as horizontal hierarchies are executed over larger areas, in faster time frame, in comprehensive details and with near-perfect accuracy, to be delivered in near-real time to longer list of force-elements. But more than that, true benefits of effective system design and architecture for network-centricity, according to General James Mattis, motivates "commander's thinking, foresight, instinct, experience and visualisation in identifying the true nature of a complex problem and devising an approach to subsequent planning and execution".

Thus having discussed the generic parameters of NCW, let us proceed to its application in the Indian military institution.

NCW in Indian Context

For the Indian military institution, network-centricity is not an option, but an intrinsic feature of military modernisation. Indeed, the Indian military had responded to the concept of NCW as early as the 1990's and has since then made considerable efforts to develop capabilities for access and sensing of wide variety of tactically relevant information, build up elaborate user-specific digitised data banks and cover operational areas with robust communication networks. There are studies carried out, goals set, resources committed, projects undertaken and military exercises conducted under the unique parameters of NCW. Much efforts have also been made to foster the entire process of automation into the operational, logistic and management functions. All the three services have undertaken many path breaking projects to promote automation and network-centricity in the fields of what are commonly referred to under the sobriquet of C4I2SR, besides creating dedicated appendages for war gaming, targeting, fire control, tracing and tracking of movements, warning and evasive measures against attack, camouflage and concealment, training and education, interlinking of logistic inputs and personnel management. In practice however, the stage when substantial advantages of harness of network-centricity may be earned with due certainty and under conditions of war, remains far away yet.

Fundamental reasons for such stagnation are the dearth of scientific temper and understanding among the military leadership, which makes them reluctant and resistant to accommodate technical expertise. Besides, strict intra as well as inter-services compartmentalisation of activities, primacy accorded to their autonomous interests and personnel policies that stifle the build-up of high-technical expertise and long experience are the other reasons that prevent growth and proliferation of network-centricity. As a result, while small pockets of stand-alone expertise – but not excellence – have developed, inter-linking, and when necessary integration, of NCW and a modern force-structure is yet to make mark in real sense. Thus notwithstanding the farsighted initiatives undertaken since the past quarter of century or so, the progress on achievement of network-centricity has seen more 'fits' than 'starts'. Resultantly, in its present state, the practice of NCW within the Indian military institution remains confined to contrived and demonstrative presentations and exercises.

The difficulties to be overcome in accelerating the process of assimilation of this modern tool of war may be elaborated by the following regressive conditions:

a) Most of the aspiring practitioners of NCW have neither had the opportunity to delve deep into its technical nuances, nor have they had the benefits of actually operating, assimilating and exploiting its core elements: assimilation of huge volumes of reliable information, process of comprehensive digitisation and operation of network-centric systems. In the former case, there is no relief from the burden of routine work to devote to new learning and experimentation, while in the second instance, there are not enough systems to work upon under realistic conditions. Therefore, technical competence among most such practitioners being but superficial, the question of operational exploitation of NCW remains hazy and distant.
b) Modernisation of the war machine and its articulation through NCW enabled 'system of systems' is contingent upon a good grounding in technical training, ready accessibility to the systems and devolution of control down to the lower rungs of the hierarchy. Such a dispensation has already pervaded the entire civil sector, public as well as private, including the traditionally fixated government machinery. Paradoxically however, in the Indian armed forces – particularly within the Army and at the inter-services level – the enabling features of NCW remain somewhat afflicted with fiscal limitations, archaic procedures, orthodox instincts and mental inertia.
c) NCW is best prosecuted with indigenously designed equipment, when the operative 'keys' and 'codes' remain classified. Unfortunately, defence research as well as the IT industry in India is yet to girdle up to produce indigenously military-customised sensors, data processing hardware, reliable software, data transmission switches, etc. Government's past policies too have been dismissive of the indigenous defence industry, which not only

prevented its development, it even sabotaged joint ventures. Availability of wherewithal of NCW is therefore limited and unreliable, import dependency adding to its vulnerability to security breach.

d) By far the most debilitating slippage of the military hierarchy has been in its neglect of building-up the digitised data-base. Just as it would be foolish to fight a war without maps or range and equipment tables, prosecution of NCW cannot even be conceived unless there is readily accessible 'data-bank' of terrain, weapon and equipment attributes in digitised form and in user-specified algorithms and formats. It would take many decades of concerted hard work by dedicated 'digitisation teams' to accomplish that stupendous task – that of creating a comprehensive and user designated digitised information data-bank. Till then, network-centricity in Indian forces may remain but a partially met aspiration, mostly limited to set-piece data and designated systems which demonstrate pre-mediated network-centric solutions, but little more.

e) At the current stage, the media of net-connectivity having been fielded under limited warlike conditions, net-centric functions within the services have proved to be reasonably effective in handling command and control (C2), target acquisition, fire control, voice communications and routine data transfer traffic. Thankfully, unlike the case of digitisation and development of sensing and processing equipment, defence planners have accorded sufficient thrust to the build-up of robust data transfer and communication network. However, to cater to situations when concurrent networks – such as wide area surveillance and reconnaissance network, intelligence network, target acquisition, designation and engagement loop, logistic net etc. – have to be activated simultaneously in tri-service dispensation, and under full warlike conditions, the current construct of net-connectivity would need to be substantially upgraded if it is to inspire the requisite degree of confidence.

To summarise, development of network-centricity so far falls short of a fully compatible, seamless, real-time or robust 'system of systems' for it to function under war-like strain. This state is exemplified by the absence of a truly comprehensive digitised geo-spatial information data bank to support all such systems, and consequently, limited exploitation of the artillery command and control, air defence control and reporting, battle field surveillance and unmanned aerial vehicle systems, to wit. Above all, officers and men have to have good science educational background and adequate on-hand exposure so that the executive level personnel have wider opportunities to learn, assimilate, think and harness the advantages that these features might offer. Only then would the nation's warriors would be able to exercise their first hand initiative and experience to apply the properties of NCW in winning wars.

For the C4I2SR systems to offer reckonable advantages in conduct of warfare, and true network-centricity to stand the test of war, the aforesaid challenges have to be addressed comprehensively in the Indian military institution, particularly in the Army and in the inter-services arena.

Fostering a Regime of NCW

Astute exercise of NCW in Indian context requires its concept and practices to be defined according to the native conditions, institutional understandings and the desired purpose. As discussed, network-centricity of a war-machine is but the articulation of hi-technology sensors, processing hardware of varying but mutually complimentary designs, custom-made algorithms and software, and robust communication linkages. Herein, the challenge lies in designing an organisational structure and finding personnel to operate the systems efficiently. This is so because the concept of network-centricity demands profound re-orientation of the prevalent theories and practices of command, control and staff work, and therefore enjoins the military hierarchy to assimilate new intricacies of organising and directing future operations, much to the divergence from their past training and experiences. Given the human instinct of resistance towards such drastic changes, particularly when it upsets the existing pecking order, that is no doubt an uphill task. Therefore to negotiate through such a profound organisational reorientation, there are cultural dispensations to be nurtured.

Firstly, military institutions are made up of professionals who interact through structured hierarchies to move towards the overall organisational goal. To that extent, military organisations possess distinct summation of collective character and a functional dynamics which exercise latent influence over the manner it performs. Therefore, organisational culture required of network-centric forces would invariably have to be revised against the traditional personnel and weapon centric chains and linkages of command, control and execution. Further, as NCW would entail activation of new elements of command and control – that is, hardware, software and data linkage – such technology-intensive elements have to be integrated into the ladder of military leadership in order to produce the expected results in war. It is this assimilation of integrated 'art' and 'science' of warfare that is most difficult to instil in a regimented set up that is brought up in 'non-science' education, given the fact that it would entail profound revision of the initial training curricula, service profiling, specialisation training and the existing equation between tactical commanders, the general staff and the technical advisors.

Secondly, institutionalisation of network-centricity has to be within the overall ambit of military modernisation which in turn would require high investments, higher design and engineering capabilities and even higher degree of the government's ready commitment. Given that there prevails a situation wherein even routine maintenance and upgrades of weapons and equipment take years to be cleared; and even when cleared, schemes take decades to fructify, the government's commitment to overall military modernisation would need to be vitalised. Indeed, the NCW regime will have to be backed up with political resolute and steered by zealous military professionals. Unless that is done, the kind of network-centricity that would finally be dispensed with might turn out to be quite different from what might have been intended in the first place (1).

Finally, in articulating network-centric processes, the military institution itself must be serious in appreciating the concept of 'errors of war', and not fall prey to the enthusiastic pre-supposition that plans would get smoothly implemented and systems would function unhindered by the enemy or technological limits, as it is usually evident in the manner field-exercises are conducted, projects are estimated and forces are assigned to task. Indeed, there are many pitfalls in perfect matching of definite technical algorithms with indefinite tactical situations, and that makes the network-centric processes prone to corruption and even failure, particularly because each of the components and steps are equally vital – failure of one is enough to trigger all round collapse. Military leadership would therefore have to be conscious of the fact that tactics, training, equipment and deployment under conditions of network-centricity have to be validated and re-tested under true conditions of unpredictability, friction and fog of war.

Properties of Indigenous NCW Architecture

Taking off from the preceding general discussion on components, systems and operational architecture for the conduct of NCW, it would be appropriate at this stage to propel the promise of network-centricity in the Indian military institution forward. To this purpose, the defining properties of an indigenous version of NCW architecture could be spelt out as elaborated in the succeeding paragraphs.

Network Architecture

A fairly comprehensive architecture for NCW with its defined vertical tiers and horizontal entities that are secure in terms of user authentication and access, and maintained by competent service support, has been build up by the efforts of the Corps of Signals and backed up, albeit tentatively, from the General Staff. The architecture is fairly advanced in terms of reliability and user confidence, and is duly controlled by empowered decision makers. As for its further development, the requirements are as follows:

a) Dedicated staff to manage and maintain the system in quick-time.
b) Extension of connectivity and control across intra and inter-service domain.
c) The present focus on routine and administrative functions of networks needs to be extended to regular tactical exploitation. For this, the range and depth of possible tactical and logistic queries needs to be met by build-up of primary and secondary digitised information data banks.
d) Incongruent procedures have to be streamlined to avoid duplication or overload of irrelevant inputs. This measure is necessary to prevent the inputs being turned into unintended interpretations, and thus causing ambiguities, direct interference of higher commanders and misplaced initiative of subordinates.
e) Need for ready back up; even the most robust systems are liable to failure.

Software

The state of development of basic, primary and secondary software that is customised to military application remains tenuous yet – as it is evidenced from the stagnation in various C4I2SR projects. Given the indigenous expertise at hand, it should be possible to develop military-conditioned software from the first principles by the integration of indigenous tactical and mathematical genius. Reliable network-centricity and digital operation may then be achieved without having to depend upon purchase of readymade, commercial, and therefore constrained, software. Lastly, just as fast paced development of increasingly powerful software requires an agency to be permanently dedicated to its update, there is also the need to institute flexible options to hire and release experts according to their usefulness from time to time (2).

Hardware

The Indian industry – defence or civil – has little to show for manufacturing capability in IT hardware. Data processors, converters, switches, gates, sensors, filters, intelligence processors etc. for military use therefore come from foreign commercial design and construction – mainly from China. This problem is exacerbated by the dependency on foreign based pre-determined algorithms, procedures and protocols with which the media for military transmission is conducted. Management of NCW hardware had also been a victim of competitive business practices of 'hard sell' of what appeared to the uninitiated military buyers as demonstrative, titillating gizmos. This had led to diversity of hardware designs among the services, arms, and branches which the conversion programmes might not fully resolve. Lastly, there is the problem of fast pace of obsolescence and the consequent high costs which our archaic system of upgrades is unable to reconcile to. With experience of hardware commerce, software development and satellite technology gained over the years, and boosted by the idea of 'Make in India', these debilities would hopefully be overcome soon.

Data Library

Operational empowerment in NCW is sustained by the system's ability to answer to unlimited range of intelligence, tactical, logistic and personnel queries, in real-time, in desired format and in perfect consistency. To be able to meet that demand, vast ranges of primary, secondary and tertiary information regarding an extensive spread and depth of objects of military interest and their attributes are required to be collected, vetted, indexed and stored through a continuous process of data mining, acquisition, update and validation. To make difference, the quality and coverage of the data library must also enjoy the unquestioned confidence of commanders and staff.

Measures Towards Network-Centricity

Presently, while the scope of net-centricity covers the field of communications and some bits of data processing, the overall NCW capability of the military institution remains confined to the realm of pre-specified operational situations in which the field formations may operate against pre-determined tactical objectives, but little more. It may therefore be in order to see as to what might help the military institution align itself for digital combat better.

To reiterate, net-centricity in the Indian military institution is effective only in patches due to inadequacies of digitised data bank, sensing hardware, optimally structured control 'hubs' and NCWCC, and rigid functional protocols within the services as well as in the joint-services mode. The inadequacy also lies in the fundamentals of net-centricity – that is, limited training and manning, partial integration of networks, inadequate hardware and narrow field of operational applications – which remain somewhat tentatively attended to. While signal communication network and its related training, experimentation and upgrade proceed well, research and development of battle worthy net-centricity equipment of indigenous algorithm have not really broken ground. More seriously, the very foundation of net-centricity – that is the build-up of military geo-spatial data bank (both primary and secondary) – remains but nascent. Lastly, as for the governing rules and regulations for specialisation of personnel and modernisation of equipment, there are much improvements to be brought about before full benefits of network-centricity are gained.

Considering the stupendous effort and time that it takes to prepare battle worthy information bank, the immediate step is to accord top priority to build up 'basic' or 'primary' as well as services and arm specific 'secondary' information data base in digitised format. In this, terrain Geo-Spatial Information System (GIS) – the fundamental plank of NCW – deserves to be accorded the prime attention. Build-up of terrain, sub-terranean and tropospheric GIS being a highly specialised field, strengthening the military survey and hydrograph units and equipping these with full range of wherewithal for recording of ground and water terrain information need to be considered, as indeed most advanced militaries have already done; some have even opted to field a mix of regular survey units and contracted vendors after due training and certification for security. To complement the build-up of the primary terrain GIS, each service and its arms and branches have to set time-lines to digitise the entire range of secondary information data that might pertain to their individual operational roles and specific queries related to the performance of these. In this manner, over a specified time, it would be possible to build up a comprehensive secondary data bank that is geared, in conjunction with the primary one, to respond to most tactical and technical queries.

Taking advantage of India's achievements in information, electronic and space technology, the second measure would be to shake the indigenous industry into developing a range of futuristic data sensing equipment, switches, routers, converters and the related paraphernalia, each customised to native conditions and programmed to function with home grown algorithm. Meanwhile, sufficient inventory of net-centricity specific equipment to equip the nominated 'test bed' field formations need to be acquired. Rather than expecting the existing staff, engaged as these are in routine matters, dedicated manpower would have to be placed to operate these equipment and experiment with these for assimilation of C4I2SR assets into the formation's NCW endeavours. Thus at least two mutually competing 'test bed formations', with full complement of headquarters and subordinate units, should be constituted to apply the theories of network-centricity and formalise appropriate functional protocols and practices. These could be structured in the manner of standard 'brigades', but staffed and equipped in conformity to modern standards. Dedicated connectivity highway and well trained staff should be specifically assigned to these formations, for them to engage in experimenting with net-centricity to start with, then generate interest in it, and follow up by experimentation and trials.

Astute management and regular maintenance of the C4I2SR systems are of paramount importance in fostering a reliable and responsive regime of NCW. Regular technology update and modernisation, ready availability of full range of ancillaries, competent maintenance and repair, validation for security and accuracy, and finally, regular training are the imperatives to insure against failure, corruption or security breach of the systems. Notably, these measures leads to cost-intensiveness of the NCW systems and since there cannot be any 'down time' in such systems, assured fund-flow is a core necessity.

To state the obvious, the terms and implications of 'Digitised Battle Field', 'Digitised Army', 'Network-Centric War', even the Chinese doctrine of 'Warfare under conditions of Informalisation', all imply the exercise of traditional art of orchestration of military forces in warfare, but with the added advantages of access to contemporary technology to gain vastly superior abilities in generating intelligence, exercise of command and control, exchange of near-real time information and feedback. However, for true benefits of the recourse to advanced technology to accrue in warfare, it would be imperative to foster certain cognitive reorientation in the functioning of the military institution. This aspect must therefore be discussed before closing this Chapter, the terms of references being, one, modernisation of the Indian military institution is a national cause, and second, network-centricity is a founding pillar of such modernisation.

Network-Centricity and Modernisation

Network-centricity calls for sweeping revisions in the manner of engaging in warfare. As a corollary, it requires restructuring of the fighting, supporting and logistic elements, which in turn necessitates application of across-the-board reforms in the management of the entire military institution. Network-centricity is therefore just one of the many components of equal salience all of which must function in synergy to bring about a native version of RMA-induced modernisation of the military structure, and consequently, achieve optimisation of national defence capabilities. These reforms have to cover the aspects of induction, training, scaling and administering military men and material, so to enable the entire war-fighting machine to remain upfront with the extensive range and scorching pace of tactical and technological developments. Indeed, net-centricity necessitates inclusive modernisation among the services, and the arms and services within each, to be level in terms of quality of training, equipment, procedures and practices. When so modernised in tune with combat role, it will be possible for each element of combat to integrate, in modular form, with task specific battle formations, and when necessary, detach to redeploy without misbalancing the order of battle.

That ordains the strategic community to push the process of full range military modernisation. The military hierarchy may do so within their own sphere of control while propagating the cause at the political level. Indeed, such efforts must manifest in comprehensive modernisation of the nation's military institution – much to the nation's benefit.

The Art and Science of Warfare

In the past, conduct of military operations was considered to be an inborn 'art' – indeed, it still is. Articulation of this art was entrusted to commanders and staff who leveraged their innate competence in leadership and tactics with due grounding in science of warfare to gain combat experience over the years spent in service. A major shift in the conceptual proportionality between the 'art' and 'science' of war however emerged in the post-industrial revolution era. Arguably, with the onset of IT revolution, that shift has further tilted towards competency in science education. Gradually a state has come today when even mundane activities in spheres military operations, logistics and administration have become captive to science and technology to an extent that even slightest breach of access to the tools of contemporary IT, would cause military organisations to be reduced to a state of utter haplessness. Warfare today, therefore, is a '50-50' affair, with techno-savvy tacticians and tactics-savvy technicians jointly bearing the cross of integration, orchestration and synchronisation of all C4I2SR capabilities – as propagated by the concept of 'team warfare'.

The Indian military institution however has been reluctant on building a leadership that is grounded in fundamentals of scientific temper and so is capable of the best exploitation of technology. While the Navy has corrected that deficiency and the Air Force has somewhat done so, the Army hierarchy, barring exceptions, remains but superficially trained in technical knowledge and skills, and it still carries on with what is termed as 'non-science' stream of curricula to recruit and train new generation of officers and men. The awareness gap is further accentuated by denial of opportunities for the officer corps to interact with advanced armies through foreign courses and exchange visits, and thus learn from their practical experiences in network-centricity – unlike China or Pakistan, such interaction are a rarity for the Indian officer corps. The deficiency is then sought to be addressed by putting them through short courses of instructions during which they are trained in the nuances of IT by rote and then left to use their shallow knowledge in planning and conducting military affairs as best as they can.

Thus, bereft of deeper understanding of the governing laws of network-centricity, the military leadership remain captive to technical personnel to design and operate network systems, even if these technicians may be unfamiliar with the range of tactical compulsions which would, as a rule, emerge under war-like conditions. As a corollary, superficial scientific knowledge among the commanders and staff permits under-performance from the technical personnel who remain unchallenged in devising innovations and alternatives in support of tactical requirements. There is therefore little to wonder as to why the Indian military C4I2SR schemes remain just about partially effective and fail to inspire confidence among field commanders and staff. Thus even after decades of time and loads of funds committed, effectiveness of IT enabled network systems remain stymied – good just for exchange of data or documents, presentations and occasional video-conferences of sundry import.

Harness of true benefits of network-centricity and NCW is contingent upon discard of fixation over 'non-science' education and training, and development of scientific temper and technology orientation among all ranks of the military institution. Even if the commanders and staff may not become mathematicians and physicists, their discomfiture over pure sciences and frontier technology must be overcome by requisite level of science education. Only then would they be able to choose between amusing demonstrations of IT-enabled gizmos from the real ones that would be workable in war, and tell between the competent developers-vendors and the glib imposters. Obviously, this initiative would entail careful selection of merit-based technocrat military leaders and advisors, not necessarily based on seniority.

Hierarchical Reorientation

Apart from near-absence of composite teams of techno-savvy tacticians and tactical-savvy technicians to run a network-centric military institution, policy-makers also have to think of cognitive reorientation of the military hierarchical attitude towards technical specialists and their expertise so as to be in tune with the regime of network-centricity. First of all, professional interaction cutting across the barrier of the rank structure has to be accepted. It needs to be appreciated that the 'boss need not always know the best'. Authority of subordinate commanders, staff and experts have to be respected and a regime of collective vetting of decision making fostered, with the overall commander confining himself to final arbitration rather that falling prey to issuance of quick-fire and personalised diktats.

Secondly, the 'generalist' leadership have to admit the technical branch leaders to the 'high-table'; there is no use having IT-enabled systems headed by someone who is untrained in fathoming scientific postulations. Similarly, there is the need to assign due manpower and funds to each service and the various arms within these, in due proportion, to ingrain network-centricity into the military system.

Thirdly, since expertise is gained by continuous exposure, the current personnel management policies in respect of technical cadres would have to be reviewed; testing a system expert or a network specialist in command of a company, to be eligible for promotion, may not be in the organisational interest.

Lastly, hierarchical reorientation to pave the way for emergence of a truly network-centric military institution would require the discard of oft parroted notions which are irrelevant in the contemporary era. It has to be accepted that modernised military institutions require larger but integrated headquarters to administer, strong logistic tails, faster procedures to attend to routine and resolve emerging issues, re-balancing between delegation and centralisation, and finally, liberal authorisations and stringent accountabilities.

The Way to NCW

There was a time when scions of aristocracy were commissioned to lead troops with little formal training, and illiterate men were rounded up to fight for their sovereign – formal training was meant for only the gunners and sappers who stood lower in the pecking order. In later periods, development of military science became a tactical compulsion. Presently, in the days of automation data processing, human brain has to delegate many of its functions to the IT-enabled systems. Consequently, while IT-enabled network-centric systems run by skilled technologists takeover the programmed functions of C4I2SR, military users across the board have to be proficient in optimal exploitation of these systems under the conditions of war. No doubt, in the coming days, technology would influence the conduct of warfare as never before, and therefore should the military institution opts to benefit from the properties of NCW – there is no option actually – profound review of human resources, material and organisational practices will have to be instituted; half measures would not do.

To summarise, development of network-centricity needs to be comprehensive, seamless across the services and their various arms, conducive to real-time response and robust under war-like strain. Only then would accrue the full advantages of developing the various elements of NCW like the artillery command and control, air defence control and reporting, battle field surveillance, and unmanned aerial vehicle systems, and a comprehensive GIS to support all these.

The order is tall. But then the Indian military institution has a tradition of overcoming challenges – it only needs to make up its mind and take the plunge.

END NOTES

(1) Three decades are a long time to make measurable and effective progress in IT, IW and NCW. But the Indian military institution remains more or less way behind in these aspects, notwithstanding its attraction towards dazzling power point

presentations and orchestrated demonstrations of its network-centricity. Besides the lack of understanding of the scientific fundamentals of NCW, the military hierarchy has not been able to rid itself of an archaic system of personnel management wherein trained experts, instead of being continuously engaged in their expertise, have to be transferred to routine work to fulfil the stipulations of 'posting profile'. The development is also stifled by the DRDO' and the industry's stranglehold which permits these to make claims of in-house development – which remain unfulfilled – to block modernisation schemes.

(2) US Department of Defence has government policies to ensure that outsourced companies do not renegade on contracts. Recently, it has revised its personnel management policy to permit recruitment of experts on long term or tenure basis. These steps are conducive to technological forward leap.

*

CHAPTER 10

TRAINING FOR MODERNISATION

> "*War is a contest between human intelligence rather than between bodies of armed men.*"
>
> – **Anon**

Modernisation: The Human Pivot

We are aware that during the last three decades or so, the levers of geo-politics have seen profound realignments, and as its natural corollary, the contemporary modes and objectives of warfare have had to undergo considerable revisions. These revisions are further influenced by far-reaching advancements in military technology, and that combination has brought about revolutionary changes in the manner of prosecuting war. The universal wave of military modernisation is a result of that development.

Military modernisation in the contemporary context signifies, not just the assimilation of high-technology in clinical prosecution of war, but also the emergence of corresponding nuances of force-structuring and innovative strategies of force-application. As however, the military institutions delved into the process of modernisation, it was realised that the prime movers behind its success had to be the quality of personnel, their education and training, and above all their cultural inclinations. In similar vein, India's possession of a modernised and cost-efficient military structure must be contingent upon, firstly, a rank and file wedded to the military culture, and secondly, high professional competence of its officers and men. After all, in the final analysis, the entire gamut of planning, processing, introducing, implementation and course corrections have to be pushed by the military personnel themselves.

It is obvious that modernisation of our military institution can succeed only when military training is rightly oriented towards that end. It is therefore proposed to discuss certain salient parameters of military training that would promote the cause of modernisation of the Indian military institution.

Objectives of Training

Appropriately, a brief recount of the implications of military modernisation may set the stage for discussion on the objectives of training.

One, under the concept of 'soldier as a system', true harness of performance enhancing hardware of war can be accomplished only if every soldier, sailor and airman is able to understand the fundamentals of technologies behind these and so assimilates such skills that would permit him to exploit his weapon and equipment to the extreme under the excruciating conditions of war. Indeed, the days of simpleton soldiery, mechanically executing specific actions in a specified sequence form memory, are over. For modernisation to work, it is imperative to prepare better educated, continuously trained to the purpose, and high initiative individuals, and so equip them to stand up to the challenges of new age soldiering.

Two, modern technology of weaponry and equipment has led to quantum advancements in observation, early warning, night operation, communication, precision fire and mobility capabilities at crew, detachment and sub-unit levels. The resultant complexity is further exacerbated by the pace and tempo at which tactical engagements would be executable in modern battle. With the nuances of seamless execution of tactical drills and battle procedures having to be upgraded thus, matching standards of collective training at sub-unit and unit and levels are also called for.

Three, the enabling features of battle-field awareness, manoeuvre, precision fire power and multi-point engagement in simultaneity have revised the practice of deployment of massed formations in battle in favour of precise manoeuvre of lean battle groups that are duly backed up with 'small team operations'. Thus the span of conventional manoeuvres of war – like defence, attack, patrolling, etc. – have outgrown the past orthodoxy. In the coming days, therefore, formations have to display the requisite flexibility to adapt to frequent changes in composition, disposition, tactics and tempo of engagements, while commanders and staff have to master larger spans of control, exercisable with compact and lethal forces, to achieve faster response to operational situations. Obviously, to conform to these modern substitutions, the parameters of training military leaders at all levels have to be revised.

Four, assimilation of 'network-centricity' into the realm of command and control has overturned the entire process of planning and execution of battles. NCW tends to dismantle narrow, vertical hierarchies while leading to 'information-overflow' in planning and monitoring, and 'time-compression' of operations, implications of which, as it was apparent in recent RMA-influenced wars, are not always desirable. Free flow of real-time information and battle instructions tend to impose dilemma and ambiguity on decision making while accelerated pace of action-reactions are liable to lead to either over or under reaction. Such ambivalences are dangerous in war and need elaborate training to control, if not eliminate altogether.

Five, the spectrum of warfare has widened considerably. Since no nation can afford to have distinct role-specific formations, the modern day soldiery at every level have to be adept at conventional, sub-conventional, irregular, and to a good extent, special and nuclear warfare. With each of these categories of warfare having inherent corollaries and exceptions, a much wider base of professional knowledge and operational acumen is imperative for the officers and other ranks to be able to stand up to their wider charter.

Six, inclusion of anti-terror actions, peace-enforcement, reconstruction and rehabilitation, and disaster relief under the gamut of military operations has led to multiplicity of the mandate of the military forces. Though such engagements are not new to military forces, the conditions in which such roles have to be performed – quick response, stringent expectations, glare of media and scrutiny in hindsight – make these tasks more onerous than ever before.

Finally, there is the widespread misconception that modern war is not as hard on physical strength and stamina as it was in pre-RMA days. Nothing could be further than the truth. Modern war, with its scorching pace, tempo, spread and continuity without the traditional phase-breaks of re-organisation and recoup, imposes severe strain on soldier's body and mind. To survive modern battles, therefore, soldiers need to be as physically fit as ever, and yet have a mind that works sharp under the fog and extreme deprivations of war. Suggestion, that such qualifications may not be so stringent in case of rear echelon or services troops is equally misplaced – as experiences of recent wars have demonstrated, military hardships do not taper with distance from the front. Notably, with modernity softening up the level of physical robustness among the people, catching up to military standards has emerged as an added challenge for the military trainers.

Of course, implications of RMA-induced military modernisation are not exceptional to past experiences; it is the profoundness and the pace of revisions in planning and conduct of operations that make the matter extra-ordinary. Wearing military uniform had never been a placid matter; it has become even more challenging today, a challenge as much for the military trainers as it must be for the society that invests on its military institution. The Indian polity as well as the military hierarchy therefore must join hands to take up the cudgels and prepare the soldiery to succeed against the challenges of modernisation if the nation has to progress under an umbrella of affordable military security.

We may now proceed to see as to how modernisation of the Indian military institution may be motivated by updated objectives of training. To do so, first, a right orientation for the training curricula, and second, the societal influence over military training, would need to be discussed.

Orientation of Training Curricula

The issue of orientation of training is afflicted with inherent contradictions which would have to be reconciled before a solid foundation for meaningful training of the officers and the other ranks, for them to be able to shoulder their mandate in modern warfare can be laid. Let us therefore see as to what these conditions might entail.

Structure of Training

The Indian military institution trains its officers and personnel fairly well. The recruitment base is large and the process is merit based and effective. The post-recruitment training emphasises on achievement of high standards of physical robustness and a fair degree of basic individual professional skills, besides imparting thorough grindings in tactical drills and battle procedures at section and platoon levels. Moreover, the curriculum gives a fair degree of exposure to knowledge enhancement and personality development opportunities by introducing the trainees to contemporary social, historical and political subjects, practical outdoor activities and engaging hobbies. Of course, the entire curriculum is underlined with a thrust on imbuement of military character and values.

Having gone through a common curriculum of pre-induction training, different types of 'entries' among officers and other ranks, who are meant to subscribe to distinct streams of service, are put through arm or service specific post-induction training curricula. Later, at different lengths of service, officers as well as other ranks are directed to various military training institutions to keep them abreast with the refrains of military knowledge and skills. Similarly, each arm and service of all the three services conduct training courses dedicated to their fields of specialisation for various service groups of offices and other ranks. Finally, professional skills so acquired are regularly honed during training camps and field manoeuvres.

Till the mid-1980s, periodic military upgrades were confined to the induction of modern weapons and equipment into a World War II era force-structure, barring some notable exceptions, of course. Some upgrades focused towards manoeuvre war and sub-conventional operations were also incorporated into the Army's training curricula. Later, following the demonstration of the effects of the RMA during the Gulf War I of 1991, advanced militaries of the world devoted to serious measures to modernise. Infusion of similar modernisation into the Indian military institution however could not proceed beyond its theoretical discourse – military modernisation not being among the nation's priorities. By and large therefore, over the past four decades, the content and curricula of military training in India – both for officers and other ranks – has seen only incremental and topical revisions.

It requires no genius to understand that the curricula of training that met the requirements of war in the pre-RMA era, cannot remain equally valid when, firstly, the manners of engaging in warfare stand drastically changed by infusion of technology, and secondly, the strategies of war-fighting stand reoriented by the contemporary dispensations, that of the means, methods and socio-political purposes of waging war. Obviously, India's military modernisation can succeed only when it is motivated by duly oriented military training, objective of which would be to impart such skills that would prepare officers and the other ranks in mastering the complexities of modern warfare. No doubt, the traditional content of military training would have to expand, and that necessitates the military institution to select competent candidates and train them to perfection.

Balance of Tactical and Science Education

By far the most significant development in the field of warfare has been the role that technology has come to play in every level of planning and conduct of military operations. These sweeping changes have been brought about by runaway breakthroughs in military technology, true assimilation of which must manifest through modern strategies and tactics of war-fighting. Indeed, no more just an 'art', warfare today is but an 'art and science'; and that calls for higher level of scientific education among the military professionals.

Advancements in military technology and advent of NCW establish the necessity for all soldiers, sailors and airmen to have mandatory benchmark levels of military competence, over and above which specialisation in one field or the other would be necessary. These fields of specialisation may be clubbed under two broad 'streams', that is, 'tactical' and 'technical'. Thus one stream of tactical experts, while adhering to the hoary principles of military command and staff work, would harness the advantages of enabling technologies to perform their functions in the fields assigned to them. Corresponding to that stream of work, the other stream of specialists would keep the technical part of military systems and structures in operation, besides devoting to the innovation of algorithms to respond to the vast range of tactical quests. Of course, modern warfare would see intense clashes and contradictions among tactical and technical options. For the commanders to take the right course therefore, there would be needed a competent 'interface' who would possess the requisite understanding of the sum total of tactical and technical capabilities and options. In other words, among the modern war-fighters, it is necessary to have one stream of technically aware tactical experts, another of tactically aware technical specialists, and an experienced interface to mediate between the two.

The departure from existing practice would be that, firstly, the notion of 'generalist' category into which the personnel had been consigned so far, would have to be revised to formally tag them as tactical specialists in their own right, and secondly, the field of military logistics would have to be admitted as an aspect of specialisation. However, in the context of logistic expertise, rather than segregating it into another stream, it may be more meaningful to start the reorientation of military training by keeping it as part of both, 'tactical' or 'technical' streams of specialisation, and manning these streams according to aptitude, work-content and experience gained by the individuals. In other words, practically if not formally, military personnel could be trained in a structured manner into tactical and technical streams, with logistic training built into both. In any case, there would have to be the flexibility of inter-specialisation mobility of qualifying individuals between the various streams – for the enrichment of the organisation.

Much of the concept of specialisation – both in respect of officers and other ranks – is already in force in the Indian military institution. However, the current practice will need to be fine-tuned and institutionalised, as discussed above, in order to orient the entire gamut of training from recruitment to release. Equally important would be the necessity to raise the level of specialisation among both the streams, tactical as well as technical; the current ends of specialisation would not be adequate to catalyse the envisioned extent of military transformation.

Tactical Specialisation

Even if the structure of current tactical training has proved to be useful so far, there is a need to add more tiers of higher operational and strategic education for selected numbers among the younger age groups. One option in this regard could be to increase the vacancies, curriculum and duration of tactically oriented training courses – both mandatory and by selection – and then to nominate selected candidates to stay back for some more weeks of advanced studies, study of 'operational logistics' included. This option would necessitate capacity-building in the training institutions, which could be accomplished by revision of training and personnel management policies. Another recourse may be to sponsor selected officers of younger age group for university education in India and abroad. Deputation of officers and other ranks with other modern armies would be another meaningful step. All these measures, however, would have to be complimented with frequent field manoeuvres at sub-unit, unit and formation levels so as to secure the goal of precise operational synergy.

In tune with the idea of 'technically aware tactical specialists', the requisite level of scientific education would have to be imparted to the tactical specialists at the early stages to enable them to fully exploit the advantages of technical feasibilities. This kind of 'user awareness' education is most essential to avoid banal expectations that are evidenced among commanders and staff who demand 'button-press' solutions from technology which, when not met, causes cynicism among them.

The dichotomy to be reconciled is that while higher specialisation calls for longer training and extended tenures of appointment, it contradicts the need for manning line units with the scaled compliment of officers and other ranks. However, as we shall see, this condition is not beyond amelioration if approached with singular intent; modern militaries have found effective answers to such problems.

Technical Specialisation

The general level of technical expertise, even in the technical arms and services of the Indian military institution, is not much to be comfortable about. This shortcoming is reflected in the prevalence of technical stagnation in almost all military endeavours: weaponry, civil construction works, electro-magnetic data communication, geo-spatial information, mobility enhancement or network-centricity etc. Even when few technical upgrades had been attempted, the progress has so far been disjointed and tenuous. To set the due modernisation in motion therefore, elaborate provisions to reinforce the current structure of arm and service specific technical training, with higher tiers of specialisation and opportunities to practice the speciality, would have to be introduced into the system. Thus, following a broad based 'basic' tier of specialisation, higher numbers of selected candidates, both among officers and other ranks, would have to be put through 'middle' and 'advanced' levels of specialisations in various fields of military science and technology. Accordingly, the content as well as duration of the successive levels of post-induction specialisation training courses may have to be revised to conform to latest technical training parameters.

Obviously, to meet higher numbers of trainees, enhancement of the capacity of the technical training institutions would be necessary. Additionally, for training on higher tiers of technical specialisations, it may be possible to tie up with the civil institutions. Appropriate provisions related to course content and financial matters could be worked out, wherein having trained on commercial syllabi in reputed civil institutions, candidates may return to military training institutions to train on military-specific exploitation of the acquired technical expertise. Even the list of 'recognised' specialisations needed by the military institution would have to be expanded to include new disciplines, such as nuclear engineering, ballistic and explosive science, electro-magnetic radiation, construction practices, nano-technology, renewable sources of energy, transportation, and so on – military customisation of new inventions cannot be left to the grace of those who do not have to fight and therefore may not understand the quest of finding scientific solutions to the excruciating burdens of soldiering.

Technical Super-specialisation

For the modernisation to bear fruition, it would be imperative to institute within the Indian military institution, an in-house 'military technology conceptualisation, research and experiment organisation'. This in-house set up could be a part of logistic specialisation under the aforementioned technical stream. The necessity arises because modern armed forces cannot place all their bets on scientists and industrialists to find ingenuous ways of harnessing emerging technologies in wining wars; presence of 'military scientists' among the soldiery is mandatory for such purpose. Though certain set-ups of that kind – the Army's Technology Development Board, for example – do exist, their competence in incorporating various sundry technological breakthroughs into enhancement of combat power remains but limited. Technical arms and services would therefore do well to nominate personnel of the right aptitude from their rolls of advanced level specialists to train in super-specialisation and commit them to tap such latest scientific developments – those at nascent as well as commercial stages – with the purpose of assimilating these into existing hardware designs, and even battle procedures, to enhance operational capabilities of combat elements.

Duration of Training

It goes without saying that for it to proceed smoothly and to reap its benefits in true sense, the process of modernisation needs to be executed by the hands of better educated, professionally well trained and motivated officers and men. Similarly, once modernisation starts taking effect into enhancement of combat capabilities, units and formations have to be manned by personnel of relatively higher tactical and technical competence. These conditions make it necessary to call for longer time and more extensive schedule of training, both for the officers and the men.

Conversely, longer training period would clash with the need to keep the defence forces young, besides intensifying the shortage of battle leadership in line units. Similarly, to reap full benefits of higher specialisation, longer terms of service, and inter alia higher age of soldiery becomes unavoidable – and that adversely affects career progression and youthfulness in the military institution. To find answers to these contradictions, we may have to find reconciliation between the social construct and military attributes.

Age, Education and Aptitude

There are three determinants in the context of age of intake into the military profession. One, divergence of values between the contemporary society and the profession of arms has widened in the recent decades – the youth today has found divergent motivations. So far, this difference was being reconciled by inducting officer cadets as well as recruits at very young age and then moulding them into the pristine military value system during the training period. But among the new generation, attitudinal hardening comes at younger age and that makes it comparatively difficult to mould them into a culture which the society finds too difficult to follow. Conversely, the nuances of fighting under contemporary conditions – when the soldiery is required to wield highly destructive capabilities while under severe scrutiny of empowered societies, media and polity – calls for more stringent observance of those military values.

Secondly, in its quest for candidates better educated and technically savvy, the military institution's answer has been to enhance the qualifying education, and correspondingly raise the age of intake at officers' as well as other ranks' levels. However, as most recruits and many of the officer cadets come from educational institutions of rather modest quality, the compromise made remains somewhat uncompensated; the military institution thus lands up with inadequately educated but higher age recruits. Out-dated afflictions with the 'non-science' stream of education further exacerbates the disconnect, since no arm or service can do better with its personnel remaining bereft of scientific temper.

Lastly, the primacy of physical robustness in war – belying the illusion of 'button warfare' – has been unequivocally proved during all the recent military engagements. Conversely, upbringing of common Indian youngsters precludes the urge – and opportunity – of build-up of physical toughness. Therefore, practically all officer and most other ranks candidates need much longer exposure to the toughening programme.

Obviously, there is the need to contrive methods to reconcile the contradictions concerning the age of intake, qualifying education, malleability of mind, duration of post-induction training and shortage of young officers.

Personnel Management and Training

Military training starts with selection of civilian recruits and cadets. Therefore, the matters of age and qualification of intake, structure, duration and funding of pre and post-induction training, and finally, reconciliation of all these aspects with the terms of military service have to be sanctified at the political level. Adequate incentives would also have to be thought of to attract the right talent into military forces if the nation does not want to consign complex and costly hardware, and of course the ultimate outcome of war, into the lap of second best men. Obviously, it would require all the guile that the managers of national defence can muster to find a system that covers the ambiguities as listed above. On the positive side, with political leadership and strategic communities playing active part, top militaries the world over have been able to find balanced and workable answers to those challenges. Modernisation, and the corresponding orientation of training in the Indian military institution, would have to be similarly backed up by right political and fiscal support. Considering that military modernisation is as much a political necessity as it is a military endeavour, such back up should be readily forthcoming.

One of the possible options to address the dichotomies as discussed above could be to recruit younger and put the candidates through quality education, character building, and physical and mental conditioning. This arrangement could be either in-house, or through specifically empanelled schools, 'Sainik Schools' included, prior to commencement of the standard schedule of pre-induction training. For post-induction technical education, empanelled civil institutes, with mutually devised syllabi, could be subscribed to, which could subsequently be supplemented by military-specific technical training at the services' own training institutions. Opening up certain categories of super-specialist entries among officers as well as other ranks to relaxed age criteria and shorter term of engagement could also be thought of under the concept of 'support cadres'.

The necessity of keeping military forces young may have to be met by the combination of regular and support cadres, as it has been under consideration for some time, albeit only at the officers' level – that provision may be extended to both, the officers' as well as other ranks levels. In case of the support cadre, customised policies on employment-oriented recruitment, shorter terms of engagement and selective extensions for rare specialities would have to be instituted. To keep the forces young and yet professional, reduction in the period of 'colour service' of the support cadre in favour of longer 'reserve liability', with, say, biennial refresher training, could be considered. This policy would have to incorporate provisions for absorption of the released and reservist personnel into appropriate grades of civil services, and public and private sectors, and that would need the Government's commitment to override bureaucratic hurdles. The purpose should be to retain in service just the minimum numbers among those who enter into that phase of life when domestic distractions start clashing against the excruciating conditions of military service. A third recourse would be to strengthen the TA with more effective legislation, so as to attract talent while arresting the truancy of civil employers against release and reappointment of embodied personnel. Of course, all these measures have to be packaged under appropriate incentives and compensations, and duly supported by legislation and government rules of business. Measures that are in vogue in advanced nations could be the reference points in this regard.

Government level measures would, of course, have to be complimented by measures within the military institution. For one, training institutions may no more be frozen in the past and restructured to meet the current criteria of candidates' entries, the pre-induction, basic-induction and post-induction trainees, and training contents and infrastructure.. Further, the scope of tactical and technical professionalism among officers and men have to be expanded by offering more opportunities for them to hone their competence. Towards this end, instructors may have to be given longer tenures including extended re-employment, and fixations that cause diversion of the highly trained wizards from their fields of expertise have to be grown out of. Indeed, to usher-in true modernisation, the system of personnel management needs to be revised.

A Purposeful Course

It is to be expected that the options discussed above would find many challenges from superficial military consciousness, bureaucratic dithering and turf-competition. Similarly, efforts to institute changes in the eligibility for recruitment, terms of service and transition to second career would have to surpass partisan machinations of political and bureaucratic detractors. Single minded intent and purposeful policy-making would therefore be needed among India's political as well as military hierarchy to tackle the challenges ahead.

The struggle for change will be a long one. Yet, rather than waiting for military modernisation to stagnate, it is wise to invest in quality manpower to further its cause.

*

CONCLUSION

MILITARY SECURITY IN PRESERVATION OF SOVEREIGNTY, UNITY AND PROGRESS

Political mentors opine that national security rests on three factors, namely, social-political security which provides for freedom and rule of law to its citizens, economic security for them to meet the basic necessities of life, and military security for the first two to prevail.

Nearly three centuries of ruthless exploitation of her national wealth had brought India down into famine, disease and poverty. Thus when India won her independence, the popular vision was euphoric on the coming of a dispensation which would free the masses from a life of abject misery. That was so when Indian leaders dreamt of promoting social-political and economic security for their masses, while consigning the third, military security, to dormancy, if not neglect. The hope was to pull it off by riding on the idea of peace, non-violence etc. and commit all resources to development. That the dream could just about proceed but imperfectly, is another matter.

Having been at the receiving end of vicious regional gangsterism, India is obliged to maintain the world's fourth largest armed forces. She does so much against the natural inclinations of her ruling establishment. The adversity is exacerbated by India's near-total dependence on war-material imported at excruciating costs. Truly therefore, it is obligatory for the nation's defence managers to shape India's military institution in a manner that not only promotes the cause of national security, but in so doing, make every penny of her defence investments count. Disconcertingly however, the situation is quite the opposite. Indeed, while India spends a high but yet insufficient amount on her defence, her military security remains below par. That allows Indian nationhood to be constantly assailed from within and without, and that diverts us from realising our much needed socio-political and economic security.

As we observe, India's military deterrence remains so weak that the stewards of the state have to discard any thought of administering even token punishments to the forces inimical to our nationhood, watching helplessly as the enemies thumb their nose to the national leadership's 'stern warnings' of 'not tolerating' any more of their base hostility. That haplessness then prompts the glib pronouncements to the effect that "war is not a solution" – as if peace is! Notably, these platitudes are mouthed by a nation that has been, and is being, trampled upon from the North and the West over most of its independent existence, and in spite of maintaining, in terms of numbers, the world's fourth largest military institution! The dichotomy is profound, and the solution lies in bringing about profound defence reforms and military modernisation. Defence reforms and military modernisation would bring maximum value for the investments made on national defence. Astutely carried out with due wisdom and by the repudiation of pseudo-strategic, partisan and motivated quick-fix solutions, this must be an initiative long overdue.

This book is an effort to focus on that long overdue revamp of management of national defence. Propositions made in the course of discussion are but the pointers to a direction, but not necessarily the only one; informed debate and discussion would bring that about. The subject is vast, requires extensive studies and experimentations to devise and perseverance over decades against systemic hurdles to apply. The dividends, of course, would be worth that effort.

*

INDEX

*